HONOR, V

S

HONOR, VENGEANCE, AND SOCIAL TROUBLE

PARDON LETTERS IN THE BURGUNDIAN LOW COUNTRIES

PETER ARNADE AND WALTER PREVENIER

CORNELL UNIVERSITY PRESS

Ithaca and London

First published 2015 by Cornell University Press
First printing, Cornell Paperbacks, 2015

Printed in the United States of America

Library of Congress Cataloging-in-Publication Data

Arnade, Peter J., author.
  Honor, vengeance, and social trouble : pardon letters in the
Burgundian Low Countries/ Peter Arnade and Walter
Prevenier.
     pages cm
  Includes bibliographical references and index.
  ISBN 978-0-8014-5346-5 (cloth : alk. paper)
  ISBN 978-0-8014-7991-5 (pbk. : alk. paper)
  1. Netherlands—History—House of Burgundy, 1384–
1477—Sources. 2. Benelux countries—History—To
1500—Sources. 3. Sociological jurisprudence—Benelux
countries—History—To 1500—Sources. 4. Pardon—
Benelux countries—History—To 1500—Sources.
5. Crime—Benelux countries—History—To 1500—
Sources. I. Prevenier, Walter, author. II. Title.
  DH175.A76   2015
  364.6'3—dc23   2014030529

Cornell University Press strives to use environmentally responsible suppliers and materials to the fullest extent possible in the publishing of its books. Such materials include vegetable-based, low-VOC inks and acid-free papers that are recycled, totally chlorine-free, or partly composed of nonwood fibers. For further information, visit our website at www.cornellpress.cornell.edu.

Cloth printing   10 9 8 7 6 5 4 3 2 1
Paperback printing   10 9 8 7 6 5 4 3 2 1

Contents

ACKNOWLEDGMENTS

Much of this book is about networks—social, familial, and institutional—and about the tug of "vrienden en magen"—friends and family. So it is fitting that we acknowledge the academic and personal help and support we have received while researching and writing this book. We owe a great deal, first of all, to our collaboration itself as authors, the result of both a friendship and a scholarly commitment to the history of the Burgundian and early Habsburg Netherlands. Conversations and work sessions between us took place globally: from San Diego to Los Angeles, from Ghent to New York City and Princeton. Second, we are indebted to our institutions, which provided much needed academic support. For Peter Arnade, these are California State University San Marcos and most recently, the University of Hawai'i at Mānoa; for Walter Prevenier, they are the Universiteit Gent and its libraries, and also, as a visiting professor, the Universities of California at Berkeley and Los Angeles, and Columbia University. Peter Arnade additionally thanks the Renaissance Society of America and the American Philosophical Society for grants-in-aid that provided crucial summer research support.

The pardon letters themselves are housed at the Archives Départementales du Nord, Lille, where we have been welcomed repeatedly and allowed to take digital photographs. For permission to reproduce illustrations from their collections, we thank Willy Van de Vijver, archivist of the city of Mechelen; Clotilde Herbert, librarian of the Bibliothèque Municipale in Cambrai; and Hendrik Defoort, librarian of the Ghent University Library. We also thank Marc P. Anderson, rights and permissions manager of Cambridge University Press (New York), for the reuse of a map from a book published in 1986. Additionally, research queries were cheerfully and helpfully answered by a number of scholars, including Tim Bisschops, Marc Boone, Marie Bouhaïk-Gironès, Frederik Buylaert, Guy Dupont, Jelle Haemers, Katell Lavéant, Jelle Koopmans, John Marino, Jeroen Puttevils, Peter Stabel, and Maarten van Dyck.

Earlier drafts of this book were greatly improved by the critical readings offered by Anne Lombard and Martha Howell, both of whom sharpened our prose, helped to clarify our arguments, and pushed us to pay close attention to matters of gender and family. Elizabeth Colwill offered extensive feedback and scholarly guidance that helped us to rethink the book's focus. We thank the students at Columbia University (2011), the University of California Berkeley (2004) and Los Angeles (2008), and California State University San Marcos (2011) with whom we shared certain pardon letters and lively discussions about them. We also had the opportunity to present our research in guest lectures in classes offered by Claude Gauvard and Elisabeth Crouzet-Pavan in Paris and Tim Soens in Antwerp, and at many international seminars and colloquia as well. Little did these fifteenth-century supplicants for a pardon know they would have a global, cosmopolitan afterlife centuries later.

The two anonymous readers for Cornell University offered much-appreciated guidance in how to recast our book and strengthen both its structure and its arguments. We are indebted to the fine and invaluable help of our copyeditor, Gavin Lewis, and to Susan Specter, our talented production editor. We also thank John G. Ackerman, the long-serving director of Cornell University Press, for his support of our work.

We dedicate this book to our friend Martha Howell, not only for her customary support and for her exacting eye for getting it right, but for something more important: years of friendship and scholarly excellence in the field of Low Country and early modern history. Without her help, our work would have been harder; without her friendship and generosity, we would be all the poorer.

Abbreviations

ADN, Lille	Archives Départementales du Nord, Lille
arr.	arrondissement
Champion *CNN*	Pierre Champion, ed., *Cent Nouvelles Nouvelles* (Paris, 1928)
cant.	canton
dépt.	département
Lancien	Eugénie Lancien, "Inventaire analytique manuscrit," 2 vols. (unpublished inventory of holdings of ADN, Lille, 1927–28)
Petit-Dutaillis	Charles Petit-Dutaillis, *Documents nouveaux sur les mœurs populaires et le droit de vengeance dans les Pays-Bas au XVe siècle* (Paris, 1908)
prov.	province

HONOR, VENGEANCE, AND
SOCIAL TROUBLE

The Forgiving Prince

Pardons and Their Origins

The power of a prince to pardon a crime in the late medieval and early modern periods was a cherished right, and in the case of the hapless Winoc de Wale, a villager of the castellany of Bergues Saint Winoc in the county of Flanders in 1492, it saved a condemned man who survived a botched execution. De Wale had hatched an ill-conceived plan with two accomplices to kidnap some wealthy local men and hold them for ransom in Ghent, a city then in rebellion against Habsburg Archduke Philip the Fair. A bailiff in Hondschoote, not far from Bergues, discovered the scheme and arrested the men, charging de Wale additionally with two minor thefts. De Wale was condemned to death and brought to the scaffold to be hanged by the town's executioner before a crowd. But much to everyone's amazement, the rope snapped during the hanging and de Wale fell to the ground, dazed but still alive. The crowd was moved by the supposed miracle, and de Wale was whisked back to prison where he was allowed to draw up a request for a pardon rather than be readied again for execution. The archduke's government freed de Wale, convinced that he had already suffered punishment and that his escape from death was a miracle.[1]

---

1. Pardon for Winoc de Wale, from the castellany of Bergues-Saint-Winoc (county of Flanders). Mechelen, January 1492; ADN, Lille, B, 1707, fol. 27r–v (Lancien, no. 1964).

Hundreds of ordinary people in the territories of the dukes of Burgundy received princely pardons in the fifteenth century, almost all for capital crimes of murder, rape, abduction, kidnapping, and other forms of hardened violence. Most petitioners claimed to be desperate—convicted of a grave offense, in jail, or hiding from arrest outside their local jurisdiction with little to no money. The administrative archives of the Burgundian court, now located in Lille, contain 2,339 legal documents overturning convictions for crimes committed between February 1386 and December 1500.[2] They range from repeals of earlier decrees of banishment to full pardons for capital crimes and cover a broad spectrum of transgressions, from theft to homicide, from kidnapping—de Wale's folly—to abduction and rape, from protracted vendettas to spontaneous and random violent confrontations, from crimes of passion to financial misdeeds like price-gouging and unpaid debts. The social background of the petitioners is equally diverse, from small-town hustlers like de Wale, soldiers, villagers, and wage laborers, to merchants, urban patricians, and even noblemen.[3] The geography of those pardoned is as varied as the heterogeneous territories the duke of Burgundy ruled, from the Francophone regions of the duchy of Burgundy, the counties of Franche-Comté, Hainault, Artois, and part of Flanders, to the more urbanized, Dutch-speaking regions of most of Flanders, Brabant, Zeeland, Holland, and other territories in the Low Countries.[4]

---

2. The 145 registers of the *Audiencier*, records of the ducal chancery, covering the entire Burgundian territories, run from 1386 to 1661, and are in ADN, Lille, Série B, nos. 1681–1824. Citations of these documents are followed by the running numbers in the unpublished inventory by Eugénie Lancien, "Inventaire analytique manuscrit," 2 vols. (1927–28). See Léo Verriest, *Les archives départementales du Nord à Lille* (Brussels, 1913), 50–55. In the pardon letters we reference, we cite both the archival document number and Lancien's inventory number, as above in note 1.

3. Given both the colorful tableau of crimes and the range of social actors, these legal documents have garnered the attention of historians of the Burgundian state, but usually in more specialized considerations of late medieval law or for the social facts they reveal in studies dedicated to other topics. See Jean-Marie Cauchies and Hugo de Schepper, *Justice, grâce et legislation: Genèse de l'état et moyens juridiques dans les Pays-Bas, 1200–1600* (Brussels, 1994); Hugo De Schepper, "Het gratierecht in het Bourgondisch-Habsburgse Nederland, 1384–1633: Vorstelijk prerogatief en machtsmiddel," in *Symposium over de centrale overheidsinstellingen van de Habsburgse Nederlanden,* ed. Herman Coppens and Karin van Hoonacker (Brussels, 1995), 44–45, 79–83; Marc Boone, "'Want remitteren is princelijck': Vorstelijk genaderecht en sociale realiteiten in de Bourgondische periode," in *Liber Amicorum Achiel De Vos,* ed. Luc Stockman and Peter Vandermeersch (Evergem, 1989), 53–59. Transcriptions of selected Audience pardons were included in Champion *CNN,* the authoritative edition of the *Cent Nouvelles Nouvelles,* and in Petit-Dutaillis, the majority of which concern vendettas and other family and factional disputes. For the sixteenth century, see the detailed consideration of pardon letters in Marjan Vrolijk, *Recht door gratie: Gratie bij doodslagen en andere delicten in Vlaanderen, Holland en Zeeland (1531–1567)* (Hilversum, 2004), and Robert Muchembled, *La violence au village: Sociabilité et comportements populaires en Artois du XVe au XVIIe siècle* (Turnhout, 1989), based on an enormous sample of 3,468 pardons.

4. See the other map in Wim Blockmans and Walter Prevenier, *The Promised Lands: The Low Countries under Burgundian Rule, 1369–1530* (Philadelphia, 1999), 175.

The Burgundian Netherlands and the Burgundies in the fifteenth century. Adapted from Walter Prevenier and Wim Blockmans, *The Burgundian Netherlands* (Cambridge, UK, 1985).

Pardon Letters and the Late Medieval World of the Burgundian Low Countries

The four chapters of our book explore the intersection between pardons and their social world, providing a close reading and interpretation of a selection of the letters of pardon issued by the Burgundian dukes and archdukes to successful petitioners who presented either an oral or written request for clemency for a crime.

We thus have organized our chapters to examine how the petitioners' stories recorded in the pardon letters expose the norms of society and lay bare its sinews, its social layers, and its gender expectations. In each chapter, we have tried to respect the text as text, acknowledging its constructedness as a product of a particular late medieval legal system and of a culture where certain rules of behavior and particular norms surrounding sex, gender, social rank, and authority prevailed. At the same time, however, we have gone beyond these texts to the many studies previous historians have made of the social and political world in which our actors lived, and to the archives where additional information about the actors and the events are sometimes available.

Together, these sources have allowed us to treat the pardon letters as social texts, though ones that construct a particular version of the social realm from which they emerged. Because these pardon texts are crafted as narratives, we will not claim that they—or any of the documents we have connected to a particular tale—accurately reflect either the true events of the case or perfectly assign cause or guilt. But we will argue that these texts can tell us a great deal about the social world they purport to describe. They can provide portraits of society's key actors, helping us understand how power was achieved, preserved, and deployed; they not only sharply reveal the society's cultural and moral norms, they show how these operated to compel behavior, and at the same time how they were constantly being challenged by ordinary people. The texts tell us a great deal about masculinity and femininity and how these two terms were mutually constructed; they provide a lively portrait of the commerce in sex in those days; they display the fragility of the social order, and the many ways it was shattered by violence. In doing so, the pardon letters help us understand what triggered violence, who was likely to resort to violence, how the perpetrators were treated, how the violence was justified, and how peace was restored.

Pardon letters are unique as sources, at once social, narrative and legal documents that capture ordinary people's voices in ways that other sources—census records, tax accounts, property documents, wills and bequests—do not. They provide glimpses into the otherwise poorly documented realm of popular taverns and inns and of drink and recreation; they expose ordinary people's passions—love, hate, revenge, and jealousy, among others—and expression of personal feelings, not to mention the intermixing of different social classes. Pardon letters are hybrid in nature—not simply fiction, although they have noticeable fictional qualities; not simply legal formulae, although they were produced in a rigid legal process; not simply expressions of princely grace and magnanimity, although they were surely that; and not simply chronicles that narrate events from the eye of a particular observer, although they were indeed that as well.

In this study, we seize on the hybridity of pardon letters to use them as access points to a social world whose larger canvas can sometimes be retrieved by other archival documents. This is also a study of how pardon letters are the product of a particular era. In one way, these letters recount seemingly timeless stories of ordinary people's habits, cultural assumptions, and social practices, and are remarkable for their recording of the customs, behaviors, and actions of often semiliterate people who left us no other forms of writing. At the same time, they record a very specific time and place: the Low Countries in the fifteenth and early sixteenth century at the height of princely power of the dukes of Burgundy, a time when sovereign rule was centralizing and when the social order was in transition to the early modern period, when the territory's many duchies and counties would become part of the composite monarchy of Habsburg rule and when its political and religious landscape would be remade by Protestantism and political rebellion. Indeed, the pardon letter was part of the expansion of state power insofar as it became a tool wielded by the Burgundian dukes to hone their executive power, a point we explore below.

In an important way, pardon letters cannot be read in the absence of a larger political narrative, just as they cannot be interpreted merely as a genre of discourse or as a legal form. It's the intertextuality of the pardon letter—its shared legal, discursive and social-political domains—that underscores its uniqueness as a source and requires attention to methodology in any discussion of its interpretation. In this book, we affirm the pardon letter's intertextual core but interpret it as a social text—one that accesses the broader social world even as it narrates a scripted point of view. We don't, however, suggest that there is a dichotomy between fiction and fact embedded in a pardon text or that the job of the historian is to peel back the clever narrative to get at the bedrock truth behind it. Instead, we insist that the pardon letter is constituted by the vocabulary and cultural and social practices of the everyday world of its petitioners, that it is formed from an accessible legal, cultural, and political set of practices that exist outside of it. A pardon can and should be read for its petitioner's presentation of his or her story, for a specific and self-interested version of what happened. But a pardon can also be compared with other archival materials, if they can be located, to shed light on the perpetrator, victim, and circumstances around the incident it recounts. In this respect, the historian is not unlike the judge whose job it was to register the pardon letter through a process of its verification. An absolute truth beyond the pardon text might not be retrievable through other texts, because these archival materials—financial ledgers, property records, related legal documents—have their own internal properties, their own constraints. But a broader social understanding of a particular crime is nevertheless possible, and our book both encourages a critical dissection of the pardon letter as a text and argues in turn how the social world constitutes it.

Princely Politics and the Pardon Letter

Rulers regularly exercised their right to pardon in late medieval northern Europe, at once a reflection of sovereign authority and of its exercise of clemency. Most pardons were for premeditated murder or unintended homicide,[5] though in principle almost any transgression was forgivable and pardon letters were also awarded for things as diverse as business fraud and kidnapping. Long before territorial rulers like the duke of Burgundy or the king of France began to issue pardons, thus substituting for or overruling decisions taken by lower jurisdictions, cities themselves and the ruler of the counties in which crimes occurred had established means of adjudicating criminal and civil offenses, including murder. As we explore in chapter 1, these generally involved a system of reconciliation between disputants, with monetary compensation to the aggrieved or murdered victim's family. Meanwhile, local rulers—counts, dukes, and other rulers—had traditionally reserved the right of superior jurisdiction to pardon some crimes, typically during such special ritual occasions as a princely entry into a city or a major religious festival like Good Friday.[6] In acquiring the Low Countries, the Burgundian dukes routinely invoked the right to issue such pardons.

---

5. Corien Glaudemans, *Om die wrake wille: Eigenrichting, veten en verzoening in laat-middeleeuws Holland en Zeeland* (Hilversum, 2004), 27, 225–80. In 1565–66, 90 percent of the French royal pardons concern charges of homicide: Michel Nassiet, ed., *Les lettres de pardon du voyage de Charles IX (1565–1566)* (Paris, 2010), xxi.

6. Jan van Rompaey, "Het compositierecht in Vlaanderen van de veertiende tot de achttiende eeuw," *Revue d'histoire du droit* 29 (1961): 43–79; Glaudemans, *Om die wrake wille*, esp. 332.

As soon as Philip the Bold, duke of Burgundy, became also count of Flanders, in 1384, he made use of pardons, a noticeable but not entirely new development. Philip's father-in-law, Louis of Male, the last local count, had used the remission system for Flemish supplicants since at least 1371.[7] The duke of Burgundy thus adopted a practice with roots in the Low Countries but whose application was more widely practiced in France, where it was tied to the practice of royal clemency. Philip the Bold was the brother of the French king Charles V, and it was during Charles's rule (1364–80) that the royal pardon system had been honed in France, permitting all convicted felons the right and means to request a remission.[8] Arrogating the right to overrule convictions from lower courts and even Parlements burnished French royal authority, yoking it to powerful religious and political concepts of *justicia* and *misericordia* while simultaneously promoting the image of the king as a *roi justicier* or bringer of justice.[9] During the 1370s, such royal pardons became part of the French royal armature, despite complaints from writers like Philippe de Mézières, whose spokesman in the *Songe du Vergier* (1378) prefers a prince who "is more strict than forgiving" ("prince trop rigoureux que piteux").[10] Despite such hesitations about the trustworthiness of royal power, French kings expanded their exercise of and monopoly over the right to pardon in the course of the fifteenth century.

As in France, the growing popularity of the princely pardon provoked concern in the fifteenth-century Burgundian Netherlands, most notably on the part of the knight and diplomat Guillebert de Lannoy, who wrote an advice manual for Philip the Good entitled *The Instruction of a Young Prince* (c. 1440). In it, Lannoy observed that pardons offered a superior legal remedy

---

7. Several of the pardon letters of de Male are kept in the ADN, Lille, B, nos. 1144–45, 1567, and some are printed in Georges Espinas, *La vie urbaine de Douai au moyen âge*, vol. 4 (Paris, 1913), pièces justificatives nos. 1277, 1316, 1380, 1392. See Marie Nikichine, "Entre rémission du prince et conciliation: L'exemple de la ville de Douai à la fin du moyen âge," in *Préférant miséricorde à rigueur de justice: Pratiques de la grâce, XIIIe–XVIIe siècles,* ed. Bernard Dauven and Xavier Rousseaux (Louvain-la-Neuve, 2012), 17–29.

8. Claude Gauvard, *Violence et ordre public au moyen âge* (Paris, 2005), 81: Gauvard uses the term "véritable inflation" for the period of Charles VI (1380–1422).

9. Claude Gauvard, "L'image du roi justicier en France à la fin du moyen âge d'après les lettres de rémission," in *La faute, la répression et le pardon, Actes du 107ᵉ congrès national des sociétés savantes,* ed. Pierre Braun, vol. 1 (Paris, 1984), 165–92. The oldest available royal remission letter dates from May 1304: Claude Gauvard, "Pouvoir de l'État et justice en France à la fin du Moyen Âge," in *Rome et l'État moderne européen,* ed. Jean-Philippe Genet (Rome, 2007), 341–64.

10. Claude Gauvard, *"De grace espécial": Crime, état et société en France à la fin du moyen âge* (Paris, 1991), 907–20.

against excessively harsh lower court decisions, but cautioned against show-ing either leniency to hardened criminals or favoritism to the rich and well-connected.[11] As we will see, Lannoy correctly suspected that pardon letters could become a political tool manipulated by a sovereign.

The Burgundian rule in the Low Countries was inaugurated in the late fourteenth century and impressively consolidated in the first half of the next century. Philip the Bold's marriage in 1369 to Margaret, daughter of Louis of Male, made him heir, after her father's death, to Flanders, Artois, and the county of Burgundy, setting into motion the rapid acquisition of territories in northwestern Europe.[12] Philip's successors grew this fledging state, acquir-ing Namur in 1421, the duchies of Brabant and Limburg in 1430, Hainault, Holland and Zeeland in 1432, Luxembourg in 1441, and Guelders in 1477. As the dukes collected these diverse territories, which were unusually rich in mid- to large-size cities, they built an administrative structure by which to govern these separate and wealthy provinces; they also nurtured a court whose hybrid Francophone and Netherlandish cultural traditions spawned a golden era of artistic patronage and lavish display.[13]

The real architect of the Burgundian state was Philip the Good, during whose long reign (1419–67) Burgundian rulership and cultural specificity were secured. It was Philip the Good who made the right to pardon into a princely monopoly by prohibiting sovereign bailiffs, his regional legal offi-cers, from awarding pardons as they had done previously. In 1515, a Flemish jurist named Filips Wielant, author of a *Short Instruction in Criminal Matters (Corte instructie in materie criminele),* put it succinctly: "Nobody other than the prince grants remission, nor forgives crimes."[14] As in France, the pardon had now become the exclusive prerogative of the prince in the Burgundian Netherlands—a new legal option open to all subjects amid a thicket of local legal codes and jurisdictions. Pardons were distinctive because they were si-multaneously an autocratic instrument—the preserve of the ruler alone—and

11. See the edition of Lannoy's text in Cornelis van Leeuwen, ed., *Denkbeelden van een vliesridder: De Instruction d'un jeune prince van Guillebert van Lannoy* (Amsterdam, 1975), 20, lines 15–20.

12. Blockmans and Prevenier, *The Promised Lands*, 17. The standard biography is Richard Vaughan, *Philip the Bold: The Formation of the Burgundian State* (London, 1962).

13. Blockmans and Prevenier, *The Promised Lands;* Walter Prevenier and Wim Blockmans, *The Burgundian Netherlands* (Cambridge, 1986).

14. Jos Monballyu, ed., *Filips Wielant Verzameld Werk,* vol. 1: *Corte Instructie in materie criminele* (Brussels, 1995), 280 (cap. 150, no. 1). Wielant's work was the textual basis for Joos van Damhouder's even more popular 1554 *Praxis Rerum Criminalium,* translated widely throughout Europe and known for its woodcut images.

a right available to any princely subject.[15] In most instances the prince's pardon does not explicitly reference the decision to overturn a verdict, except in rare cases like that of Francesco Spinola in chapter 1 (letter no. 4).

The pardon fit nicely into the larger arena of princely forgiveness that had always been a visible component of late medieval statecraft; as with lords and kings elsewhere, the Burgundian dukes used special ritual occasions such as their inaugural entries to pardon local prisoners.[16] But more generally, because Burgundian rulers since the onset of their rule in the Low Countries faced regular urban protests and rebellions—sometimes scattershot rioting over local matters and sometimes broader and deeper challenges to their economic or political policies—they had to settle rebellions with both military and diplomatic means. To impose peace after urban rebellion routinely involved financial penalties coupled with a blanket pardon of the malefactors once the small cluster of rebel leaders had been rounded up and executed. In such instances, the duke would award clemency as part of the diplomatic treaty that ended the conflict. The largest and most violent urban revolts, however, earned elaborate princely rituals of punishment meant to memorialize a city's defeat. Such was the case with Bruges in 1440 and Ghent in 1453. After a serious rebellion, and in Ghent's case, outright warfare, duke Philip the Good threatened to destroy the city as punishment, and relented only after imposing harsh terms of peace and demanding that guilty townsmen literally strip down to their undergarments to beg his forgiveness in person in a religiously saturated ritual known as the *honorable amends*.[17]

For a rebel to be literally forced down on his knees to beg the prince's forgiveness, bareheaded, barefoot, in white undergarments, and holding a

---

15. For Frédéric Lalière, the pardon system was indeed a "juridical instrument of the centralization of power" because it gave the duke a new manner to overturn a number of decisions of the urban courts by outright annulment; see Frédéric Lalière, "La lettre de rémission entre source directe et indirecte: Instrument juridique de la centralisation du pouvoir et champ de prospection pour l'historien du droit," in *Violence, conciliation et répression,* ed. Aude Musin, Xavier Rousseaux, and Frédéric Vesentini (Louvain-la-Neuve, 2008), 21–65.

16. On Burgundian ceremonial entries, see Elodie Lecuppre-Desjardin, *La ville des cérémonies: Essai sur la communication politique dans les anciens Pays-Bas bourguignons* (Turnhout, 2004); Hugo Soly, "Plechtige intochten in de steden van de Zuidelijke Nederlanden tijdens de overgang van middeleeuwen naar nieuwe tijd: Communicatie, propaganda, spektakel," *Tijdschrift voor Geschiedenis* 97 (1984): 341–61; Peter Arnade, "The Emperor and the City: The Cultural Politics of the Joyous Entry in Early Sixteenth-Century Ghent and Flanders," *Handelingen der Maatschappij voor Geschiedenis en Oudheidkunde te Gent* 54 (2000): 65–92.

17. On these rebellions and their punishments, see Jan Dumolyn, *De Brugse Opstand van 1436–1438* (Kortrijk-Heule, 1997); Jelle Haemers, *De Gentse Opstand, 1449–1453: De strijd tussen rivaliserende netwerken om het stedelijke kapitaal* (Kortrijk-Heule, 2004).

penitential candle, predicated forgiveness upon a theatrics of submission. It was, in fact, a larger-scale version of what every individual petitioner for a ducal pardon had to do in a more private setting: literally supplicate the prince's goodwill, and "humbly" request forgiveness and pardon. In this way, every offer of a ducal pardon was a political act staged on a small scale. Thus the pardon vaunted the image of the prince as a supreme leader, one endowed with an almost religious authority to redeem souls and set people free.

If colored with politics, princely pardons were neither an appendage of royal conceit nor slipshod affairs. They required careful judicial oversight, prompting some legal historians to interpret them as fairer than the loosely jointed realm of customary law, where the accused might confront local officials without formal legal training or haphazard and sometimes uncodified rules.[18] The pardon, by contrast, lay within the jurisdiction of the prince and his chancery officials and legal officers; their job, as Filips Wielant pointed out in his 1515 manual, was to ensure that all claims in a request for remission of a crime were verifiable and true.[19] "If anyone introduces an application [for a pardon] that is false and beneath truth," Wielant confidently explained, "his request becomes invalid [and] the pardon [is] canceled."[20]

Indeed, Wielant had reasons to boast about the pardon as a legal instrument, even if its practical applications sometimes bent too easily to political winds. When someone petitioned the duke for a pardon in oral or written form, the request was fact-checked by an official, usually a bailiff, sheriff, or judge, from the jurisdiction in which the crime had occurred. If the petition passed this first legal check, the duke either denied or granted a pardon, ordering a notary of the chancery to record it. These pardons still had to be ratified (*entériné*) after a second review, usually by one of the Burgundian regional courts.[21] When the claimant submitted the pardon letter to this court, its notaries usually also drew up a second document called the *intendit* that enumerated the case's facts and laid out the petitioner's argument for dismissal.[22] The officials of the court might chose to order a new investigation,

---

18. See, for example, Vrolijk, *Recht door gratie*, 457; De Schepper, "Het gratierecht in het Bourgondisch-Habsburgse Nederland," 52–53.

19. On the Audience as a section of the ducal chancery, see Pierre Cockshaw, *Le personnel de la chancellerie de Bourgogne-Flandre sous les ducs de Bourgogne de la maison de Valois (1384–1477)* (Kortrijk-Heule, 1982), 60–68.

20. Monballyu, *Filips Wielant,* 249, cap. 125, no. 2.

21. The French king used the same procedure of entérinement; see Louis de Carbonnières, "Les lettres de rémission entre Parlement de Paris et chancellerie royale dans la seconde moitié du XIVe siècle," *Revue historique de droit français et étranger* 79 (2001): 179–95.

22. Vrolijk, *Recht door gratie,* 395.

as they did with the actor Mathieu Cricke's pardon for abduction and rape in 1475 (see chapter 4). Cricke's case included a *recollement*, the redeposing of witnesses from the preliminary investigation conducted at the time of the petition's submission. This second level of judicial review gained added weight if, as happened here, a pardon request was contested by the counter-claimants in the case.[23]

Such judicial fact-checking might discover the omission or suppression of damning evidence, or it might ferret out false statements, either of which would lead to the rejection of the pardon request and the formal pardon letter. If the reviewing judges or counter-claimants discovered that crucial information had been hidden or omitted, either the pardon request would be denied or the pardon letter not validated (*subreptice*). If they found false statements or the twisting of facts, the pardon letter was formally rejected as untrue (*obreptice*). If the checks did not reveal fraud, lies, or mistakes, however, the court validated the pardon letter.[24] While our study demonstrates several clear examples of pardon letter procedures being altered for some clear political goal of the Burgundian dukes, it also reveals that for the vast majority of ordinary petitioners, the pardon process adhered to its standard rules.

In principle, a pardon was attractive exactly because it ignored social standing, age, status, or gender—a rare unrestricted option in an age rigidly structured along social hierarchies. Yet however broad its accessibility, a pardon letter was not always free. First, much as customary law that predated Burgundian rule had required, most successful petitioners were ordered to pay compensation to the victim or the victim's family, in much the same way that capital offenses were traditionally settled in the cities. Second, petitioners also had to pay a "civil amends" to cover a pardon letter's administrative fees.[25] Whereas the amount of compensatory damages owed to the victim depended on the seriousness of the crime, the court fees varied according to the petitioner's status and financial standing. For many indigent petitioners, the administrative fees were waived; for example, 40 percent of all pardon

---

23. Ibid., 42–52 on the general legal procedure for a pardon, 303–36 on the request for a pardon, 337–75 on the preliminary first check of a pardon's veracity, and 375–406 for the pardon's ratification and second review.

24. On the definition of *subreptice* and *obreptice*: Gauvard, "*De grace espécial*," 67–68; Vrolijk, *Recht door gratie*, 381–84.

25. Lalière, "La lettre de rémission," 34–36. Compensation money to the victims usually came embedded in the following language: "satisfaction faicte a partie premierement et avant toute oeuvre se faicte n'est civilement tant seulement." Court fees typically are described as an "amende civile, selon l'exigence du cas et la faculté de ses biens," the phrasing thus permitting the sum to be adjusted to the seriousness of the crime and the financial status of its perpetrator.

letters awarded in the provinces of Namur and Hainault during the fifteenth century omitted such fees.[26] At the opposite end, this price could be stiff for such prominent or rich petitioners as the nobleman Jan II van Gavere in 1460 or the urban patrician Dirk van Langerode in Louvain in 1476. As we shall see, both had sought pardons for abducting women in order to marry them against the wishes of the families of their intended brides.[27] The nobleman paid a whopping "civil amends" of one hundred gold lions (the equivalent of nearly two years' wages for an unskilled laborer), while the merchant paid over eight times as much: five hundred pounds of forty Flemish groats (the equivalent of sixteen and a half years' wages for an unskilled worker). Pardon letters do not regularly specify the exact amount required. For those petitioners who were neither exempted because of poverty nor gouged because of their resources and circumstances, the amount owed was probably similar to the average amount for a French royal pardon in the sixteenth century: the equivalent of about two months' wages for an unskilled worker.[28]

One of the most controversial juridical distinctions in the pardon procedure was the difference between homicide and murder. Corien Glaudemans's analysis of a large sample of court texts from the late medieval Low Countries demonstrates how French jurists applied a distinction between "murder," in which the perpetrator does not admit to the crime, and "homicide," in which he or she does so admit.[29] Glaudemans's definitions parallel those formulated by the Flemish jurist Filips Wielant in his 1515 legal manual.[30] "Homicide" (*dootslach*) is excusable for four reasons: self-defense, defense of one's goods, defense of honor, and defense of friends. Murder, by contrast, is never pardonable.[31] In this book we adhere to this late medieval

---

26. Ibid., 36.

27. For van Gavere's 1460 pardon, see chapter 1, letter no. 5 ; for Langerode's 1476 pardon, see chapter 3, letter no. 17.

28. In the 1530s in France, fees for pardon letters were about six livres, but increased to ten livres by the 1550s. See Natalie Zemon Davis, *Fiction in the Archives: Pardon Tales and Their Tellers in Sixteenth-Century France* (Stanford, CA, 1987), 10 ; and Hélène Michaud, *La Grande Chancellerie et les écritures royales au seizième siècle* (Paris, 1967), 335–36, 341–43.

29. Glaudemans, *Om die wrake wille*, 27; Claude Gauvard asserts that in late medieval France "murder" referred to a premeditated killing while "homicide" was involuntary, and therefore regarded as committed in self-defense; see Gauvard, *"De grace espécial,"* 798–813.

30. Monballyu, *Filips Wielant*, 213, cap 87, no. 1: "moorde: es yement dootslaen, bedectelic, uut den weghe, . . . zonder roupen of waerscuwen . . . verswijghende ende niet te kennen gheven."

31. Ibid., 192–96, cap. 68–75. The fourteenth-century French jurist Philippe de Beaumanoir applied this same distinction: homicide is always without premeditation, murder never without treason. See Amédée Salmon, ed., *Philippe de Beaumanoir, Coutumes de Beauvaisis*, vol. 1 (Paris, 1900), sections 825–28.

distinction between "homicide" and "murder" while recognizing that late medieval jurists and legal scholars never drew a clear distinction between the two.[32]

The Boundaries Between Law and Literary Artifice

As much as they provide a window onto the petitioners and their lives, pardon letters are narratives, artfully constructed legal texts.[33] The pardon letter, as Natalie Zemon Davis made amply clear in her 1987 study of French royal pardons, is at once a legal text and a story, an act of narration in which the petitioner and the notary join forces, with the former supplying the storyline and the latter adding his training in rhetoric and jurisprudence with which to adorn it.[34] Scholars like Pierre Bourdieu argue that a genre like a legal document constructs its own internal reality, a symbolic world that is its own truth.[35] For this reason to interpret a pardon as a narrative device and also as a legal source are not incompatible approaches. As a text, the pardon letter deployed standard legal protocols while constructing a compelling, unified narrative with literary elements of emplotment. To be successful, a pardon letter followed a basic script: it had to recount a tale of misfortune that typically began with the petitioner's daily business and built to a confrontation that turned violent even though the petitioner neither intended nor initiated it—a crime narrative that strove, and sometime strained, for verisimilitude,

---

32. The lack of this distinction might explain why some historians such as Pieter Spierenburg prefer the use of the term "murder" as a general category, and as a "shorthand for all forms of private and non-accidental killing"; see Pieter Spierenburg, *A History of Murder: Personal Violence in Europe from the Middle Ages to the Present* (Cambridge, UK, 2008), 1–3. By contrast, Natalie Zemon Davis underscores that "Pardon tales were mostly about homicides, claimed to be unpremeditated, unintentional, in self-defense, or otherwise justifiable or excusable." See Davis, *Fiction in the Archives*, 7.

33. On narratives, see Mieke Bal, *Narratology: Introduction to the Theory of Narrative*, 3d ed. (Toronto, 2009), 5. Bal describes a narrative as a "text in which an agent relates a story. A story is a fabula that is presented in a certain manner. A fabula is a series of logically and chronologically related events that are caused or experienced by actors."

34. Davis, *Fiction in the Archives*, 15–25.

35. Pierre Bourdieu, *Ce que parler veut dire: L'économie des échanges linguistiques* (Paris, 1982), 21. This point is reinforced by Shannon McSheffrey, "Detective Fiction in the Archives: Court Records and the Uses of Law in Late Medieval England," *History Workshop* 65 (Spring 2008): 65–78, especially how the legal archive constructs a narrative reality, and in doing so, suppresses as much as reveals, for which see Jacques Derrida, *Archive Fever: A Freudian Impression*, trans. Eric Prenowitz (Chicago, 1996), 4. On the contrast between "plural truth" and "single reality": Martha Howell and Walter Prevenier, *From Reliable Sources: An Introduction to Historical Methods* (Ithaca, 2001), 21, 103–4, 146–50; on the problems with decoding the individual recounting of an event: Donald P. Spence, *Narrative Truth and Historical Truth* (New York, 1982).

what Roland Barthes dubbed the "reality effect."[36] The anthropologist Lawrence Rosen has studied the use of lies and semi-lies in communication as a rhetorical strategy he termed "bargaining for reality."[37] Pardon letters are full of such microbargaining, edited disclosures of what transpired that are strategic rather than purely factual, requiring readers to pose several interpretive scenarios, as we do with the case of Lieven de Zomer in chapter 2 (letter 9). The legal form of a pardon letter is fundamental for structuring its content. It required a notary's hand in preparing it, the invocation of certain legal formulae, and dictated the latitude of an admission of a crime.

As narratives, pardon letters were not impermeably sealed within a realm of discourse, and our book differs from Davis's in its effort to study pardon narratives within an archival register of social life. Pardons were legal instruments embedded within a broader judicial procedure that required external means of verification, and in doing so, they connected their textual narrative to a verifiable social world. In his essay about the study of culture as a system of cultural signs and signifiers, the anthropologist Clifford Geertz famously described the social person as "suspended in webs of significance he himself has spun."[38] As a genre, the pardon letter captures two distinct sides of the petitioner: as an individual with a self-crafted story, with the subjective self and the legal quandary the pivot, but also as a social being with a wider arc of affiliations and obligations.

It is true that even if they tell a person's story, pardon requests are not personal letters, but appeals written by an educated jurist or notary. That said, the Burgundian pardons are less confined to impersonal storytelling than the French royal pardon. Many letters have a sometimes vibrant vernacular flavor, and they incorporate pungent direct quotes, like the insult hurled against a Flemish innkeeper in1459 calling him a "false son of a whore and a ruffian."[39] The frequent use of literal quotes demonstrates, among other things, a concern for verisimilitude. In a conflict with Italian merchants in Antwerp in the Spinola case (chapter 1), insults in Italian are rendered in French to

---

36. Roland Barthes, "The Reality Effect," *French Literary Theory Today,* ed. in Tzvetan Todorov (Cambridge, UK, 1982), 11–17. On embedded speech and the reality effect, see also Michael S. Kearns, *Rhetorical Narratology* (Lincoln, NE, 1999), 152–61.

37. Rosen's analysis is based on a completely different context, the techniques of communication employed by twentieth-century Moroccan villagers: Lawrence Rosen, *Bargaining for Reality: The Construction of Social Relations in a Muslim Community* (Chicago, 1984), 1–5, 18–19, 180–81; see also Peter Berger and Thomas Luckmann, *The Social Construction of Reality* (London, 1971), and McSheffrey, "Detective Fiction in the Archives," 65.

38. Clifford Geertz, "Description: Toward an Interpretive Theory of Culture," in *The Interpretation of Culture: Selected Essays* (New York, 1973), 5.

39. ADN, Lille, B, 1689, fol. 20v.

demonstrate the seriousness of the dishonor. Some pardon narratives recount in direct and tangible form the locations, goods, and buildings of the petitioners' daily lives: inns, marketplaces, public squares, homes, and the materials and people in them. These surroundings are presented in a linear narrative and ordinarily in French—the first language of the many petitioners in the Walloon areas of the Low Countries and in the two Burgundies. French is also the language of the pardon letters that feature Dutch speakers; only a small minority of the pardons are in Dutch, and most of the Dutch petitioners knew French well.

Even though pardon letters are strategically crafted texts, they remain crucial sources for the reconstruction of the late medieval and early modern past. They offer the petitioners' point of view and also give us tantalizing access to ordinary people of that time. But as Davis reminded us, they are hardly transcripts of an external reality, much less factual templates, and in fact should be judged more candidly as narrative devices. Cultural historians of medieval and early modern Europe recognize that there is no direct access to the subject's voice, even in a source as close to it as a pardon.[40] Even the archives themselves, as repositories of official documents that compile a society's social, political, financial, and institutional history, aren't an open book but rather the mandates of a governing body—city, country, duchy, or kingdom—about what to collect, how to order it, and how to record it.[41] No source, therefore, is innocent of those who created it and their intentions.

However, the archives themselves sometimes offer the historian a way beyond the formalism and formulae of many pardon letters when they house documents that record either separate accountings of the conflict or factual details about the parties involved. A pardon letter of 1460 in chapter 1, for example, identifies the petitioner as "our beloved and loyal knight messire Jan van Gavere, lord of Heetvelde," and explains that he had been banished

40. For legal documents, both in Latin and in the European vernaculars, see Carlo Ginzburg's celebrated *The Cheese and the Worms: The Cosmos of a Sixteenth-Century Miller,* trans. John and Anne Tedeschi (Baltimore, 1980); Emmanuel LeRoy Ladurie, *Montaillou: The Promised Land of Error,* trans. Barbara Bray (New York, 1978); Natalie Zemon Davis, *The Return of Martin Guerre* (Cambridge, MA, 1983), among the best known of a much larger microhistory genre pioneered in the 1970s, for which see Giovanni Levi, "On Microhistory," in *New Perspectives on Historical Writing,* ed. Peter Burke (University Park, PA, 1991), 97–119. For a shrewd consideration of the ethnographic possibilities and limits of historical sources concerning ordinary people, focusing on Ladurie's classic, see Renato Resaldo, "From the Door of His Tent: The Fieldworker and the Inquisitor," in *Writing Culture: The Poetics and Politics of Ethnography,* ed. James Clifford and George E. Marcuse (Berkeley, CA, 1986), 77–97.

41. For a good introduction to the literature on archives, see Antoinette Brown, ed., *Archive Stories: Facts, Fictions, and the Writing of History* (Durham, NC, 2005), but also Arlette Farge, *Le goût de l'archive* (Paris, 1989).

for homicide during a prolonged vendetta (letter no. 5). But the text does not reveal his rank as a nobleman, his prominence, or his networks of close family and distant kin. Only the city and ducal archives can reveal the petitioners' social status and broader world, sometimes only by a small footprint, and sometimes by making it possible to reconstruct the political or social context. In such cases, the self-contained narrative of the pardon is pierced, and we are able to get glimpses into a richer, messier, and more complicated storyline. While we may not be any closer to reality—for that is lost in the incompleteness of the past and the multiple claims upon it—we see the supplicants embedded in the social, political, and familial ties and obligations that defined them as social persons in the urban world of their ordinary lives.

Pardon letters' micronarratives are not a self-contained world encased in miniplots. To begin with, not all petitions for pardon are cleverly or even capably written; for example, the case of the convicted kidnapper Cornelis Boudinzoon in Zeeland in 1449 in chapter 3 is both wooden in its narrative and brazen in its admission of raw violence. Such weakly justified pardon requests that nevertheless earn a full remission highlight the importance of the extratextual world: of the circumstances—especially the social context and political considerations—that can affect a case's outcome. So far as possible, we have turned to archival and literary sources to give context to the legal cases we explore, tracking, where sources permit, how these specific texts can be fruitfully interpreted when their social and political framing is exposed.

Despite legal phrasings, the French of the pardon letters is strikingly familiar in style and syntax to Burgundian vernacular literature, literary tales as well as chronicles and annals. It is interestingly close to one work in particular, the *Cent Nouvelles Nouvelles*. Written around 1462 during the reign of Philip the Good, each of the hundred comic tales in this Burgundian court cycle was assigned to one of thirty-five different mock authors, though the real number or names of those who composed these stories is unknown.[42]

---

42. The author was identified, erroneously, as the French writer Antoine de la Sale. The best edition of the original manuscript is Champion *CNN*, with a good English translation in *The One Hundred New Tales (Les Cent Nouvelles Nouvelles)*, trans. Judith Bruskin Diner (New York, 1990). The one extant illuminated manuscript of the text is found in Glasgow University Library, Hunter ms. 252, celebrated for its illustrations, for which see Alison Adams, "The Cent Nouvelles Nouvelles in MS Hunter 252: The Impact of the Miniatures," *French Studies* 46, no. 4 (1992): 385–94. A thorough consideration of the *Cent Nouvelles Nouvelles* and its textual history is Roger Dubuis, *Les "Cent nouvelles nouvelles" et la tradition de la nouvelle en France au Moyen Âge* (Grenoble, 1973), and a brief but substantial analysis can be found in Mary J. Baker, "Spinning Out the Story in the Cent Nouvelles Nouvelles," *Le moyen français*, no. 44–45 (1999): 21–28. Dubuis dates the original manuscript to 1462, corresponding to the estimated date of the Hunter ms. Champion, however, thought the manuscript was prepared between 1456 and 1461 (Champion *CNN*, lvii).

The *Cent Nouvelles Nouvelles* is easily mistaken for a northern European version of Giovanni Boccaccio's celebrated *Decameron,* also with one hundred novellas, especially since Philip the Good owned it in French translation. In genre and language, however, the *Cent Nouvelles Nouvelles* owes much more to French *fabliaux*, borrowing from their bawdy, scatological, and sexual comic tales that feature a stock association of social types. But as we shall see in chapters 2 and 3, some tales in the *Cent Nouvelles Nouvelles* seem to shadow Burgundian pardon letters; in other words, the inspiration for these tales comes less from literary tradition than from current local events.

As long ago as 1928, Pierre Champion offered a sample of pardon letters in the preface to his text edition of the *Cent Nouvelles Nouvelles;* he was so impressed with how closely the *Cent Nouvelles Nouvelles* matched the *lettres de rémission* that he became convinced that these archival texts had inspired the authors of those comic stories.[43] Champion was among the first (the French medievalist Charles Petit-Dutaillis had preceded him in 1908) to dip into the Burgundian pardon letters housed in the archives of Lille.[44] The social world evoked in the *Cent Nouvelles Nouvelles* indeed paints in comic form the misfortunes of people we encounter in the pardon letters—merchants, clergy, noblemen, political officials, townspeople, husbands and wives, family and neighbors—and often revolve around the same themes in a world of sin, sex, and human folly. Given these similarities, it's tempting to view the boundaries between the literary and the legal as porous and even interlaced. After all, two people involved in a pardon's authorship, the petitioner and the preparer, often a notary, had storytelling skills, with the notary steeped in the written word and in the larger arena of theater and literature.

Yet there is never an exact match between a Burgundian pardon letter and a tale from the *Cent Nouvelles Nouvelles,* even if there are strong parallels; for example, between the pardon for abduction in 1469 after the urban patricians Dirk van Langerode and Katharina Meulenpas had eloped in Louvain and tale 26 of the *Cent Nouvelles Nouvelles,* which recounts the love between Gérard, a nobleman of lower status, and Katherine, daughter of a richer noble family, emphasizing the social barriers that prevented their union.[45] We can also find affiliations and correspondences between legal text, language, and cultural assumptions. Most of the pardon letters we consider predate the era of print, and none was well enough known to have been recounted in

---

43. Champion *CNN,* lxii.

44. Petit-Dutaillis, v–vi.

45. Chapter 3, letter no. 17; Champion *CNN,* 77–86, tale no. 26.

broadsheets, much less ballads or other popular media. But the Burgundian court milieu that handled these legal cases was the same social setting in which the *Cent Nouvelles Nouvelles* were recounted orally as entertainment to the duke and his entourage. If one didn't duplicate the other, they inhabit the same social and cultural spaces, and their relations are best seen not within a mechanical cause-and-effect or borrow-and-copy model, but in one in which shared sensibilities and a fund of stories, fiction, fact—and some combination of both—found room to coalesce.

The Stories to Come

Chapter 1 uses a group of pardon letters to explore the ruler's efforts to cultivate political allies and curry favor and, more generally, to expose how the bonds of family, kin, and occupation that knit society in those days could be fractured. Here we see the pardon letter at work in many arenas—in warfare, in work disputes, in family quarrels—and among people of all ranks, from the poor to the well-heeled. We consider the pardon as an instrument that the dukes of Burgundy could employ to resolve legal logjams that traditional means of arbitration could not, and also as a means to dole out favors. But we also look just as carefully at the petitioner's point of view, and at his or her ability to make a request to seek pardon from crimes stemming from conflicts with neighbors, kin, fellow townspeople, and others.

One of the striking tropes to emerge from the pardons is the term "hot anger" (*chaude colle*), almost ritually deployed as an explanation for a violent act. Even today, extreme anger is invoked as a legal defense "as a passion that overrides reason and defeats self-control," but in the world of our pardon letters, hot anger had a very specific connotation.[46] It was a component of the humoral theory of the human body and its physical balances.[47] Filips Wielant understood the sudden rise of heat ("hitte") as a mitigating factor in a crime.[48] Medieval and early modern writers and jurists formulated very similar proposals,[49] citing the classical medical origins of the idea in the

---

46. Raymond W. Novaco, "Anger and Psychotic Disorders," in *International Handbook of Anger: Constituent and Concomitant Biological, Psychological, and Social Processes,* ed. Michael Potegal, Gerhard Stemmler, and Charles Spielberger (New York, 2010), 471–72.

47. Merril Singer and Pamela Erickson, eds., *A Companion to Medical Anthropology* (Oxford, 2011), 387.

48. Monballyu, *Filips Wielant,* 196, 197, 268, cap. 76, no. 2, 77, no. 4, 140, no. 5.

49. Davis, *Fiction in the Archives,* 36–37, 170 n. 7.

humoral theory of Hippocrates of Kos (fifth century BC) and Galen (second century AD).[50]

Self-defense mattered almost equally as an explanation for a sudden, murderous crime, with antecedents in both theological and legal traditions that dated far back in the Middle Ages.[51] Wielant repeatedly cited self-defense, enumerating all circumstances legitimating it against aggression, especially after verbal threats of bodily harm.[52] In fourteenth- and fifteenth-century France and England the notion of "excusable homicides" is closely linked to self-defense.[53] Perhaps more surprising to us today is how verbal aggression also factored into a petitioner's case for a pardon. Verbal violence was often a prelude to hot anger,[54] and was routinely accepted in the Middle Ages as legal cause for a suit.[55] Wielant has a full chapter on verbal assaults, with several examples of terms considered injurious.[56]

Chapter 2 centers more directly on issues of male aggression, adultery, sexual scandal, and gender hierarchy, all linked to honor. The chapter's cases help us see what threatened honor and how, in which circumstances it had to be defended, its gendered dimensions, and the wide cultural swath it cut, so much so that its defense became critical to legal appeals for clemency. Not unlike personal, familial, social, corporate, and political ties, honor was an essential component of male self-worth in the Burgundian Low Countries, and in Europe more generally. It compelled men to comport themselves in ways to maintain and defend it. As often as not, the social perceptions of a man's worth by neighbors, friends, and family prompted him to act in honor's name. The notion of male honor shapes and informs many of the cases in this chapter, and we consider how honor bound men in scripted ways and how it served also as a rhetorical device to be strategically invoked in emergencies. Honor's wide reach as a social norm was repeatedly touted by late medieval and early modern authors, who knew enough about its potency to covet its value while admitting its complexity.

---

50. Paul Blaney and Theodor Millon, *Oxford Textbook of Psychopathology* (New York, 2009), 8–12.

51. Frederick H. Russell, *The Just War in the Middle Ages* (Cambridge, UK, 1975), esp. 95–98, 164–65, 175–76.

52. Monballyu, *Filips Wielant,* 183, 197–99, cap. 58, no. 11, cap. 77.

53. Gauvard, "*De grace espécial,*" 798–806.

54. Jean-Pierre Leguay, *Vivre en ville au Moyen-Âge* (Luçon, 2006), 216–23.

55. On verbal violence and its typology: Karen Jones, *Gender and Petty Crime in Late Medieval England: The Local Courts in Kent, 1460–1560* (Woodbridge, UK, 2006), 94–128, esp. 105; Spierenburg, *A History of Murder,* 32–38; Glaudemans, *Om die wrake wille,* 73–77, 122–125.

56. Monballyu, *Filips Wielant,* 267–270, cap. 140.

Chapter 3 focuses on a small subset of pardon cases concerning forced abductions of women, widows especially, revealing the less studied use of pardon letters to settle marital quarrels. As cases not involving violent death, this category of pardon letters might be secondary to tales of hot anger and murder, but they shine a bright light on the social work pardon letters did as instruments to solve kidnappings, family conflicts, and marriage disputes more generally. This chapter foregrounds five pardon cases involving the real or supposed abduction of aging and young widows, as well as cases of eloping couples, ranging from violent kidnapping and rape to voluntary evasions of legal parental authority. These pardons illustrate how marriage conflicts became family dilemmas, and underline the usefulness of pardons as sources for the history of social institutions and practices. But they do so with a singular perspective, that of the male petitioner, even for one case that has a newly married husband and wife from Louvain as copetitioners. Although about the relation of men to women and of couples to families, the pardons in this chapter feature an insistently masculine cast, with women and other dependents scripted in ways that obscure or deny their perspectives.

Many pardon texts in chapter 3 chart the inner workings of late medieval familial partnership and marriage, especially contemporary perceptions of civic and ecclesiastical marital rules, to which the texts are sometimes sympathetic but often oppositional. They reveal the persistent efforts of parents and families to exercise a strong hand in the choice of marriage partners for their children and kin. The numerous elopements and seductions, however, suggest that young people often did not bend to such exerted pressures, invoking their own criteria that ran the gamut from material support to emotional interest. A second window on late medieval society is opened in these cases: the tug of clientism, exercised by urban elites and Burgundian officials as a tool of political power and social influence.

Our final chapter explores a single pardon for abduction and rape in depth—one that generated a larger archive, allowing the reader to compare the pardon text with other legal documents that describe the case, and in the process, helping to hear other voices besides the dominant one of the male petitioner. This 1475 case pitted an actor, Mathieu Cricke, against both Maria van der Hoeven, a former prostitute and fellow performer in his small company, and Jan van Musene, a townsman from Mechelen. It resulted in fuller documentation, both because it was contested by Cricke's opponents as counterclaimants and because the recently created Parlement of Mechelen deposed a series of witnesses to the supposed abduction and rape. This richer harvest permits us to delve more thoroughly into a dispute involving people otherwise hard to locate in fifteenth-century sources. It also raises especially difficult questions about how to decode and evaluate a pardon letter both empirically and rhetorically by presenting us with three different readings of the conflict between Mathieu Cricke, Maria van der Hoeven, and Jan van Musene. Its multiple recountings of what occurred, and the social antagonisms the sources detail, give the reader privileged access not only to the people at dispute with one another, but with the interpretive process itself. Its most intriguing protagonist is certainly Maria van der Hoeven, a woman fought over by two men. The case offers us rare glimpses of an actress and former prostitute in a late medieval city; even though she herself neither brought the suit nor influenced its twists and turns, these legal documents construct her as the central person in the dispute.

Although each chapter concentrates on a particular set of issues revealed by or addressed by the pardon itself, certain themes are threaded through all of them, none more central than the concept of male honor and its link to gender, sex, family life, and the social world more generally. The cases themselves will allow readers a close inspection of what the term meant to people in this society, how it both motivated and justified violence, and how it functioned to preserve or establish power relations among men and between women and men. Another issue that links all the cases are the bonds of solidarity—how are they achieved, among whom, and on what basis. As we shall see, none is stronger than the ties of family, especially those of blood, although the bonds of marriage can also link people in ways that compel action. But we will also see how networks of clientage, a direct product of the political hierarchy of the day, cut across and sometimes cancel out the social realm of family and blood. Finally, we will see alliances among men who shared a trade or a profession, and we will see that men in that society could also be divided by age, into adults on the one hand, which implied a secure household and control of it, a secure trade or profession or standing in the elite political order, and adolescents on the other, which meant none of the above. These groupings cut across and could fracture the traditional bonds of family, lineage, and clientage.

In today's digitally saturated world, crime stories and legal woes feed an insatiable appetite for transgressions and scandal packaged into tantalizing narratives, sliced up, rethreaded, edited, and increasingly distributed in electronic snippets. Our pardon stories are far removed from our digital moment, predating, for the most part, even the first media revolution of print. They might appear like desiccated old tales excavated from the big folio volumes of a provincial archive in northern France. But they offer human dramas comparable to today's instantly downloadable crime dramas—with the vital difference that a defendant's life might literally depend on the way his story was packaged. More importantly, these condensed narratives can instruct us about matters of life and honor—family disputes; male anger over work, honor, and sexual self-worth; status; marriage and its social choices and constraints; the problem of random, spontaneous violence—in a past age when even Europe's leading king, Francis I of France, could say "all is lost save honor."[57] The worlds they invoke are of an entirely different tempo and order than ours. But the protagonists and their voices in these late medieval stories are still largely recoverable, and their themes and their woes remain recognizable in our contemporary world, even if the settings where many took place long ago are not.

---

57. Quoted in Garrett Mattingly, *Renaissance Diplomacy* (1955; New York, 2010), 174, from a famous letter penned after the French king's capture at Pavia in 1525.

CHAPTER 1

Social Discord

Disputes, Vendettas, and Political Clients

What befell Christiaen van der Naet on January 12, 1489, as he sat outside a tavern in his small Flemish town of Deinze, eating and drinking with friends, was more akin to a satire-laced tale from the Burgundian *Cent Nouvelles Nouvelles* than a trigger to a killing. But it ended with a man dead and van der Naet in a panic, seeking shelter from his enemies by fleeing the county of Flanders and preparing a request for a ducal pardon to evade homicide charges, the confiscation of his goods, perpetual banishment, and perhaps even execution.

Van der Naet was an ordinary citizen of Deinze, a town recently devastated by warfare. With fewer than a thousand inhabitants, the little city lived in the shadow of Ghent, eighteen kilometers to its northwest. Although self-governing, with its own aldermen and jurisdiction, the city had the misfortune to be on a main road that led friends and adversaries to its powerful, often troublesome urban neighbor, and for that it paid a high price. Over the course of the late Middle Ages, Deinze had been a punching bag for larger forces in conflict with Ghent and its allies, repeatedly damaged and pillaged, sometimes by Ghent, as in 1328 and 1452, and sometimes by the dukes of Burgundy and their armies in their campaigns against Ghent and other rebellious cities, as in 1382. In 1488, just a year before the incident discussed here, German mercenaries in the service of Archduke Maximilian of Austria burned Deinze almost completely down in their military campaign against rebellious Flemish cities.[1] The city suffered grievously from these continual scourges, its citizens seeming to live fear of the next wave of violence. In 1436, for example, a particularly difficult year, Deinze's aldermen conducted a house-by-house survey to ensure that its inhabitants had the bare essentials to survive a cold winter.[2] In 1489, the same year that Christiaen van der Naet ran afoul of the law, Deinze's aldermen paid for two pitchers of wine for the celebrations of the Feast of the Holy Innocents on December 28, to "cheer up the people from the troubles they found themselves in"—a reference to the city's destruction the year before.[3]

The misery inflicted by war and Deinze's woeful state formed the backdrop to Christiaen van der Naet's troubles. His pardon letter makes explicit reference to these challenges, describing how he and other families took up residence in the Saint George hostel because their houses had been burned down in "this war"—an overt reference to the intractable conflict between Archduke Maximilian and the rebels of Ghent (letter no. 1).[4] While eating with several other neighbors also forced to lodge there, van der Naet had a chamber pot of urine and feces emptied on his head from a window above. It soaked him from head to foot, but more consequentially, it humiliated him before his friends, who, as van der Naet admitted, mocked him. These men were certainly drinking with their meal, and the sight of the contents of an upended chamber pot covering their friend provoked ribbing and guffaws. Van der Naet was furious, both embarrassed and dishonored in a social environment in which citizens were suffering already from the loss of home and income.

It is no surprise then that van der Naet went after the person who had exposed him to mockery by the careless emptying of a chamber pot. The culprit turned out to be the daughter of a fellow lodger in the Saint George hostel named Rogier de Marscalc. Neither her name nor her age is given by van der Naet, probably a sign that he wanted to downplay his retaliation against a young child or teenager. Van der Naet admits hitting the girl twice

---

1. Walter Prevenier, ed., *Geschiedenis van Deinze,* vol. 1: *Middeleeuwen en Nieuwe Tijden* (Deinze, 2003), 123–26.

2. Ibid, 221.

3. Algemeen Rijksarchief, Brussels, Rekenkamers, Reg. 33.952, fol. 15r (accounts of the city of Deinze, 1488–89).

4. The Saint George hostel was affiliated with the town's local chapter of the Guild of the Crossbowmen, one of many popular shooting clubs found throughout the cities of the Low Countries. The guild had its own house on the town's central marketplace, and membership in it, as elsewhere, was a badge of male social prestige. On the shooting guilds, see in general, Peter Arnade, *Realms of Ritual: Burgundian Ceremony and Civic Life in Late-Medieval Ghent* (Ithaca, 1996), 65–94, and Theo Reintges, *Ursprung und Wesen der spätmittelalterlichen Schützengilden* (Bonn, 1963).

Throwing a chamber pot of urine out of a window of the Saint George hostel in Deinze. Etching from the treatise by Joost de Damhoudere, *Praxis rerum criminalium* (Antwerp, 1554), p. 499. Copy in the Library of Ghent University, Jur. 011275/1. Courtesy of the University of Ghent.

with the backside of a small axe as punishment, though he adds two qualifying points: first, that he regretted his actions, and second, that de Marscalc had afterwards accepted his personal apology. The father reassured van der Naet that his daughter merited her punishment, so much so that he had also struck her himself, especially because she had a habit of dumping chamber pots out of the window.

At play, but never discussed in the pardon request, was a man's right to discipline individuals under his authority as head of a household. An ordinance of 1320–1340 from the city of Aardenburg in Flanders permits "that a husband may beat his wife, since the wife is part of his household effects."[5] When van der Naet struck de Marscalc's daughter he could not claim this right, because she was the daughter of another man, and he ran the risk that de Marscalc might interpret his actions as a violation of his paternal authority. That is why van der Naet apologized: "He bid Rogier forgive him and not consider him poorly because he, the supplicant, had hit his daughter since everything had been done in jest."

In van der Naet's recounting of the incident, trouble broke out even though he had made amends to Rogier de Marscalc. His pardon letter recounts how he went to sleep that night in the church instead of the hostel where he lodged, fearing an attack by some enemies. It is not clear just who these enemies were or why they were a threat. Perhaps "enemies" referred to the extended Marscalc family, but perhaps the word recalled another set of adversaries, like the soldiers who were still in Deinze in 1489. Whatever the case, the very next day things came to a head. It was January 13, and van der Naet describes a day of piety—he was going to church to attend the evening service of vespers—and errands, including visiting a home that he had previously owned. On the way to church, Rogier de Marscalc confronted him as the two passed in the street. De Marscalc was visibly angry and armed with a pike in his hand; he excoriated van der Naet for attacking his daughter. Van der Naet attempted to diffuse de Marscalc's agitation, asking why he was now mad after his supposed display of conciliation the day before. But de Marscalc lunged ahead at van der Naet, who struck back in self-defense. In the heat of anger—the pardon letter invokes the humoral theory of *chaude colle* to justify the sudden spike in emotion—Christiaen van der Naet stabbed Rogier de Marscalc with a dagger, cutting his left arm and piercing his chest. Afterwards, as if nothing had happened, van der Naet left the scene to attend vespers. In the days that followed, de Marscalc continued to hound him, even

---

5. Raoul C. van Caenegem, *Geschiedenis van het strafrecht in Vlaanderen van de XIe tot de XIVe eeuw* (Brussels, 1954), 49. Van Caenegem refers also to a second regulation text, which he considers as exaggerated: "the husband may split the woman from the bottom to the top, and warm his feet in her blood." See also Willem Kuiper, "Over het slaan van vrouwen in de voorhoofse epiek," *Tijdschrift voor sociale geschiedenis* 10 (1984): 228–42.

though, according to van der Naet, he was wounded—thereby proving himself a man whose drive for vengeance outweighed reasonable attention to his medical needs. Although he finally consulted a local surgeon at the urging of his friends, de Marscalc died eight days later. Christiaen van der Naet had no choice but to flee Deinze and Flanders, hounded by his victim's "friends and relatives" who sought his arrest. Fearing his seizure by the bailiff, he prepared a formal plea for pardon, hoping to be excused for the murder of his neighbor. In June 1489, five months after the events, the archduke awarded van der Naet the remission, pending, as was customary, the verification and ratification of its narrative of events, and the payment of an unspecified sum for legal fees and a civil penalty.

Dispute Resolutions and Ducal Pardons

Public violence among private individuals was among the most disruptive of social problems facing legal and political authorities of territorial and civic jurisdictions in the late Middle Ages. The frequency of civil disputes, of vendettas, and of stories of private vengeance in our pardon letters shows just how often a killing involved more than just a perpetrator and a victim, and just how often, too, the individual petitioner was involved in a broader social conflict.[6] The ducal pardon to prevent or end vendettas was a fifteenth-century development in the Burgundian Netherlands, part of a broader effort found elsewhere in Europe to use sovereign authority to crack down on feuds (conflicts between groups) and vendettas (conflicts between individuals)—the tenacious medieval practice, enshrined in customary law, that private vengeance was an appropriate response to a violent attack,[7] and that adversaries' families and male associates were fair targets.[8] In England blood feuds were still a legally recognized practice in the eleventh and twelfth centuries, but ceased by the reign of Edward I (1272–1307). In Scotland and Wales, however, blood feuds survived until the early sixteenth century.[9] Paul Hyams claims that after

6. For a definition of vendetta, see Keith F. Otterbein, "Feuding," in *The Encyclopedia of Cultural Anthropology,* ed. David Levinson and Melvin Ember (New York, 1996), 492–96.

7. On vengeance in the Middle Ages: Susanna A. Throop and Paul R. Hyams, eds., *Vengeance in the Middle Ages: Emotion, Religion and Feud* (Farnham, UK, 2010); Claude Gauvard, "*De grace espécial": Crime, état et société en France à la fin du moyen âge* (Paris 1991) 753–88.

8. Edward Muir, *Mad Blood Stirring: Vendetta and Factions in Friuli during the Renaissance* (Baltimore, 1998), xxii, claims that in Renaissance Italy the term vendetta had both the traditional connotation of a conflict between individuals and that of a feud (conflict between groups).

9. R. R. Davies, "The Survival of the Blood Feud in Medieval Wales," *History* 54 (1969): 338–57.

1200 English kings, like most late medieval rulers, asserted their legal power to resolve disputes but failed nevertheless to dislodge the traditional means of doing so through compromises, settlements, and arbitration.[10]

What was a popular sport of violence among aristocratic families widened out by the high Middle Ages among the urban middling sorts, as cities, especially in Italy and in the Low Countries, grew wealthier and more populated, and as families became enmeshed in conflicts and social and political factions. Most historians until recently have asserted that judges and city magistrates in medieval Italy explicitly tolerated vendettas and their private resolution through compensation. Trevor Dean, however, has proven, at least for the city-state of Bologna, that this wasn't necessarily true. Revenge was treated in fourteenth- and fifteenth-century Italy as an ordinary crime. Pacification was no longer, as in earlier days, a private system of dispute resolution but instead was settled as a formal addition to the judicial sentence and ban. A convicted offender could no longer lift his ban if he did not comply with the court's procedure of reconciliation between assailant and victim.[11]

Like northern Italy, the Low Countries were among the urbanized zones where vendettas and private vengeance were enacted, and there developed in these territories a multitiered system of tackling such violence. During the Middle Ages, the dukes and counts of the different territories at various times began to exercise the right to intervene to stop feuding. In Flanders, such interventions started as early as the twelfth century while in Holland and Zeeland, princely intervention to offset private vengeance began in earnest only in the late fourteenth century.[12] In the legal realm, formal systems of resolution developed through both the office of the bailiff and the city aldermen, a subgroup of whom met separately in session as *paysierders* (peacemakers) to adjudicate disputes. Violent offenders in a feud could be summoned or arrested either by the bailiff in his capacity as ducal law officer or by the *paysierders* in their role as local aldermen. But an offender could also initiate

---

10. Paul R. Hyams, *Rancor and Reconciliation in Medieval England* (Ithaca, 2003), 111–54, esp. p. 132; Hyams offers an excellent overview of the evolution of the concepts of wrong and redress, rancor and reconciliation.

11. Trevor Dean, *Crime in Medieval Europe* (London, 2001), 96–108; Trevor Dean, "Marriage and Mutilation: Vendetta in Late Medieval Italy," *Past and Present*, no. 157 (November 1997): 3–36; Trevor Dean, "Violence, Vendetta and Peacemaking in Late Medieval Bologna," in *Crime, Gender, and Sexuality in Criminal Prosecutions,* ed. Louis A. Knafla (Westport, CT, 2002), 1–18.

12. For the Low Countries, see Bernard Dauven, "Composition et rémission au XVe siècle: confusion, concurrence ou complémentarité? Le cas du Brabant," in *Préférant miséricorde à rigueur de justice: Pratiques de la grâce, XIIIe–XVIIe siècles,* ed. Bernard Dauven and Xavier Rousseaux (Louvain-la-Neuve, 2012), 31–52.

a resolution. When an offender "composed" with a bailiff, he or she paid money to forestall further legal action and end a case. The two quarreling parties could also choose to approach either the bailiff or the *paysierders* together, offering compensation for the victim and the payment of a financial penalty to the legal authority.[13] If the bailiff organized a settlement, it was referred to as a composition (*compositio*). If the *paysierders* settled matters, the procedure was called a *zoen* (reconciliation), and was recorded in the so-called *zoenboeken* (reconciliation books).

Only when the traditional means of reconciliation or composition failed to yield peace and a deal between the fighting parties could not be brokered did the case come before an urban or a ducal court. The parties in dispute had the right to take their grievance before a full session of the city aldermen themselves. Or the public authorities could summon the disputants to appear before the local court, or before the comital or ducal court, such as the Council of Flanders in Ghent.[14] Cases that came to court were by far the minority. In Ghent, only 10 percent of all conflicts became criminal cases before the aldermen's court in the second half of the fifteenth century; the *paysierders* settled a whopping 90 percent.

The *paysierders* proved popular because they were fellow townsmen of the offending parties with the same cultural orientation and urban sensibility, men who would often know the two parties better than any outsider. During the second half of the fourteenth century in Ghent, for example, the *paysierders* handled an average of 325 cases a year; in the *zoenboeken* of Leiden in Holland between 1370 and 1390, 722 sentences are recorded involving either deaths or serious injuries.[15] The settlements of feuds and vendettas also kept bailiffs busy, not just with cases of violent death, but with other capital offenses such as rape, abduction, and robbery. In the year 1370 alone, the sovereign bailiff of Flanders handled seventy-six settlements, fifty-two of which were linked to either banishments or capital offenses.[16]

If the disputants could not reach an agreement, or if a peace agreement had been broken, the ducal pardon letter became a cherished third option.

---

13. On the differences and the connections between the two types of payments, see Guy Dupont, "Le temps des compositions: Pratiques judiciaries à Bruges et à Gand du XIVe au XVIe siècle," in Dauven and Rousseaux, *Préférant miséricorde à rigueur de justice*, 55–61.

14. Van Caenegem, *Geschiedenis van het strafrecht*, 301–5.

15. Ibid., 320–23, and Corien Glaudemans, *Om die wrake wille: Eigenrichting, veten en verzoening in laat-middeleeuws Holland en Zeeland* (Hilversum, 2004), 221.

16. Jan van Rompaey, "Het compositierecht in Vlaanderen van de veertiende tot de achttiende eeuw," *Revue d'histoire du droit* 29 (1961): 43–79; Van Caenegem, *Geschiedenis van het strafrecht*, 311–319.

That men resorted to pardons for vendettas suggest, however, that these other legal avenues either worked imperfectly or were supplemented, perhaps even superseded, by this newer option to appeal for princely clemency.[17] It was a ducal pardon letter that resolved the conflict between Christiaen van der Naet and the relatives of Rogier de Marscalc, ending the dispute—at least in a legal sense. Many others caught in the crosshairs of feuds would also resort to ducal pardons to settle violent, ongoing conflicts between family members and their kinfolk and others or to blunt them before they intensified. The pardon letter did not dislodge the well-oiled system of composition and reconciliation, but it did add, as in Bologna, another legal venue, sometimes short-circuiting the more traditional route and sometimes resolving problems when efforts at peace broke down with either the bailiff or the *paysierders*. More importantly, it affirmed the duke as the ultimate arbitrator of justice, and as the final and best adjudicator of violence when local and regional legal venues were rejected or failed—burnishing his image as the forgiving father and the restorer of social peace. Because the ducal pardon still required compensation to be paid out to the victim's kin, it replicated the compensatory damages the bailiff and *paysierders* traditionally required. Of no small importance, a pardon additionally required a fee to be paid to the ducal treasurer, thus enriching the prince's revenues.[18] Frédéric Lalière observed that the pardon system was a clever blend of the traditional civic *zoen* and the bailiff's composition. The pardon system came in competition with these traditional procedures, and in many ways superseded them, though the *paysierders* and bailiffs still kept busy.[19]

Most striking in these cases of vendettas and feuds are the ways in which the wider world of family and friends either sparked a specific conflict or later complicated and prolonged a simple fight. These tightly wound coils of blood and propinquity shaped choices and informed decisions, with

---

17. For the Low Countries, see Wim Blockmans, *Een middeleeuwse Vendetta: Gent 1300* (Houten, 1987); David Nicholas, "Crime and Punishment in Fourteenth-Century Ghent," *Revue Belge de Philologie et d'Histoire* 48 (1970): 289–334, 1141–76; Lorenza Vantaggiato, "Civil Disputes in Fourteenth-Century Ghent: The Case Study of the Feud between the Rijn and Alijn families," *Handelingen der Maatschappij voor Geschiedenis en Oudheidkunde te Gent* 64, no. 1 (2010): 57–85; and the essays in *Tijdschrift voor Geschiedenis* 123, no. 2 (2010), including the general introduction by Peter Hoppenbrouwers, "Bloedwraak en vete in late middeleeuwen," 158–77.

18. Frédéric Lalière, "La lettre de rémission entre source directe et indirecte: Instrument juridique de la centralisation du pouvoir et champ de prospection pour l'historien du droit," in *Violence, conciliation et répression,* ed. Aude Musin, Xavier Rousseaux, and Frédéric Vesentini (Louvain-la-Neuve, 2008), esp. 33–34.

19. Ibid., 36.

individuals playing out their conflicts in consultation and collaboration with family, peers, allies, and neighbors.[20] The feud cases are a reminder that inhabitants of the Low Countries settled scores by means of private vengeance, even as city officials and ducal officers offered the means of conciliation before feuds and vendettas spun out of the control.

In the Neighborhood: Street Violence

Christiaen van der Naet's case recounts the woes of a small-town man during a time of warfare and social distress (letter no. 1). But it is a typical pardon story in deed, narrative device, and legal dimension. Van der Naet is guilty of a "homicide," a killing that occurred in self-defense against an unreasonable adversary—the most common justification for the unintended killing of an opponent. His narrative is exculpatory, admitting to the crime while padded with justifications for the events. Explaining away violence is the narrative essence of any successful pardon letter. In this particular instance, the mitigating factors are van der Naet's outright humiliation, his open apology to the girl's father, his verbal assurance from his adversary that all was forgiven, and his right to defend himself when he was attacked the next day. What is more, the pardon indicates—whether true or not—that Rogier de Marscalc confessed on his deathbed that he had provoked the fight. Van der Naet also referenced the wider social context—the destitute situation in Deinze—as a technique to elicit sympathy. He, de Marscalc, de Marscalc's daughter, and others were crammed together at the Saint George hostel because they were victims of war, having lost their homes to the predatory actions of mercenaries. The essence of this pardon letter, however, is van der Naet's suffering from public shaming by means of a chamber pot dumped on him in public and before his friends, a deed made all the worse because a young woman had committed it. Christiaen van der Naet had nonetheless sought peace and exhibited piety, having been attacked on his way to vespers. He was a good man, a victim of warfare, of a humiliation, and of a particularly vengeful neighbor. In self-defense and in anger, van der Naet had wounded the

---

20. On this network of "family and friends," see a discussion of the social reach of this web of blood, kin, and association in Marianne Danneel, "Vrienden en Magen in de bronnen van de laat-middeleeuwse Brugse Weeskamer," *Handelingen Koninklijke Zuidnederlandse Maatschappij voor Taal- en Letterkunde en Geschiedenis* 36 (1982): 33–39. On similar conditions in Italy, see Christiane Klapisch-Zuber, "Kin, Friends and Neighbors: The Urban Territory of a Merchant Family in 1400," in *The Italian Renaissance*, ed. Paula Findlen (Malden, MA, 2002), 97–123, and for France: Juliette M. Turlan, "Amis et amis charnels d'après les actes du Parlement au XIVème siècle," *Revue historique de droit français et étranger* 47 (1969): 645–98.

man who had ambushed him. Rogier de Marscalc died from these wounds because he was tardy in seeking medical help and, the pardon letter implies, because he was a thoughtless patient of an unskilled surgeon.[21]

Christiaen van der Naet exemplifies the typical petitioner for a pardon. He is an ordinary man, presenting himself as a blameless citizen who has a good explanation for how he fell afoul of the law. Immediately after the death of de Marscalc van der Naet, "fearing the rigor of justice, absented himself in neighboring territories. Some time thereafter, friends and relatives of the aforesaid dead man made efforts to have him arrested by Deinze's bailiff so as to bring him to the court's criminal justice." Van der Naet feared arrest and conviction for murder. Like most inhabitants of late medieval Flanders, van der Naet was well aware that he could recover his status only by a direct request to the highest official in the land, the duke of Burgundy. From an un-identified location outside Flanders, van der Naet requested clemency. Such a context for a petition to the prince is not atypical. Some were penned from prison, before or after a formal conviction, but most came from locations outside the territory in which they occurred, with the petitioner in hiding.

Van der Naet's pardon letter demonstrates an economy of style that is typical of this legal genre. Tightly sequenced and shrewdly economical, it concisely narrates events that led from the chamber pot incident to the deadly encounter with Rogier de Marscalc. In two folio pages, van der Naet gives a complete account of how his raw humiliation led to an unintended fight with a neighbor and lodger. The request is a model of self-defense, but it also provides partial access to the social domains that he inhabited. For if, from a legal point of view, van der Naet is an individual supplicant pleading a case in his own voice, all else about his story is in the plural, from its social foundation to the very conflicts upon which it turns. Van der Naet's striking of the girl who drenched him with a chamber pot triggered the beginnings of a feud. Inhabitants of van der Naet's world, like their counterparts elsewhere at the time, lived within networks and clusters of collective associations, from family to guild to confraternity to social club to parish to political community, among others; to paraphrase Clifford Geertz's observation, they were "suspended in webs of significance they themselves himself had spun."[22] Men like Christiaen van der Naet lived enfolded in such webs, not only spun from their cultural vocabulary and practices, but also from the broader social

---

21. Prevenier, *Geschiedenis van Deinze*, 1:247 and 346. De Marscalc had probably consulted Jan van de Perre, Deinze's official city surgeon between 1473 and 1489.

22. See introduction, note 38.

groups that gave them purpose and definition. If the petition of an individual supplicant like Christaen van der Naet reveals voice, plot, and narrative style, the setting of the story shows the individual enmeshed within social institutions and forces that compel and restrain choices and actions.

Christiaen van der Naet's case also captures two of the most commonplace themes of a pardon narrative: how affronts to honor breed revenge and how such revenge proves intractable and dangerous to other family members and more distant kin, often triggering cycles of attacks. Van der Naet's dishonor is the easiest to discern—a case of a girl assaulting a defenseless older male in public and of human waste dumped over one's body, offenses to both corporal integrity and cleanliness. The potential for a conflict among two warring groups of kin and friends is, however, more subtly announced. It is hinted at when van der Naet seeks shelter and asylum in Deinze's church fearing unspecified enemies, undoubtedly a reference to Rogier de Marscalc's friends and relatives. It is these same kinsfolk whose attempts to arrest van der Naet force him to flee Deinze after de Marscalc's death. While never named, these foes become the collective adversaries of van der Naet, shadow opponents who seek punishment for his killing of Marscalc.

Van der Naet's is one of countless cases in which the dukes of Burgundy exercised their prerogative to solve a conflict and a potential or full-blown feud when customary legal remedies were not invoked. In other cases, the ducal pardon became essential when city *paysierders* were unable to contain violence. In 1434 a neighborhood conflict in the city of Mechelen between two neighbors, Jan Spaen and Jan van de Putte, ended in a killing: "Words arose between the supplicant Jan Spaen and his neighbor Jan van de Putte, such that many times after hours during the night Jan van de Putte flung and threw rocks against Jan Spaen's house door, threatening to kill him."[23] The case was referred to the city's *paysierders* since verbal and physical violence could be cited to justify acts of self-defense and the preservation of honor:

> the aldermen . . . formally commanded the parties upon penalty for the violation of the peace not to continue under any circumstances to use force, with the intention of arriving at a compromise and peaceful settlement of the dispute. Nevertheless, before the urban court had pronounced a peace, Jan van de Putte came on a certain day with a chamber pot full of urine and threw it at Jehan Spaen's house while pronouncing many injurious words.

---

23. Pardon for Jan Spaen and Arnoul Spaen, Brussels, August 16, 1438. ADN, Lille, B, 1682, fol. 16 (Lancien, no. 202). Published in Petit-Dutaillis, 143–44.

After these provocative taunts, van de Putte suddenly attacked Jan Spaen with an axe as he came out of his house to investigate the noise. Spaen's son saw the danger his father was in and jumped into the fray, pulling a knife and stabbing van de Putte to death: "On July 16, 1437, the supplicants [father and son]and all their accomplices and adherents were perpetually banished for breaking the peace. The supplicants dare not return or live in our lands and seigneuries. On the contrary, they are forced to live in foreign border-lands in great misery and poverty."

While the precise nature of the tension between Spaen and Jan van de Putte remains a mystery, the pardon letter recounts the conflict as a simple story of self-defense, in which Spaen was saved by a son quick on his feet. It was probably Spaen's initial effort to broker peace, as well as the portrait of himself and his son as victims of a violent neighbor, that netted him a pardon on August 16, 1438. Both he and his son are depicted as reasonable men, suffering the violence of a dangerous acquaintance who dared to hurl a chamber pot against their home precisely when Mechelen's aldermen were meeting to resolve the conflict. That the son came to the father's rescue, and that both suffered banishment on a capital charge as a result, added filial piety to their plea of innocence—polishing the image of a good family disturbed by a bad man.

A related example from Bruges in 1455 concerns a feud that intensified even as compensation was being brokered between the two parties. A dispute had flared up between Jan Rutghers van onder de Linde together with his friend Jossequin Richart, and an innkeeper named Denis Deilz (letter no. 2). The two sides had had a fight—over what is not specified—but the letter opens not with their quarrel but with its consideration by officials in Bruges, including one of the burgomasters. Financial compensation had been offered to Deilz by Rutghers and Richart for wounds they had inflicted and the costs of a physician's treatment, but the amount, ten Flemish pounds, was unacceptable to Deilz. As negotiations over a different sum were pending, Rutghers and a servant were ambushed by Deilz and three other men as they were running errands. In dramatic fashion, Rutghers describes the bloody attack:

> They ran to the supplicant and his servant and assailed them, shouting and striking them. The supplicant pleaded and begged with Denis and offered again to give him a larger amends [compensation] than previously had been offered, and asking if he would leave him in peace. Denis ignored [this plea], and Wiltfranc immediately threw the supplicant's servant, named Coppin van Hoorne, to the ground and cut his

throat. They next came after the supplicant, who had his hand cut below his arm. After this, with his servant killed, and to escape the danger he was in, he started to defend himself the best he could, such that he wounded the principal [aggressors] Denis Deilz and Wiltfranc, so severely that, since then, both went from life to death. He also wounded Pierquin, Jan Yver's servant, in one of his feet, so that he remained crippled.

Rutghers then fled the scene and sought immunity in a church outside Flanders, living in "great poverty and misery" while his wife and children suffered. His case for a pardon is built around his good-faith effort to negotiate compensation with Deilz, only to become the victim of an ambush that killed an innocent servant. His version raises some obvious questions about its description of the central attack, particularly how a wounded and outnumbered man managed to kill his two opponents and maim a third. But its tale of how an ambush ruined efforts at mediation was compelling enough to earn Rutghers the duke's clemency.

In this particular incident, the archives help to shed light on the actors, thanks to the surviving accounts of Bruges' bailiff. However small these tidbits of information, they remind readers that a pardon letter, whatever its factual basis, is both a stylized narrative and inevitably incomplete, framed according to its own narrative logic and legal strategy. The history revealed in the bailiff's records paints a more complicated, and troubling, portrait of Rutghers. In 1452, three years before his unfortunate quarrel with Denis Deilz, Jan Rutghers van onder de Linde had paid a sum of three pounds Parisian to resolve an unspecified conflict with Godevaert van den Kerkhove. Twelve years later, a Jan Rutghers—either the same man of the pardon letter or perhaps his son—once again had to pay, this time six pounds Parisian for—of all things—insulting his father. In 1460, a certain Jacob Breydel had to pay the bailiff six pounds Parisian in compensation for unspecified violent behavior, as well as giving a pledge of sixty pounds to Jan Rutghers van onder de Linde.[24] Rutghers's companion Jossequin Richart appears twice in the bailiff's records as a man of violent impulses. In 1456, he paid thirty-three pounds compensation for a murder he described as committed in self-defense, and sometime between 1475 and 1476, he shelled out eighty pounds for another murder.[25] Finally, the setting of the original quarrel between

---

24. Algemeen Rijksarchief, Brussels, Rekenkamers, 13776, fol. 25v, 13778, fol. 30r, and 13777, fol. 61r. We thank Guy Dupont for sharing these archival citations with us.

25. Algemeen Rijksarchief, Brussels, Rekenkamers, 13776, fol. 83r, and 13780, fol. 22v.

Rutghers, Jossequin Richart and Denis Deilz, the hostel Paon that Deilz ran, crops up in city records as a place frequented, as many hostels were, by prostitutes. It was located in Bruges' Noordzandstraat, and apparently functioned as both a bath house and a tavern. Its innkeeper paid fines in 1417, 1429, 1433, 1448, and 1451 for prostitution, which, while not officially legal in Bruges, was openly tolerated by city authorities eager to serve the city's male population of foreign and resident merchants and traders.[26]

These fines tell us two things: that Rutghers and his friend Jossequin Richart were quarrelsome, violent men and hardly innocent victims, and that the system of compensation for verbal and physical violence that ranged from insults to murder was apparently considered as routine business in cities like Bruges, where familial, guild, neighborhood, and work conflicts were part of life's daily fabric. What is more, in none of these incidents was a ducal pardon necessary because the compensation system stemmed, or at least managed, the violence. But the killing of Deilz and Wiltfranc required a pardon request because the victim, Deilz, refused the financial compensation offered twice by Rutghers.

How did a man of dubious background like Rutghers succeed in his pardon request? First of all, at the time of the pardon of 1455, Rutghers's other misdeeds, and most of his violent behavior had not yet happened, nor had the two murders by his companion Jossequin Richart. Before 1455 Rutghers had not much more than a fine for one unspecified conflict. We should also consider the potential of a good narrative to help win clemency. In their appeal, Rutghers and his associate admit they had fought with Deilz and injured him. Their defense was less their innocence than their good-faith effort to seek compensation for the victim, an effort that broke down because Deilz responded with violent revenge, violating the norms of the traditional reconciliation process by continuing a vendetta whose resolution was under adjudication. If Rutghers's life is viewed as a whole, we see a man guilty of frequent violent behavior, proof positive that the quarrels of 1455 were not standalone incidents, as the pardon narrative would have us believe. As often as not, such incidents were spikes in longer, murkier tales of factional and family disputes whose source might range from political alliances to neighborhood or work quarrels.[27]

---

26. Guy Dupont, *Maagdenverleidsters, hoeren en speculanten: Prostitutie in Brugge tijdens de Bourgondische periode (1385–1515)* (Bruges, 1996), 151, 224. The tavern was also fined four pounds Parisian in 1448 for selling beer for less than the set price. See Algemeen Rijksarchief, Brussels, Rekenkamers, 13775, fol. 50r.

27. A good analysis of the range of factionalism in late medieval Flanders, from political blocs to local quarrels, is Jonas Braekevelt, Frederik Buylaert, Jan Dumolyn, and Jelle Haemers, "Factiestrijd in laatmiddeleeuws Vlaanderen," *Tijdschrift voor Geschiedenis*, 123 (2010): 202–25.

Of the many sites where violence and feuds might flare, none surpassed the tavern, locus of male sociability. A typical case is what befell Philippot de Boneffe, a village inhabitant who supervised the manorial oven[28] in the ducal fief of Noville outside Namur.[29] His pardon narrates a mundane barroom brawl that spawned a conflict.[30] As de Boneffe recounts, he, his wife's stepfather Colart Willot, Willot's son, and a friend Jean Japotte were in a tavern sharing a pitcher of wine after work one day in 1449 when they spotted some men they knew:

> One of Philippot's companions, in jest and out of affection, and to drink some more, threw a cake of wax at the other men, saying that this was a piece of their salted meat so they could drink more. One of them named Girart Toppet was greatly furious and asked them why they mocked them, saying that they were scoundrels. The person who had thrown the cake of wax pleaded with him not to become angry because he had done this in jest, and he would be glad to please their wishes.

A fight broke out, and using a pewter jug Boneffe blocked a knife thrust at him by Toppet. The scuffle ended with neither side hurting the other, and Boneffe returned home. In Boneffe's account, he went to take water to his horse when Toppet and one of his brothers suddenly appeared, brandishing weapons. They attacked Boneffe, who had only a bread knife on him to defend himself, though he managed to land a fatal blow against Toppet.

Boneffe's feud unfolded in typical fashion: drink laced with insults led to fisticuffs and a fatal injury. Unlike many such conflicts, it proved impossible to resolve using traditional legal forms of mediation because Toppet's son refused to agree to a brokered resolution with financial compensation for his father's death. He instead opted for a full-blown feud, becoming "head" of a party opposing Boneffe and his friends—"party" in this case referring to family:

> Since this misadventure, the supplicants, especially Philippot, were very sorrowful about this case. As a defendant, he [Philippot] had offered to arrange amends with the party of the deceased, which was not

28. A manorial oven was one that was owned by the lord of an estate, and to which the tenants were required to bring their bread for baking. For his part, the lord was to maintain the oven (as well as the mill, etc.). For that maintenance he had a responsible tenant in charge of the maintenance of the oven; see François Olivier-Martin, *Histoire du droit français* (Paris, 1948), 152–54.

29. Noville-les-Bois, Belgium, province and arrondissement of Namur.

30. Pardon for Philippot de Boneffe and accomplices, from Noville (county of Namur), Bruges, October 1449. ADN, Lille, B, 1689, fol. 39 (Lancien, no. 459). Published in Petit-Dutaillis, 149–51.

accepted. On the contrary, the son of the deceased, who was the chief and head of the opposing party, went away from the city, and insisted on holding the supplicants longer in danger, which caused great grief, prejudice, and damage to them.

Since Boneffe and his friends were still in danger of prosecution and conviction for murder, and since the traditional means of reconciliation had failed, they sought a ducal pardon as another way to resolve their dilemma. Such an appeal was, however, risky. Boneffe had to admit that his party—unintentionally of course—had provoked the fight and what is worse, he had to admit to killing Toppet. Nonetheless, Boneffe presented a coherent tale of self-defense that earned him a pardon and the restoration of his own and his men's property. That he ran the manorial oven on ducal property might have also helped his case, as he could present himself as a loyal subject. In the end, it was more likely his tale of a vengeful and unreasonable opponent that got him, Colart, Colart's son, and Jean Japotte off the hook, pending the registration of their pardon and payment of the legal fees involved. Boneffe's case shows how the ducal pardon yet again could resolve a conflict when the proposal of a deal by the suspects was not accepted by the opposite party.

Protracted Conflicts

Scuffles and feuds often were efficiently resolved by aldermen seated as *paysierders*, but some turned into intractable conflicts that likewise needed a duke's intervention to halt—prolonged affairs that had no single moment of resolution, like the bitter quarrel in which the nobleman Jan van Gavere found himself embroiled. In July 1460, van Gavere received two simultaneous pardons from Duke Philip the Good: the first for a feud with his family's enemies that had begun with the murder of his father thirty one years earlier (letter no. 5), and the second for having abducted and then eloped with the woman now his wife twenty-one years earlier.

The van Gaveres were a prominent noble family, and Jan, who bore the formal name of Jan II van Gavere, was a minor scion of the Hérimez branch. When his father, Jan I, was murdered by enemies in 1429, Jan II was on pilgrimage in Jerusalem, as was customary for men of his status and wealth if time and circumstances allowed.[31] Not only did his absence at the time

---

31. Raoul De Liedekerke, *La maison de Gavre et de Liedekerke: Histoire de la ligne directe depuis l'origine jusqu'à nos jours*, vol. 2 (Bruges, 1969), chart 1; Stanislas Bormans, *Les fiefs du comté de Namur*, vol. 1 (Namur, 1875), 313. See also Félix-Victor Goethals, *Dictionnaire généalogique et héraldique des familles nobles du royaume de Belgique*, vol. 2 (Brussels, 1849), s.v. Gavre, xiv.

Drawing from *Chronique des comtes de Flandre*, Master of Mary of Burgundy (1477), of warring factions in Ghent in 1342. Holkham Estate Library, Ms. 659. © Holkham Estate.

of the initial attack absolve him of any role in the outbreak of the vendetta, his spiritual journey spoke to his knightly stature and his desire to envelop it with Christian devotion. What transpired afterwards cast him as a devoted son pursuing vengeance against his father's murder, yet a man reasonable enough to settle violence legally. His pardon request to the duke makes it clear, however, that the vendetta against Daniel van de Werde, Wouter van Bouchout, and their male associates, the men who had murdered his father, was serious business, leading to what the pardon request called a "big war and conflict" in which opposing sides ventured in public only with armed retinues, eager to settle scores and to come to blows. Daniel van de Werde, the leader of the opposing clan, was a prominent nobleman in Zeeland who was also active in Flanders.[32] A major escalation of the conflict occurred in 1438 when friends who where traveling with Jan II happened upon Heyne van Bouchout, son of one of the men who killed his father, and managed to pin him down and murder him. Jan II's pardon letter was careful to point out

32. Dirk van de Perre and Rik van Hauwe, "De geschiedenis van Denderwindeke, II: De middeleeuwse heren, ca. 1100–1487," *Het Land van Aalst* 44 (1992): 1–62. Daniel van de Werde (or van den Waarde) became lord of Wedergrate (in Flanders) and Meerbeke (in Brabant) by his marriage in 1426 to Maria, widow of Hoste V de Trazegnies, lord of Wedergrate. See Frederik Buylaert, *Repertorium van de Vlaamse adel, ca. 1350–ca. 1500*, Historische monografieën Vlaanderen, no. 1 (Ghent, 2011), 777.

that he was not one of the attackers; on the contrary, he had tried to come to Bouchout's help, although he arrived on the scene conveniently too late. For this attack, he and his men were banished from Flanders. Still, they took the initiative to arrange a peace settlement and pay compensation to their victim's kin. They were also lucky enough to receive a pardon, not from the duke, but instead from his sovereign bailiff of Flanders, Colart de Comines. The document was, however, lost during the Ghent war of the 1450s. Now gone, it could no longer serve as certain evidence that a pardon had been granted, and that might have been one of the reasons Jan II sought pardon from the duke. But his request may also have had to do with the fact that the original document had been granted by the sovereign bailiff and not by the duke himself. After 1448, the dukes of Burgundy disallowed any legal officer other than themselves from issuing pardons.[33] All good reasons to seek confirmation of legal remission of any crimes with which he had been directly or indirectly associated.

That van Gavere's motive in 1460 was to clean up old business with an official ducal pardon is underlined by his separate request for a ducal pardon for kidnapping and marrying his wife of twenty years.[34] Here again the networks among nobility were essential. In 1439, Jan II had arranged the abduction of Maria van Schoonvorst[35] when she was a young canoness in Mons after he had become infatuated with her but could not secure her father Konrad II van Schoonvorst's approval for a marriage. This was certainly because Jan II, though from the van Gavere clan, was not as prominent as van Schoonvorst, who was very active as a ducal councilor and chamberlain of the dukes of Brabant John IV and Philip of Saint-Pol.[36] As the pardon recounts:

> Fearing that messire Konrad would not be happy with this marriage, the supplicant convinced another demoiselle, named demoiselle of

---

33. Boone, "'Want remitteren is princelijck,'" 55. In his 1460 pardon request, Jan II also obliquely mentioned one other attack linked to the ongoing cycle of vengeance and vendetta, between one member of the Gavere clan and one member of the van de Werde clan. Someone named Roelquin, bastard of Gavere—probably a bastard son, cousin or nephew of Jan II—wounded Daniel Donckerberre in the face, but later settled with him. The accident reveals that the Gaveres suspected that peace treaties were never fully safe.

34. Pardon for Jan van Gavere, lord of Heetvelde (county of Hainault). Brussels, July 1460. ADN, Lille, B, 1690, fol. 9r (Lancien, no. 897). Published in Champion CNN, LXXXIX–XC.

35. Maria van Schoonvorst married Jan II van Gavere before 1435. When Maria's sister Margarethe died in 1458, she inherited the seigneuries of Elsloo and Diepenbeek; when Konrad II died in 1458 she inherited the seigneuries of Zétrud and Sint-Agatha-Rode, province of Brabant-Wallon: Florian Gläser, *Schönau-Schönforst: Eine Studie zur Geschichte des rheinisch-maasländischen Adels im Spätmittelalter* (Trier, 1999), 364–65. Maria died in 1473 or 1474.

36. André Uyttebrouck, *Le gouvernement du duché de Brabant au bas moyen âge, 1355–1430*, vol. 2 (Brussels, 1975), 180, 684; Gläser, *Schönau-Schönforst*, 360.

Wickrath, a legal aunt [of Maria],[37] and Renault, bastard of Schoonvorst, demoiselle Maria's uncle, to send a man called Regnier van Velkem, at that time a valet and servant of the demoiselle of Wickrath, to bring Maria before them at the court of Vrekkem in the parish of Denderwindeke in our county of Aalst,[38] where they would meet her. The valet did this.

From Vrekkem they brought her to Heetvelde, where the two were married before relatives: "Even though fifteen days later the marriage was consummated, the married [couple] went before messire Konrad, father of the demoiselle, and her other relatives, and did such that from then on they were very content with the marriage." Although they had finally secured the legal blessing of Maria's father, and had lived together as husband and wife for over twenty years, because their match was the result of a prearranged abduction, a pardon was necessary to clear up any chance of a legal challenge to their marriage.

The two van Gavere pardons point out how long vendettas could last and how an old crime—an elopement staged as an abduction—needed formal legal resolution even if an agreement was struck among the families shortly after it had occurred. They are proof positive that a pardon had legal validity only as long as the document itself survived; this is no longer a world in which oral agreements and oral testimony suffice. But they also put the shadow world of social and familial networks in the nobility within which our protagonists lived more firmly under the magnifying glass than our other vendetta cases. Van Gavere intersected, negotiated, and fought with two other prominent circles of families and their associates: the clan led by Daniel van de Werde and that led by Konrad van Schoonvorst. If van de Werde was the murderous enemy whose enmity spawned years of conflict, van Schoonvorst became a relative, but only through a forced abduction of his daughter when Jan II's request to marry Maria van Schoonvorst had been originally refused by her parents and kin. One additional set of key players threading through both letters are van Gavere's servants, men and women who, as the death of Jan Rutghers's valet proved, could pay dearly for their work on behalf of their employers. Jan II van Gavere's servants Pieter van den Abeele and Willem

---

37. The "demoiselle of Wickrath" was Mechthild van Schoonvorst, a sister of Konrad II, explaining why she was called in this pardon a legal aunt of Maria van Schoonvorst; she married Dietrich von Wickrath (Gläser, *Schönau-Schönforst*, 366–367, 409). Wickrath was an imperial fief of the Rhenish-Westphalian Circle, now a suburb of Mönchengladbach, Germany, Rheinland-Westfalen.

38. Vrekkem was the name of a family of the lower nobility, living in the Court of Vrekkem, a still extant small fortress located in Denderwindeke, now in Ninove, Belgium, province of East Flanders; see van de Perre and van Hauwe, "De geschiedenis van Denderwindeke," 51.

Vierendeel were involved in the abduction of Maria van Schoonvorst. Pieter van den Abeele was also involved in the vendetta against the van de Werde clan, as was another Vierendeel named Gillis. Neither kin nor friends of equal status, servants nonetheless were woven very tightly within the family fabric, exhibiting loyalties that matched those of blood even if their bond was sealed by wages and contracts. Finally, Jan II van Gavere's pardon for murder committed during his hotly pursued vendetta points out an element entirely lacking in the other cases: overt financial gain for the duke of Burgundy. Van Gavere was a nobleman with resources. Philip the Good's chancery officials knew this, and took advantage of Jan II's desire to replace the lost pardon and officialize a marriage compromised by a staged abduction long ago by charging him a much higher fee for his clemency: one hundred golden lions, the equivalent of nearly two year's wages for an unskilled worker, for the pardon of the vendetta murder. They did so brazenly, by forgoing the usual procedural language at the pardon's conclusion that required the verification and ratification of the letter. Instead, they simply required payment of the sum specified in exchange for affirming Jan II's narrative, and for renewing an original pardon that he had somehow lost. In essence, van Gavere bought his new pardon, guaranteeing that the normal procedures of careful scrutiny were waived. He also got the new pardon with a good story and, at the same time, received a second pardon to compensate for the illegal way he had se-cured his wife in marriage. In return, Philip the Good netted more money than was usual for a pardon, and gained yet another nobleman in his corner, a friend he could call on when politics required him to do so.

Ordinary Vendettas

The long vendetta and the need to substitute a ducal pardon for a lost pardon issued by an earlier bailiff that characterized Jan II van Gavere's case were not exclusive to his situation, nor were they closely associated with men of his social rank. The same features characterized the case of Parcheval van de Woestine, an ordinary inhabitant of Ypres in the mid fifteenth century, who found himself jailed in the ducal prison of the castellany of Ypres in 1458 for a crime committed forty years earlier when he was just sixteen years old.[39] The case involved a classic vendetta complicated by a lost pardon, several ju-risdictional layers, and reform legislation that the duke of Burgundy enacted

---

39. Pardon for Parcheval van de Woestine, from Ypres (county of Flanders). Lille, August 23, 1458. ADN, Lille, B, 1688, fol. 21 (Lancien, no. 793). Published in Petit-Dutaillis, 173–74.

in 1457 to better manage his financial officers and his political domains. No matter that four long decades had passed, the pardon request Woestine put together as he sat in custody at the age of fifty-six for the sins of his teenage years vividly recalls the quarrel's beginning. As Woestine puts it, he was still a boy when he got ensnared in a feud between two of his illegitimate brothers and Hellin and Mahieu Annesen and "their accomplices and allies." Like many other pardons concerning such disputes, what sparked this feud is unknown, though it was obviously a serious, tenacious affair that involved more than just the immediate siblings of each family. Woestine's involvement in the feud came after a near fatal attack against him by his brothers' rivals:

> The supplicant [Parcheval] was on a small horse which conveyed his late pregnant mother in a wagon that passed before the door and house of the late Jan Willays, uncle of Hellin and Mahieu Annesen. Hellin and Mahieu, accompanied by around twelve people, came outside this house when they saw the supplicant, who was a young boy and who had never done them harm or misspoke to them. They threw him down, doing what they could to kill him, which they would have done if by the grace of God he had not escaped from them. The supplicant's late mother was so startled with fear from this argument and conflict when she saw Hellin and Mahieu and their accomplices making efforts to kill the supplicant that in a few brief days afterwards she and the child with which she was pregnant very piteously both died. She left behind the late Roeland van de Woestine her husband, father of the supplicant, and seven little children and minors, of whom the supplicant was one, with little money and goods.

However incredible the link between the attack and his mother's death may sound, Woestine builds on it to elicit empathy before describing the murder to which he was party:

> A brief time afterwards [Woestine], who was very regretful about the piteous death of his late mother, tempted and instigated by the devil, and seduced by his youthfulness, simplicity, and the instigation of his bastard brothers and others, innocent and not knowing what he was doing, moved with them to the parish of Deulémont[40] in the seigneury of the religious abbess and abbey of the church of Messines.[41] There and in the presence and with the knowledge of the supplicant, the late

---

40. Deulémont, France, dépt. Nord, arr. Lille, cant. Quesnoy-sur-Deûle.
41. Messines (Mesen), Belgium, prov. West Flanders, arr. Ypres.

> Jan Willays, uncle of Mahieu and Hellin Annesen, was so beaten and
> wounded that he ended his life and died.

Woestine fled the scene to take asylum in a church in Ypres.

What transpired next was a several-layered process of attempts to resolve
the conflict legally. The lord of Merkem—a minor nobleman probably connected to Woestine's family through some sort of local clientage network—
helped to arrange a *zoen* between the two warring families, prompted by
Parcheval's "relatives and friends." At the same time, because Jan Willays's
murder had taken place in Deulémont, located within the seigneury of the
abbey of Messines, its religious authorities had the right to prosecute Woestine separately for murder. They chose not to do so, probably because the
two families had already arranged a settlement, and instead issued an "au-
thentic letter," that is, a legal recognition that a valid peace had been reached,
one that was now confirmed within their jurisdiction. Given that peace had
been made, why then did Woestine find himself in trouble forty years later,
arrested for a crime that had been resolved? Although, like Jan II van Gavere,
he had actually lost the old letter that confirmed the *zoen* his family had
negotiated, this cannot explain why he needed a new letter, for the loss was
not discovered until after he had already been arrested. Instead, Woestine was
caught in an administrative reform effort Philip the Good had implemented
the year before.[42] The duke had appointed six experts to improve the fiscal
management of his territories, with a particular eye to rooting out incompe-
tent and corrupt local officials. These appointees also held the right to clean
up local abuses and badly handled legal or political cases. That they took
their job seriously and had an eye for minutiae is evident in their decision to
apprehend Woestine for an old crime, but their intention is hardly clear, especially since this was a case that had been officially settled long before. Perhaps
old grievances lingered decades later, and someone in the Annesen clan had
the ear of one of the commissioners, or perhaps they thought the case poorly
or wrongly handled. A hint that the later might be case is the fact that the
bailiff of Ypres was one among a number of ducal bailiffs the commissioners in their investigations suspected of embezzling part of the fines they had
collected for the duke. In the end, however, Woestine got the ducal pardon
he sought, the duke's councilors overriding the decision of their own reform

---

42. For its commissioning, see the text in Jan van Rompaey, *Het grafelijk baljuwsambt in Vlaanderen
tijdens de Boergondische periode* (Brussels, 1967), 584–88. The Woestine case in referenced ibid., 465
n. 4. On this commission's atypically large scope, see also John Bartier, "Une crise de l'Etat bourguignon: La reformation de 1457," in *Hommage au Professeur Paul Bonenfant* (Brussels, 1965), 501–11.

commission. As for why, we are in the dark, as the answer never addressed this issue. Woestine told a very good story, one that exemplified the pardon request's tactic of self-defense and mitigating circumstances. He was an innocent boy long ago, attacked undeservedly for a quarrel between two of his illegitimate brothers and another family. He escaped an ambush only to lose his pregnant mother and spent the years that followed in poverty. While he helped his two brothers kill his principal attacker, he admitted to the wrongness of this, then affirmed that he settled the case twice, covering all his legal bases. It was a solid appeal, and what is more, at age fifty-six, what transpired was a very long time ago in a different world. Ducal forgiveness ultimately trumped the careful eye of his own reform commission as it painstakingly reviewed old cases and current abuses.

Work, Craft, and Professional Identities

In 1459 in the small Flemish city of Nieuwpoort, a heated quarrel broke out between rival innkeepers for which one of them, Vincent Zoetart, sought redress.[43] The pardon's specificity comes not from the nature of the violence it recounts but instead from the professional jealousies and rivalries it reveals that could divide small communities. The pardon tells a familiar story of insults flung, tempers flaring, and a violent reckoning to settle a falling-out between rival innkeepers. Its narrative is richer in direct quotes than most, perhaps to emphasize the particular sting of the invectives Zoetart suffered. In the hands of Zoetart, the story is one of an unhinged rival,

> a certain Gerard Rosin, also a hosteler living in this same town, who was married but repudiated his married wife. Separate from his spouse, he publicly maintained a hostel and home with Margareta van de Mote, also married, despite the fact that the aldermen and the city tribunal of Nieuwpoort had forbidden the two of them from dwelling, residing, living, and running a hostel together, which they ignored. Gerard developed a great hatred and envy toward the supplicant, as did Margareta too.

Both had contempt for Zoetart, perhaps because he was a successful competitor, perhaps because he was now an alderman, or perhaps because of earlier

---

43. Pardon for Vincent Zoetart, from Nieuwpoort (county of Flanders). Brussels, May 1459. ADN, Lille, B, 1689, fol. 20v (Lancien, no. 853). Published in Petit-Dutaillis, 181–84; and in Champion *CNN*, lxxxvi.

tensions. In his pardon request, Zoetart portrays himself as an upright citizen and good professional: "that since a very long time many good people and merchants visit and stay at the supplicant's hostel. It is with great effort that he earns his living, and he serves his guests the best and most diligently he can."

By Zoetart's own account, one evening around April 18, 1459, when his inn was bustling with guests, he had run out of white wine and went into town to buy some more. Advised by one Jacop de Bil that white wine was plentiful at the Saint George inn of his rivals Gerard Rosin and Margareta van de Mote, he headed there empty jug in hand, only to be greeted by their open vituperation. Everyone chimed in against him, first van de Mote, then Rosin, and then de Bil, who, as it turned out, was married to Rosin's illegitimate daughter. The words slung against him were nasty:

> She responded with malignant determination and disapprovingly that she would love it more if the jug would be in his stomach than that she should give him some and that he had come for no other reason than to lure away her guests. She replied, "I will tear the life out of your body, whatever that may cost me," shouting and screaming very hideously, "False traitor, false son of a whore, ruffian, I'll have you killed by the dirtiest rascal that I can find." Because of these impolite words the supplicant left the hostel and went somewhere else for the wine.

Rosin himself threateningly brandished a crossbow against him for trying to steal business. As with the case of Jan Spaen and his neighbor Jan van de Putte, Zoetart initiated a suit against Rosin and van de Mote for verbal violence and threats against him. But as the pardon letter indicates, it went nowhere. Zoetart described this frustrated attempt to seek compensation against his adversaries as prelude to his violent retaliation against them weeks later on May 12 when he was returning from the city of Thérouanne on business.[44] He encountered Jacop de Bil and Margareta van de Mote on a wagon, and, seized by hot anger, attacked them with a javelin. De Bil ducked the blow, getting struck on the shoulder, but van de Mote, Rosin's partner and mistress whom Zoetart had identified for her earlier invectives against him, was viciously attacked, her nose disfigured as a result. As Zoetart admitted in the pardon request, he had singled her out:

> Previously you had said I was a false son of a whore and a ruffian, that you would destroy my body, having me killed by the dirtiest villain you could find, or that you would burn me in my own hostel. And because

---

44. Thérouanne, France, dépt. Pas-de-Calais, arr. Saint-Omer.

of that it's time for you to be punished. He gave her a blow across her face, above her nose, with his knife so that from the blow the nose is damaged and deformed, because they waited too long to attach the flesh and sew it back.

While we don't know why Zoetart got a ducal pardon, the decision probably rested on the pardon letter's narrative of threats and harassment. Zoetart had cast himself as a good townsman, both an alderman and a diligent innkeeper. His adversaries were shadier sorts: a married man and woman living with one another rather than their spouses and with an illegitimate daughter, whether theirs or not is not specified. They were guilty of unprovoked verbal heckling and physical threats against which Zoetart tried to seek a resolution with the local court. Although it was actually Zoetart who resorted to real violence—and against a woman—and lost his temper, the pardon letter had introduced him as an honorable burgher before it recounted the attack on the road back from Thérouanne. Forced to be separated from his wife while in exile, cut off from his inn and any livelihood, Zoetart won the duke's clemency for the portrait of himself as a good man who had temporarily lost his cool under pressure.

For men like Zoetart and Rosin, and especially the many craftsmen and artisans of the vibrantly commercialized Low Countries, work and its affiliation equally shaped one's profile, cultural appetites, political commitments, and social niche. In fact, to judge from the records we have, the more general landscape of violent quarrels routinely centered on work and sociability, with craftsmen, artisans, traders, and merchants often the social types involved. These men inhabited the same social universe, and if in the same guild or profession, often the same organizations, be it a guild or a confraternity.

Work disputes ranged enormously, from minor fracas over prices, debts, and delivery of goods to murderous confrontations. They also covered a range of social types, from workaday artisans to more prominent merchants. In some instances, they shed light on people for whom the historical record is often murky, like itinerant artists. Our examination of the richly documented dispute that divided the actor Mathieu Cricke and the actress Maria van der Hoeven will be taken up later in chapter 4, but a simpler case in 1489 concerning the musician Jan Claeys still affords a glimpse in this often obscure world of the small-time performer (letter no. 3). That year, Claeys had a pardon request prepared after he killed a tambour player in a fight in Middelburg in Zeeland during a clash between the two. The fight itself is less interesting than the social context within which it occurred. For Claeys was a troubadour who sang and played the rebec, a stringed instrument that derived from the *rabāb*, a Spanish Moorish instrument. Originally from the French-speaking county of Hainault, Claeys had settled in the port city of Middelburg in Zeeland. On January 12, 1489, "the supplicant came with some jongleurs whom he brought into Middelburg, to play the rebec before them on the Dam in front of the Ter Platte hostel. At this place, several Spanish merchants were holding a big festival among themselves where there were several burghers and ladies from the city." The Spanish merchants in Middelburg had hired Gheerkin Jans, a tambour player from Nivelles, and his group, to entertain them. The setting is revealing, not only for its glimpse into the world of a midwinter festival with musicians and merchants, but also for its cosmopolitan setting: artists from Walloon Brabant and Hainault performing French-language songs like *Savoynne* for Spanish merchants and local guests, described as "honorable people . . . burghers and ladies," in a Dutch-speaking port city.

The winter cheer, however, took a turn for the worse when, according to the pardon letter, Claeys entered the Platte hostel, where one of the Spanish

Harbor and Dam in Middelburg, copper engraving from Mattheus Smallegange, *Nieuwe Cronijk van Zeeland* (Middelburg, 1696), p. 443. Copy in the Library of Ghent University, Acc. 002649. Courtesy of the University of Ghent.

merchants invited him to play a piece. When Claeys began to play, Gheerkin Jans mocked and then attacked him. Claeys recounts his incredulity at the assault, suffering verbal insults and shoving by Gheerkin and his two musician friends as he tried to maintain composure while he performed a song. Claeys gives no real explanation for the attack, except for a cryptic threat Claeys slung against Gheerkin, whose meaning is unclear, about how he had already "ruled out" three or four persons, and Gheerkin might be the fifth. Had Claeys previously insulted him, or had he upstaged Gheerkin, who turned jealous? Whatever the reason for the confrontation, Gheerkin challenged Claeys to fight him. Soon the two men, plus Gheerkin's two companions, were outside in a scuffle, with the Spaniards—or so Claeys recalled—trying to help him out, one of them suffering a wound in an attempt to stop the fight. Claeys was himself badly beaten and woozy, but after a short spell to regain his wits, he recovered. Armed with a dagger and inflamed with "hot anger," Claeys struck back, this time wounding Gheerkin. Gheerkin died shortly thereafter, and Claeys fled the territory for fear of arrest, with a pardon awarded in June of the same year. Both Gheerkin, the assailant, and Claeys, the defender, were in the same line of work, itinerant and local musicians hired to play at the same celebration for their social superiors. Jealousies and competitions over attention and perhaps wages led to their fight, played out in public on the Dam. As the defender, Claeys cast himself as the good musician, nimbly finishing his performance even as he was heckled and shoved by Gheerkin and his two associates.

Merchants higher on the social ladder than itinerant artists also crop up in the pardon letters for their work disputes, even though guilds and trading companies had their own methods and courts to resolve disputes. A particularly revealing case in 1492 concerns the Genoese merchant Francesco Spinola[45] in Antwerp who was in a dispute with Jacques du Puis, a merchant from the county of Nice, in the duchy of Savoy, over money and undelivered goods (letter no. 4).[46] Antwerp's international setting—the city was in transition to becoming the Low Countries' greatest merchant center—and its bustling realm of commerce provided the setting for the dispute that

---

45. In 1489 Francesco, son of Baldo Spinola, is mentioned as an international businessman together with his brother Teodoro Spinola: Giovanna Petti Balbi, *Negoziare fuori patria: Nazioni e genovesi in età medievale* (Bologna, 2005), 205.

46. ADN, Lille, B, 1707, fol. 43r-44v (Lancien, no. 1989). See also Stadsarchief Antwerpen, Privilegekamer, no. 3441, fol. 161r, 1492, the names recorded as Franciscus Spimule and Jacques de Funto, for the city's order of banishment. For their patient help tracking down this citation in Antwerp's archives, we thank Peter Stabel, Maarten van Dyck, Tim Bisschops, and Jeroen Puttevils.

left Jacques du Puis dead.[47] The case sheds light on the careful attention Antwerp's city fathers paid to business disputes and on the corrosive effect of debt between two merchants in dispute, but it also reveals yet again how the world of competitive international business spawned deadly conflicts. Guilty of killing Jacques du Puis at Antwerp's stock exchange, Spinola faced perpetual banishment by a court in Antwerp. Although a foreigner in Burgundian territory, he resorted to the ducal pardon to exonerate himself. Spinola apparently had business contacts at the Burgundian court, a probable sign that clientelism, however modest, might have had a role in his appeal to Archduke Maximilian.[48]

In Spinola's telling of events, the quarrel began as a routine legal dispute over a debt for forty-two crates of Greek wine that was owed to Juan de Saint Jean de Barondo, a Spanish business partner of Jacques du Puis.[49] Spinola paints Antwerp's officials in an unflattering light, portraying them as inconsistent. The aldermen first heard the case as part of their routine business and absolved Spinola of the money owed, but then reversed their decision. Spinola appealed the verdict before the Council of Brabant, the duchy's regional court, only to change his mind and pay the debt and the legal fees associated with it. But du Puis wanted a better settlement, including compensation for damages and interest, and initiated another suit for these, winning this new claim while Spinola happened to be out of town. Friends and business partners of Spinola protested the decision because the judges had failed to give Spinola fifteen days to contest the decision, which was all the more difficult because he was in the county of Holland handling yet another business dispute. Taking this new information into consideration, the aldermen decided to appoint arbitrators to negotiate an agreement between Spinola and du Puis, and the two men appeared twice before this specially appointed board. It was after their second appearance before the arbitrators that trouble broke out. Both men were at Antwerp's stock exchange amid a crowd of others that included one Alberto Spinola, also from Genoa and

47. For introductions to Antwerp, see Karel van Isacker and Raymond van Uytven, *Antwerp: Twelve Centuries of History and Culture* (Antwerp, 1986), and Inge Bertels, Bert De Munck, and Herman van Goethem, eds., *Antwerpen: Biografie van een stad* (Antwerp, 2010).

48. Giovanna Petti Balbi, *Mercanti e nationes nelle Fiandre: I Genovesi in età bassomedievale* (Pisa, 1996), 88.

49. Louis Gilliodts van Severen, *Inventaire des archives de la ville de Bruges*, vol. 6 (Bruges, 1876), 276, refers to a Spanish merchant Juan de Barando, captain on a ship sailing between Bruges and Bilbao in the Basque country; he may have been Basque or Castilian, because Bilbao was used by businessmen of both countries.

probably a relative of Franceso Spinola. According to the pardon letter, du Puis lambasted his opponent:

> Talking about their dispute there, the deceased Jacques said to the supplicant in front of Alberto Spinola—the only other one present— several injurious words, calling him in Italian "rubado, grosso, trayto" and "homo dapoche" which is in French, "ribald, ruffian, traitor, and bad man," and other such words in substance. The supplicant was so troubled and affected because of these words that in hot anger he pulled his dagger and struck Jacques du Puis in the chest with one blow, from which he died the following Thursday.

Spinola then fled Antwerp, had his goods confiscated by the aldermen, and prepared his pardon letter. Even after his pardon, Francesco Spinola probably never returned to Antwerp, cautious to avoid more trouble. In 1497, Francesco became a citizen in Naples, and early sixteenth-century sources indicate that, together with Battiste Lomellino, he was one the most active members of the colony of Genoese merchants in that city.[50]

Spinola's pardon is relevant both for the social context it highlights and for the nature of the dispute itself. Much like Jan Claeys's pardon, Spinola's affords us access to the daily life of the international merchants whose trading colonies and busy involvement within commercial life were the economic lifeblood of the Low Countries. Spanish merchants holding a festival in Middelburg, entertained with French-language ballads, and merchants from Italy, Spain and Nice, conducting business, quarreling, and using local courts to resolve business differences tell us much about the international character of these cities. At the more specific level, the feud between Spinola and du Puis, like the vendetta cases already sketched, shows how a dispute whose legal resolution was either frustrated or protracted could easily spawn open violence, and how the ducal pardon was a practical option once blood had been spilled and lives lost. As is often the case, it is not clear why a pardon was awarded, in this instance by the ducal administration of Archduke Maximilian. Apart from the small fees netted, the incentive was more likely a broader political interest in urban social peace and, on a narrower front, an attempt to defuse conflicts among valuable foreign traders when the normal mechanisms to address these—merchant courts and local aldermen—failed to work. The archduke overruled Antwerp's edict of banishment against

---

50. Giovanni Brancaccio, *Nazione genovese, consoli e colonia nella Napoli moderna* (Naples, 2001), 33 and 66.

Spinola, an action that was perhaps made easier by the Genoese's depiction of their unfair handling of his case.

Pardons, Political Allies, and Expressions of Burgundian Loyalty

Burgundian pardon letters reveal the dukes' double ambition: on the one hand, to restore social peace and cohesion in communities both big and small where they had broken down, and, on the other hand, to build up networks of loyalty by securing clients and allies—the pardon as a tool to bargain for loyalty.[51] In both instances, political considerations loomed large. Settling feuds and disputes, whether small quarrels or intractable vendettas, helped to stabilize the social order, and reminded petitioners and magistrates alike of the power of the duke and his pardon to resolve legal logjams and ensure civil tranquility. Helping important noblemen like Jan van Gavere was a more explicit political maneuver: acquiring allies to build networks of support. Such pardons had as their recipients petitioners both big and small—the elite like van Gavere but also ordinary citizens who had in one way or another demonstrated loyalty to the Burgundian dynasty and for whom a pardon was an expression of ducal gratitude as much as it was a calculation that allies in the often tense world of city and state relations came from many different social backgrounds.

The pardon story of Gilles Brayman, a native of Brussels, is a case in point. It might be short and unadorned, but it is deep in political resonance, a good example of how a seemingly minor fracas in a tavern encapsulates larger conflicts (letter no. 6). The case, recording events of 1466, seems fairly simple; Brayman and a friend were traveling from the city of Mons when they stopped to dine in a tavern in the Hainault village of Nimy. Drinking at a table nearby were Herman Steexkens and some friends from the territory of the imperial bishopric of Liège, and Brayman and his friend decided to

---

51. On this double function of pardons: Walter Prevenier, "The Two Faces of Pardon Jurisdiction in the Burgundian Netherlands: A Royal Road to Social Cohesion and an Effectual Instrument of Princely Clientelism," in *Power and Persuasion: Essays on the Art of State Building in Honour of W.P. Blockmans,* ed. Peter Hoppenbrouwers, Antheun Janse, and Robert Stein (Turnhout, 2010), 183–86. On clientage and clientelism as systems in the late Middle Ages: Willem P. Blockmans, "Patronage, Brokerage and Corruption as Symptoms of Incipient State Formation in the Burgundian-Habsburg Netherlands," in *Klientelsysteme im Europa der frühen Neuzeit,* ed. Antoni Mączak (Munich, 1988), 117–26; Gunnar Lind, "Great Friends and Small Friends: Clientelism and the Power Elite," in *Power Elites and State Building,* ed. Wolfgang Reinhard (Oxford, 1996), 123–47.

join them. All was fine until the bill came. A fight broke out, not over the tab but over doodling on the bill itself:

> After they had eaten and drunk together and their bill was tallied and paid, it happened that one from their company drew the sign of the cross of Saint Andrew on the spot where their bill had been signed, blotting out the symbol that had been on the bill. This made the aforesaid Herman unhappy, saying that he would want to take away the cross of Saint Andrew and replace it with that of Liège's Perron because he was Liégeois.

Saint Andrew was patron saint of the Burgundian dukes, and his symbol in the form of a saltire cross was closely associated with their military force and with their chivalric order of the Knights of the Golden Fleece; the heraldic device often complemented the flint-and-fire-steel badge that Philip the Good made his personal emblem.[52] Steexkens and his men were from the prince-bishopric of Liège, a principality not part of the Burgundian lands but in a heated conflict with their ruler, and the Perron with which Steexkens wanted to replace the cross was a public column in Liège that had long been a symbol of the city's independence.[53] In Brayman's account, Steexkens repeated this wish a second time, even though he had warned him that it was politically ill advised to want to flaunt a symbol that had taken on anti-Burgundian overtones. Steexkens ignored Brayman's advice, and instead provoked a fight over which drawing would prevail: the cross of Saint Andrew or the Perron. "For honor" Brayman decided to defend himself—and by extension, Burgundian political loyalty—outside the tavern. Once in open air, Steexkens pulled a knife and uttered several other contemptuous remarks, including that he didn't care where Brayman or his friend hailed from, be it Hainault or Brabant—both Burgundian territories. For his hot temper, Steexkens certainly paid the price, since Brayman stabbed him to death.

---

52. Charlotte Denoël, *Saint André: Culte et iconographie en France, Ve–XVe siècle* (Paris, 2004), 101–2; D'Arcy Jonathan D. Boulton, "The Order of the Golden Fleece and the Creation of Burgundian National Identity," in *The Ideology of Burgundy: The Promotion of National Consciousness, 1364–1565,* ed. D'Arcy Jonathan D. Boulton and Jan R. Veenstra (Leiden, 2006), 21–97.

53. The Perron is located at the place du Marché in Liège. The monument represents the freedoms of the city and of the principality of Liège. Charles the Bold of Burgundy had demolished the original Perron; Mary of Burgundy allowed it to be rebuilt. The present Perron, designed in 1697 by Jean Delcour, consists of an octagonal fountain with arcades in which a column, carried by four lions, supports the Three Graces who carry a pine cone. See Albert Dandoy, *Le Perron de Liège* (Liège, 1954); on its political importance: Jean-Louis Kupper, "Aux origines de la cité de Liège: Sur deux chartes inédites de 1171 et 1266," *Bulletin de la Commission royale d'histoire* 175 (2009): 331.

Although guilty of murder, Brayman got his pardon, on the surface of things because he had simply defended himself against an enraged opponent. But his pardon narrative obviously played to princely disdain for Liège, one of Philip the Good's and his son Charles the Bold's biggest headaches, while unambiguously touting Brayman's pro-ducal political sentiment. For the conflict between Philip the Good and the city of Liège in 1465 was no minor affair, nor an entirely new episode in town-state relations. Philip's father had wrestled with Liège's independence, and in 1408 after a conflict, John the Fearless had confiscated the city's Perron and installed it in Bruges as part war booty, part memorial of Liège's defeat.[54] While it was later returned, troubles intensified in midcentury, especially after Philip the Good installed his eighteen-year-old and obviously inexperienced nephew Louis de Bourbon as bishop in 1456 in an attempt to gain control over this important bishopric. A radical coalition of urban patricians and guildsmen forced Bourbon's exile, and eventually the conflict led to warfare. An important settlement was reached on December 22, 1465, when Liège and its allies signed the Treaty of Sint-Truiden, which called for the performance of an honorable amends before the duke, imposed financial reparations on Liège and its allied cities for its maneuvers against Burgundian authority, confirmed anew Bourbon as bishop, and put the city under ducal guardianship.[55] It was a tough peace, and it soon unraveled. By1467, a year after Brayman's pardon, warfare broke out again. Liège was not subdued until 1468 when, after two military campaigns, the new duke Charles the Bold destroyed much of its center in a spectacular punishment meant to set an example of the price of stubborn rebellion.

The fight between Brayman and Steexkens happened just four and a half months before the Peace of Sint-Truiden was imposed on Liège and before the new cycle of intense warfare began. Its storyline is something of a barometer of the intensity of the conflict between the dukes of Burgundy and the city of Liège, and a pointed illustration of the power of symbols to evoke deeply felt political and emotional attachments. Symbols like the cross of Saint Andrew and Liège's Perron might seem trivial, but like national flags, anthems, and other appurtenances of the modern nation-state, they were bearers of enormous meaning. They stood for specific bundles of personal and political identity in a premodern world suffused with the power

---

54. Richard Vaughan, *John the Fearless: The Growth of Burgundian Power* (London, 1966), 63–64.

55. For the treaty of Sint-Truiden, see Stanislas Bormans, *Recueil des ordonnances de la principauté de Liège* (Brussels, 1878), 590–601; Wim Blockmans and Walter Prevenier, *The Promised Lands: The Low Countries Under Burgundian Rule, 1369–1530* (Philadelphia, 1999), 179–81.

of cultural signifiers—badges, emblems, heraldic devices, flags, livery, and clothing more generally—to denote familial, personal, civic, group, and political affiliations, among others. In 1465, the cross of Saint Andrew bespoke ducal power and Burgundian military exploits while the Perron, always a representation of Liège's civic makeup, had come to signify its defiance and its opposition to Burgundian hegemony. No wonder Steexkens reacted as he did to Brayman's doodling on the bill, and no wonder too that he evoked the Perron as an image to blot out the cross of Saint Andrew. His stubborn allegiance to Liège's cause cost him his life, much as it would cost the city its independence and urban integrity as it lay in ruins after its destruction in 1468, the beloved Perron once against confiscated by the Burgundian state.

Brayman's pardon appeal touted a pro-Burgundian stance in a time of warfare, a winning strategy we find in two pardon letters that concern soldiers. Like other late medieval rulers, those of the Burgundian lands were constantly at war. Like other rulers, too, they had less a permanent standing army than an assemblage of different fighting forces upon which they could call, a heterogeneous mix of noblemen with their own companies (*bandes d'ordonnances*), city militias, and other conscripts. Since preparing for a military campaign meant the slow process of summoning these different groups, in 1471 Duke Charles the Bold issued a reform measure to begin to replace this patch-quilt, feudal system with a more easily assembled army of mostly mercenary forces. But his efforts to create a more stable military were never wholly complete. They only intensified a perennial problem Europeans of this era confronted: warfare conducted by soldiers who were poorly and irregularly paid, and who bullied, pillaged, stole, and raped during military occupations, campaigns, and—as the so-called laws of wars permitted—after sieges.[56]

In a pardon unusual for its collective petition on the part of an entire community, the small town of Hulst in 1485 earned forgiveness for allegiance to the Burgundian prince and opposition to soldierly misbehavior.[57] Hulst's pardon concerns citizens and a military garrison, with the citizens in this case the defenders of social order and the Burgundian state. Collective pardons are themselves unique, but so too is an appeal on behalf of the entire

---

56. Maurice H. Keen, *The Laws of War in the Late Middle Ages,* 2d ed. (London, 1993). For a rich case study of soldierly violence during Charles the Bold's reign, see Franck Viltart, "Exploitiez la guerre par tous les moyens! Pillages et violences dans les campagnes militaires de Charles le Téméraire, 1466–1476," *Revue du Nord* 91 (2009): 473–90.

57. Pardon for the citizens of the city of Hulst (county of Flanders). Ghent, July 1485. ADN, Lille, B, 1703, fol. 95r–96r (Lancien, no. 1727).

population, both the "male and female citizens" of the town, and the "male and female legal inhabitants" of the territory and "office" of Hulst, that is, those residing in both the town and the countryside around it.[58] As noted, diplomatic settlements after urban revolts often involved a treaty with a pardon part of the stipulations, and there are also several cases in the registers of the Audience of the Chamber of Accounts in Lille of individual rebels receiving pardons. But neither scenario matches that of an entire citizenry submitting a collective appeal for a remission, as Hulst did in 1485.[59]

The narrative submitted on behalf of Hulst's citizens and inhabitants is dramatic, a tale of a collective decision to rid themselves of the violent occupation of the English captain Robert Long. The political facts closely mirror Hulst's account of its travail. In 1484, Hulst had sided with the Burgundian Archduke Maximilian of Austria in his campaign against Ghent and other rebellious Flemish cities, even though it was a municipality in one of the castellanies of the Ghent Quarter, called the *Vier Ambachten* (Four Offices), located north of Ghent, a hinterland of smaller towns and territories politically subordinate to the great city.[60] Convinced that Maximilian would scale back urban legal rights, Ghent had led a coalition of Flemish cities against him after he assumed the regentship for Philip the Fair in 1482. To clamp down on Hulst's actions, Ghent had sent two different sets of garrisons in January 1485, but neither managed to subdue the town, despite their violent harassment of its citizens and despite the damage they caused to the area's peat industry by their territorial raids. On July 2, 1485, Ghent dispatched the English captain Robert Long to secure the town with some one hundred

---

58. Together with the city of Axel and the villages of Assenede and Bouchoute the Office of Hulst formed the Four Offices (*Vier Ambachten*), an administrative subdivision of the county of Flanders, and a union of jurisdictions constituting a castellany. See David Nicholas, *Medieval Flanders* (London, 1992), 82–83; Marie Karoline Elisabeth Gottschalk, *De Vier Ambachten en het Land van Saaftinge in de middeleeuwen* (Assen, 1984), 16–26.

59. Most diplomatic treaties to conclude a rebellion did not require the pardon to be separately recorded in the Audience's registers in the Chamber of Accounts of Lille. An exception is Charles the Bold's forgiveness of a rebellion against him during his inaugural entry into Ghent on June 29, 1467—a pardon that was later revoked. See ADN, Lille, B, 1693, fol. 7v. (Lancien, no. 998). On the revolt, see Peter Arnade, "Secular Charisma, Sacred Power: Rites of Rebellion in the Ghent Entry of 1467," *Handelingen der Maatschappij voor Geschiedenis en Oudheidkunde te Gent* 45 (1992): 69–94. Another example is Mary of Burgundy's pardon of Ghent's rebellion against her in 1477. See ADN, Lille, B, 1699, fol. 13, March 18, 1477, B, 1699, fol. 13 (Lancien, no. 1472). On this pardon, and on other collective remissions to the Ghent rebels: Jelle Haemers, *For the Common Good: State Power and Urban Revolts in the Reign of Mary of Burgundy (1477–1482)* (Turnhout, 2009), 234–35.

60. On this area, see Nico Bastien, "Tussen autonomie en centralisatie: De Vier Ambachten in het graafschap Vlaanderen," in *Over den Vier ambachten: 750 jaar keure, 500 jaar Graaf Jansdijk*, ed. A. M. J. De Kraker et al. (Kloosterzande, 1993), 531–44, esp. 543.

men.[61] Hulst's pardon recounts the brutality of these forces when they mustered on the central marketplace on July 2:

> Once there, the captain, first, and also his men, shot their crossbows and struck with their clubs at all the city's inhabitants and others, who had gathered with so many on the marketplace as well as on the place before the church and in the streets. They injured and wounded around 130 or more from the city, seven or eight of whom died days later and the rest who are still either languishing or in great danger of death.

This violence, however, failed to quench the garrison's aggression, and they headed to the bailiff's house to demand the keys to the town gates, intending to pillage the city. They threatened the bailiff's wife when they learned that her husband was temporarily in Ghent, then shot a bolt through an open window. Hulst's citizens took action, weary after three separate garrisons and their outrageous behavior:

> In order to have the greatest assistance and aid from all the inhabitants and the peasants, their neighbors and friends, they rang the city bell. Its ringing caused so many to come and assemble in such numbers and strength in the city that the captain and his men did not dare wait for them and stay on the marketplace. To be safer, they retreated to the town hall, which they held and reinforced.

Certain that the very fate of the town lay in their hands, leaders of Hulst's rally decided on a surprise attack with torches and pitch against the town hall, the very symbol of a late medieval city's political order and civic rights. Long, his concubine, and many of his men were consumed in the flames, and those soldiers who managed to stumble outside through the heat and smoke were cut down by the angry crowd of citizens outside.

In their collective action, Hulst's defenders had decimated the garrison Long had brought, and were guilty of a remarkable slaughter. To defend their actions, they resorted to the standard rhetoric of other townspeople who confronted violent military occupations. They had acted to defend their town, their wives, and their children, a common justification for violent reprisals against soldiers, as it would be a century later during the most violent years of the Spanish occupation of Dutch cities, when precisely the same image of the inviolable family was invoked to safeguard a city under

---

61. Peter J. Brand, "De stad Hulst in strijd tussen aartshertog Maximiliaan van Oostenrijk en de Vlaamse steden," *Jaarboek van de Oudheidkundige Kring De Vier Ambachten* (1962–63): 52–216, esp. 57–73.

siege.[62] The townspeople's decision to seek a legal pardon for their uprising against Long and his men, however, was entirely unique. It suggests that Hulst's authorities were concerned that their rebellion would provoke a serious punishment by Ghent. They also plainly worried that they could be prosecuted for collective murder, admitting in a highly novel plea that they had all—men and women—acted in *chaude colle*.

Hulst's archival sources shed considerable light on its town leaders' decision to exterminate Long and his men and seek an official pardon for their actions. The archives largely confirm the pardon's description of the collective decision of Hulst's leaders—aldermen, guildsmen, and civic militia most importantly—to go on the offensive. On the evening of July 2 and into the early morning hours of the next day, several burghers gathered in the house of one Jan Grobbe to plan their revenge following an earlier vote by a majority of its citizens and peasants from the nearby countryside to use arson as their weapon. In their planning efforts, they fortified themselves with eleven barrels of beer, and came armed with wood, pitch, and torches. Having rallied a huge number of inhabitants and residents of the outlying area, they carried out their attack. They were equally organized in their political actions after the fire. They sent two aldermen the next day to Ghent, where Archduke Maximilian of Austria was in residence, securing from him a promise to treat their actions as pure self-defense. Maximilian issued a charter in French furnished with his seal officializing the pardon, and Hulst's town secretary prepared a Dutch translation for those citizens who could not understand French.[63] The charter—and Maximilian's personal promise of it before the Hulst aldermen—was a stinging rebuke to Ghent, issued in the very city that had ordered Long to secure Hulst. But Hulst's actions were themselves extraordinary. While political rallies were common, exterminating a whole garrison by the ruse of trapping them in the town hall then setting fire to it, was not. Burning their own town hall came at quite a cost since it took Hulst' citizens forty years to rebuild it. But it was a clever tactic of revenge, as Long and his men had probably assumed that a town hall would never be attacked by the town's own citizens, for whom it stood as the political pulse and symbol of its urban life. Just as unusual was the decision of Hulst's citizens to admit collective "hot anger," and seek a legal pardon even while

---

62. Peter Arnade, *Beggars, Iconoclasts, and Civic Patriots: The Political Culture of the Dutch Revolt* (Ithaca, 2008), 212–59.

63. G. Stadermann, *Regestenlijst, bewerkt van de charters in het oud-archief der gemeente Hulst: 1199–1763*, (n.p., n.d., [1965]), no. 58; Gerardus Cornelis A. Juten, "Lijst van charters berustend in het stedelijk archief van Hulst," *Archief Zeeuws Genootschap* (1909): 59.

they simultaneously secured a legal charter of forgiveness: "These supplicants have committed and perpetrated the above stated things in hot anger, and in defending themselves, and also to avoid and prevent the total destruction of themselves, their women, children, and goods, and similarly to safeguard our city's very existence." As we have noted, registering a legal pardon to duplicate a political one was highly unusual, an indication that the city recognized its vulnerability at the hands of nearby Ghent, whose English captain and garrison Hulst's citizens had violently wiped out.

The ties that bound the dukes of Burgundy to important allies, such as their regional nobility, and the way in which mutual political interests colored the consideration of their legal misdeeds is perfectly illustrated by a trio of pardon letters concerning a nobleman from Zeeland, Clais van Reimerswaal, and his illegitimate adult son. The Reimerswaal family—father and son especially— were active in the political life of Zuid-Beveland, Yerseke, and the town of Reimerswaal from which they took their name in the late fifteenth century. Big fish in a small pond, they were guilty of haughty behavior and intemperate outbursts—frontier lords who were far enough away from the center of royal power to wield influence with a measure of independence. The fact that the Reimerswaal lords were not particularly prominent men, nor at the center of power in court cities such as Bruges, Brussels, or Mechelen, is noteworthy. It was exactly these aristocrats in provincial locations like the islands of Zeeland whose loyalty and help in the administration of Burgundian rule the dukes viewed as valuable.[64]

Clais van Reimerswaal first got in trouble in 1473 during the reign of Charles the Bold for what he thought would be a night of celebrating with drink and prostitutes (letter no. 7). Besides his local status and landholdings, he had some other holdings also in Flanders. He held several local offices, including that of bailiff of the town of Reimerswaal, and was married to Antoinette van der Zickelen, daughter of a patrician from Ghent.[65] On January 8, 1473, he had come to Middelburg in Zeeland as a member of the Estates of Zeeland and Holland, the region's parliamentary body, to discuss

---

64. For the position of the Reimerswaal lords within the nobility in Zeeland, see Arie van Steensel, *Edelen in Zeeland: Macht, rijkdom en status in een laatmiddeleeuwse samenleving* (Hilversum, 2010), 304–7; on Clais van Reimerswaal, also 199 and 334.

65. For a study of this case with social, prosopographical and political context, see Walter Prevenier, "De Zeeuwse adel in de ban van Bourgondië in 1473. Loyauteit als motief voor gratie na doodslag," in *Uit diverse bronnen gelicht: Opstellen aangeboden aan Hans Smit ter gelegenheid van zijn vijfenzestigste verjaardag,* eds. Eef Dijkhof en Michiel van Gent (The Hague, 2007), 265–276. On the Reimerswaal family and Clais van Reimerswaal, see Adriaan W. E. Dek, *De heren van Reimerswaal en het Zeeuws geslacht Blok* (The Hague, 1957), esp. 15–29.

the collection of an "aid"—that is, a one-time tax—that Duke Charles the Bold had requested a year earlier to defray his excessive military costs. Van Reimerswaal was therefore in town for political work on behalf of his prince:

> And soon after arriving in Middelburg, accompanied by his servants, he found his cousin the knight messire Jan van Heenvliet there, who asked him if he would like to join him for dinner with the lord of Veere, to discuss how to handle the murder perpetrated and committed against the person of the late Michiel van Heenvliet by the populace of our city of Zierikzee. He responded that he would gladly accompany him. In fact, they and many other noblemen and important men dined with the lord of Veere, who received them well and had an excellent meal with them. As a result it was late when they finished dinner and discussion of their business.

Michiel van Heenvliet had been one of two commissioners seized and murdered by a crowd of angry protestors in the town of Zierikzee when they had tried to collect the duke's unpopular tax, which had been levied on basic foodstuffs like beer, wine, salt, and flour.[66] It was a tense political environment, with popular agitation against the ducal tax pressing hard against noblemen like van Reimerswaal and van Heenvliet who had supported its collection. The violent uprising in Zierikzee had underscored the unpopularity of the ducal tax that the Estates had earlier agreed to and now had to reconsider.

While Zierikzee was duly punished, with ringleaders executed, tensions still were high.[67] Clais van Reimerswaal's trouble, however, had nothing to do with the political fallout of this unpopular tax. It was instead triggered by his hankering after a good time following the dinner at Heenvliet's residence, specifically by his desire to hire a prostitute for the evening. His pardon letter is unusually long as it lays out the circumstances, including a misunderstanding, that led to a surprise ambush by a group of other men at a brothel. For all its detail, however, van Reimerswaal's account fails to explain clearly why he was suddenly attacked, or the reasons for the assault, though some of the men involved are identifiable in other sources, and their affiliations and status suggest they may have belonged to rival elite networks. Noblemen might

---

66. The murder happened at the town hall of Zierikzee; an engraving of this building is in Mattheus Smallegange, *Nieuwe Cronijk van Zeeland* (Middelburg, 1696), 490.

67. Frans Westra, *Het oproer te Zierikzee, 20 november 1472*, Scriptie Middeleeuwen (Universiteit Groningen, 1979), 4; Jacobus Johannes Westendorp Boerma and Cornelis Albertus van Swigchem, *Zierikzee, vroeger en nu* (Bussum, 1972), 33–38.

stand together against rioters in towns like Zierikzee but rarely, if ever, did they band together as a united front, divided as they were by factionalism and jockeying for resources and political offices and favors.

If nothing else, van Reimerswaal's tale recounts the social privileges and personal conduct of the noble elites in the Burgundian Low Countries. He found it perfectly normal, after a day of political work, to dine with his peers, then pursue a prostitute for "some fun" at his hostel. Surprisingly, the woman is identified by name: Jehenne Rassens. She was so tired that she declined his proposition, sending him instead to the house of Grietkins Bier, where some servants of another nobleman in town, the lord of Ravenstein, were cavorting. The pardon letter gives us access to this realm of privileged male sociability, a world of political bargaining, noble cheer, the exchange of sex for money, and personal and familial connections to the Burgundian duke. Clais van Reimerswaal is characterized as "our beloved and loyal knight" in the pardon's prologue. The lord of Ravenstein, Adolf van Kleef, is likewise described as "our good cousin," on account of a family connection to Duke Charles the Bold both through his mother, a daughter of the duke's grandfather, and through his marriage in 1470, after the death of his first wife, to the duke's illegitimate sister Anna of Burgundy, herself a widow.[68] Of the two men, Ravenstein obviously had the closer relationship to the Burgundian court, not only because of these blood ties, but also because he held several senior appointments and offices, including knight of the Golden Fleece and a captaincy in the Burgundian army.[69]

It was Ravenstein's men, particularly Adriaan van Gavere and Heyne Peck, who, according to van Reimerswaal, provoked trouble when he arrived at the doorstep of Grietkins Bier's home. Eager for sex and fun, van Reimerswaal and a few servants asked to be led up to where Ravenstein's men were relaxing. Even though doors were closed, at first all went well, with van Gavere greeting van Reimerswaal with the salutation "cousin," here meant not as a tie of blood but as a badge of group solidarity and noble privilege. But amid a series of closed doors and dark passageways partially illuminated by candlelight, van Reimerswaal was attacked. Two men armed with a lance and sword appeared: "But the messire Clais, not thinking they meant harm and thinking they were joking, responded lightly, 'Companions, take your time!'

68. Hans Cools, *Mannen met macht: Edellieden en de moderne staat in de Bourgondisch-Habsburgse landen (1475–1530)* (Zutphen, 2001), 238–40.

69. Willem Blockmans, "Adolf von Kleve," *Lexikon des Mittelalters* 5 (Munich, 1991), 1214; Richard Vaughan, *Charles the Bold* (London, 1973), 240–41; Arie De Fouw, *Philips van Kleef* (Groningen-Batavia, 1937), 10–17; Haemers, *For the Common Good,* 105–9, 130–36.

To these words they began to shout 'Ravenstein!' Because he did not know if they knew him or not, messire Clais was not worried. He said, 'I'm also at Ravenstein's, like you. Be content.'"

Telling them to take their time was perhaps a reference to the prostitutes they had hired. Despite a few more exchange of jovial words, they attacked nonetheless, drawing blood, and cutting off half of van Reimerswaal's finger. Thinking himself already dead, he ordered his servants Aerne Spierinchk, Dankart Henriczone, and Josse de Palfrenier to counterattack. They did so, striking one Pierre Agit's head with a hammer, with van Reimerswaal himself delivering a fatal blow with a dagger to the dazed Agit as he fell. Guilty of murder, van Reimerswaal and his three servants fled the scene, and soon thereafter prepared their case for a pardon.

Besides van Reimerswaal and Ravenstein, the latter of whom was never personally at the hostel, the only other person in the conflict whose trace can be found elsewhere is Adriaan van Gavere. Although a "servant" of Ravenstein, he was of moneyed background, the son of the lord of Liedekerke, Colaerd van Gavere, a Flemish nobleman. More interestingly, four years after this incident in Middelburg he found himself in hot water after he tried to force a marriage with the widow of the senior Burgundian official Guy de Brimeu by abducting her, a case we shall later consider.[70] And yet van Gavere was the least aggressive of van Reimerswaal's adversaries in the Middelburg brothel, and his precise role in the ambush is hardly clear. What is certain is that we don't know why Ravenstein's men attacked Clais van Reimerswaal and his servants, despite the detail offered and despite the careful context the pardon letter sketches. This is no doubt strategic on van Reimerswaal's part, a desire to craft his story as a tale of reverse expectations—a night of fun and noble conviviality inexplicably morphed into a fight for his very life.

Politics, and especially proximity to Charles the Bold and his court, frames the entire story of van Reimerwaal's night of pleasure gone wrong. Politics, van Reimerswaal is quick to emphasize, was the reason he was in Middelburg, and political factionalism—his own in Zeeland and that of the lord of Ravenstein—is apparently what fractured an evening of male sociability with drink and women. But if rewards and personal ties are a measure of one's access to the Burgundian prince, then van Reimerswaal's tale makes no sense, because it was he, and not the better connected lord of Ravenstein,

---

70. Walter Prevenier, "Geforceerde huwelijken en politieke clans in de Nederlanden: De ontvoering van de weduwe van Guy van Humbercourt door Adriaan Vilain in 1477," in *Beleid en bestuur in de oude Nederlanden: Liber Amicorum Prof. Dr. M. Baelde*, ed. Hugo Soly and René Vermeir (Ghent, 1993), 299–307.

who carried the day. After all, as Jelle Haemers has noted, Ravenstein was the most prominent noble at the Burgundian court in 1477.[71] Given Ravenstein's prominence, van Reimerswaal had to magnify his own political fidelity to the Burgundian duke in the pardon request, taking the emphasis off the actual crime of murder. In this task, van Reimerswaal had real ground beneath him. Perhaps it was because of the social troubles arising out of the issue of the aid that the Estates had approved and were now reconsidering that van Reimerswaal netted his pardon for his violence against the servants of the lord of Ravenstein, even though this *grand seigneur* was Charles the Bold's cousin. The duke plainly needed van Reimerswaal's help, for he was part of a noble faction in Zeeland that was both more distant and more independent than the Ravenstein network. Van Reimerswaal had stumbled into a party of probably drunk and rowdy men, stupidly so, but not with violent intentions. He had been ambushed and wounded, and in response, he and his servants had killed one of Ravenstein's servants. The fact that it was not a nobleman like Adriaan van Gavere who died that night, nor a politically important individual, made the duke's decision all the easier. So too did the fact that this conflict was not, as it might first appear, a vendetta between two factions of noblemen, but instead a one-off drunken confrontation. To award a pardon to a man who had killed someone of minor status was an easy way of buying goodwill and loyalty from him. While no explicit reason is given for van Reimerswaal's pardon, surely it was his status as the duke's "beloved and loyal knight" that helped to influence the outcome. Van Reimerswaal's case for pardon was his claim to have been of service and shown loyalty to the duke of Burgundy. In the final analysis, it was this commitment to the Burgundian cause that made the pardon a smart bet on future loyalty.

Clais van Reimerswaal and his family would, it turns out, test the Burgundian court's newly sealed investment in them. For he turns up in two more pardon letters, with an illegitimate son also a supplicant in a separate incident.[72] This itself is an unusual legal footprint in the registers of the Audience in Lille's Chamber of Accounts, an indication of van Reimerswaal's arrogance and sense of entitlement. In one of the requests from 1481 that narrates a brawl at the bailiff's house in the small town of Arnemuiden, Reimerswaal made only a cameo appearance and was not himself the petitioner. But in August 1494 he found himself once again the protagonist of

---

71. Haemers, *For the Common Good,* 107.

72. See ADN, Lille, B, 1702, fol. 12 v–13 r (Lancien, no. 1583). This case concerns a drunken fight that involved a soldier.

a pardon narrative, this time having to do with an outburst over two different lawsuits against him for debts unpaid and for quarrelsome aggression.[73]
Although van Reimerswaal was no young man—his birthdate is unknown
though he died in 1503—he was full of bluster, and it is this personality
trait, more than the storyline itself, that makes the pardon letter of interest. The letter is not flattering to van Reimerswaal, even if it proclaims his
good intention. As he explains, he was at home with his wife at his castle
in Lodijk[74] when his privacy was disturbed by an impolite officer from the
Court of Holland, Marinus Janszoon, who came to his house:[75] "The supplicant seeing this, and with his blood rising, got up and went over to him
at the door, thrust his fist in his chest and got in front of his face and asked
him why he had appeared in his house. Marinus answered the supplicant
that he had received a warrant for him from lord Lodewijk van Schengen."[76]
Van Reimerswaal was incensed; the Court of Holland's jurisdiction did not
extend across the border to Zeeland: "The supplicant answered Marinus
that he did not owe anything more to Lord Lodewijk than from this current year, requesting Marinus to show him the warrant, which Marinus
willingly did. After the supplicant had seen the warrant, Marinus beseeched
him to return it, which the supplicant refused to do, but instead took the
same warrant, rolled it up, and put it in his breast pocket." The warrant was
"contrary to the truth," burdening van Reimerswaal, as he puts it, so that
he reluctantly opted to appear in person to settle the matter. But once at
the court in the Hague, his troubles were compounded. Not only did he
lose his suit, he was charged with a violation from an incident seven years
earlier in Lodijk when he had verbally badgered another court officer, Jacob
van Nyenlant, who had also come to issue a warrant.[77] While he was not
arrested on this second charge, he was fined for the van Schengen debt, and

---

73. ADN, Lille, B, 1708, fol. 47r–48r (Lancien, no. 2064).

74. Lodijk, The Netherlands, prov. Zeeland, Zuid-Beveland. Eighteenth-century print by Andries Schoemaker of the Reimerswaal castle in Lodijk: Jacob Pieter van den Broecke, *Middeleeuwse
kastelen van Zeeland* (Delft, 1978), 253; copper engraving of 1696: Mattheus Smallegange, *Nieuwe
Cronijk van Zeeland* (Middelburg, 1696), 737.

75. Marinus Janszoon was a messenger both of the Estates of Holland (1494) and the Council
of Holland; see Hendrik Kokken and Marjan Vrolijk, eds., *Bronnen voor de geschiedenis der dagvaarten
van de Staten en steden van Holland voor 1544,* vol. 4: *1477–1494* (The Hague, 2006), 1236, no. 956a.

76. Lodewijk van Schengen, knight from Zeeland; see van Steensel, *Edelen in Zeeland,* 37. He
had been convicted for physical violence in Goes in 1484; see Jan van Herwaarden, *Opgelegde bedevaarten: Een studie over de praktijk van opleggen van bedevaarten in de Nederlanden gedurende de late Middeleeuwen, ca 1300–ca 1550* (Assen, 1978), 387.

77. Jacob van Nyenlant was a messenger tasked with distributing official documents of the
Council of Holland; see Kokken and Vrolijk, *Bronnen,* 1071, no. 863b.

his goods declared confiscated. Given the seriousness of the matter, van Reimerswaal prepared his request for a pardon, and for a second time was awarded a favorable judgment.

The reasons for the success of van Reimerswaal's second pardon are obscure—perhaps Maximilian of Austria wanted to continue to curry favor with his Zeeland noblemen, and perhaps van Reimerswaal had a good case, having had to contend with two separate warrants from across the border in Holland. This said, the pardon shows an older van Reimerswaal in a different light from his portrait of himself as ally of Charles the Bold and victim of an unfair attack in the 1473 Middelburg letter. He is clearly more angry and hot-tempered in this second case, lashing out twice against warrants issued against him for a debt and in connection with an unknown earlier legal matter.

As an ironic coincidence, much of Clais van Reimerswaal's personality comes through in a pardon letter concerning his illegitimate son Adriaan van Reimerswaal, who as a "young nobleman" and bailiff in the small village of Bath[78] on the island of Zuid-Beveland got into hot water.[79] Just like his father, Adriaan had offended a ducal official sent there to issue a warrant against someone in the town. The general receiver of Zeeland, the lord of Kruiningen, had dispatched an officer named Coppin Lauwe to collect what must have been debt owed by Lauwerens Christoffels:

> Coppin Lauwe arrived early in the parish of our village of Bath with a large group of heavily armed men. They went to the door of Lauwerens Christoffels, and so rashly and hurriedly pounded on it that they broke the lock and some household objects. When the neighbors heard the commotion, they went over to the house of Lauwerens's brother and woke him, and they also woke the supplicant [Adriaan van Reimerswaal], in his capacity as bailiff and officer of this place. This supplicant never heard anything but good about Lauwerens. He knew nothing more than that he was a good, upright man, and that his wife was so pregnant that she would not have tried to do anything if she had not been so rudely pushed by these people, or by some of them, so that she sank lower to the ground.

In the pardon letter's histrionic recounting of the incident, Adriaan, like his father, portrayed himself as a victim of an aggressive ducal officer, an

---

78. Bath, The Netherlands, prov. Zeeland, Zuid-Beveland, municipality of Reimerswaal.

79. Pardon for Adriaan van Reimerswaal, bastard son of Clais van Reimerswaal. Brussels, January 1499. ADN, Lille, B, 1710, fols. 10r–11v. (Lancien, no. 2228).

impatient outsider with armed men who had invaded the space and privacy of a fellow citizen. He also emphasized his role as mediator. When Coppin Lauwe challenged van Reimerswaal's loyalty to the Burgundian administration given his attempt to stop him, van Reimerswaal proclaimed his fidelity to his prince: "Why should I oppose my lord? All my life I risked my life and property for him. Should he require my service I would still risk my life and goods for him." Van Reimerswaal also suggested that the matter was best mediated by the laws and customs of Zeeland. Further, in a suggestion that echoed his father's conviviality, he counseled everyone to lay down their arms and share a pitcher of wine together. But the mood only soured more: Lauwerens Christoffels failed to hold his tongue against Coppin Lauwe, who himself scoffed at van Reimerswaal's offer to resolve the situation in his role as bailiff. Frustrated, Lauwe left angry and empty-handed, so bitter about what happened that he apparently filed a brief against van Reimerswaal at the Court of Holland. Like his father, Adriaan van Reimerswaal won his pardon, explaining away his "harassment" of Coppin Lauwe as the effort of a small-town bailiff to amicably settle a confrontation that had almost turned violent.

The three van Reimerswaal pardons tell us much about regional noblemen, from their social world to their cultural tastes. They also capture these men's compound of political sentiments: a fierce pride in their regional authority, a kinship to other noblemen in their network, and a wariness of outsiders and competitors, especially officers who threatened their juridical or financial prerogatives. But despite the swagger and independence of these nobles, their loyalty to the Burgundian court was hardly in question, especially in these letters in which they were positioned as supplicants. Adriaan Reimerswaal put it succinctly when he proclaimed that all his life he had risked his life and property for his prince. If he was angry at a lower official, or if he jealously guarded his privileges as a nobleman in Zeeland, this didn't mean that he wasn't a faithful, obedient subject. Clearly, the van Reimerswaal men, both father and son, were full of male braggadocio and political self-importance, rich men of minor distinction. And clearly, too, they were troublesome, but not in any deeply threatening way to the Burgundian duke, who could afford to impart his grace to keep them loyal. After all, the nobles' pardon narratives make decent cases for self-defense and political honor, just as they nakedly show that the pardon process could—as we have seen in all the cases with a political cast—fall prey to the pressing demands of alliances and factions.

Pardons and the Social World

For miscreants ranging from self-important noblemen like Jan II van Gavere and Clais and Adriaan van Reimerswaal to ordinary men like Deinze's

Christiaen van der Naet, the pardon letter was a godsend. Although it sometimes cost money and required civil penalties to be paid, it saved these men's
necks, absolving them of capital crimes, ending their banishment, and restoring their confiscated goods. The pardon requests' narratives vary considerably in style and length, some more prolix than others, some enlivened with
direct quotes, others favoring sparse details and a sober storyline. But what
they share is the common denominator of a plea for clemency built around
claims of self-defense and allegations that unreasonable, intemperate adversaries pushed the protagonists to "hot anger." With the exception of Hulst's
collective plea, all are from individual supplicants, sometimes, however, jointly
with an accomplice, like Jan Rutghers, or servants, like those in Clais van
Reimerswaal's 1473 pardon. But no matter how individualized and subjective
the voice of the supplicant, the social and political domain of his larger world
is never far from the surface, nor the social trouble—disputes, political factionalism, neighborhood tensions, vendettas, and political woes—that often
clouded that world. The networks petitioners inhabit, and the social institutions and practices in which they participate, form the broader context of
the pardon letter. Whether in the city archives or in the richly documented
history of the Burgundian state and its cities, a pardon letter's narrative might
be fleshed out, sometimes only by dint of a small footprint, sometimes by the
ability to reconstruct the political or social context. In such cases, the self-
contained narrative of the pardon is pierced, and we are able to gain glimpses
into what usually is a messier, more complicated storyline. While we may
not be any closer to the truth—for that is lost in the incompleteness of the
past—we see the supplicants embedded in the ties and obligations, social,
familial, work, and among the strongest also political, that defined them as
social persons in the urban world of their daily lives.

THE PARDON LETTERS

Letter no. 1

Pardon for Christiaen van der Naet of Deinze (county of Flanders). Ghent,
June 1489. ADN, Lille, B, 1705, fols. 1 r–3r (Lancien, 1889).

Philip by the grace of God, archduke of Austria, duke of Burgundy, etc. Let
it be known to all those present and to come that we have received the humble
supplication of Christiaen van der Naet, charged with a wife and a child, stating
how this past January 12 in the afternoon the supplicant was sitting together with
his other neighbors in the city of Deinze[80] before the hostel and tavern of Saint

---

80. Deinze, Belgium, prov. East-Flanders, arr. Ghent.

George,[81] where they ate and drank daily because their houses had been burned and destroyed by this war.

It happened that the daughter of Rogier de Marscalc, who was lodged in the Saint George hostel, threw a chamber pot of urine, or other stinking and smelling water, out of a window of the hostel upon the company of the supplicant right in the middle of them, from the top down, in such a way that the supplicant was soaked from head to foot. Seeing what happened to him, his companions mocked him. And he, the supplicant, desirous of revenge and seeking a remedy, did what he had to do to seize the daughter in his hands. He gave her two or three blows on her back with the backside of a small ax that he had in his hand, without, however, hurting her in any way because he was not angry. And shortly thereafter he heard that her father was angry with her about what she had done and had also struck her, as the supplicant presumed. The supplicant regretted that he himself also had struck [the daughter] as described. He had told Rogier that he did not want to hit her any more because he, the supplicant, was well enough satisfied. He bade Rogier forgive him and not consider him poorly because he, the supplicant, had hit his daughter since everything had been done in jest. Rogier answered that he was quite content about the blow, and that he had wished that she would have received more blows from the supplicant than she got, because in the past she had also thrown urine or stinking water as she did on the supplicant. And finally the supplicant, who cared no more about the aforesaid matters, went to eat in the evening with his company in the Saint George tavern.

After dinner he went to sleep in the church in Deinze for protection against some enemies, who came daily there and around the church. In the morning of the next day, being January 13, the supplicant heard mass in Deinze's church,[82] and after that he went at the request of Jacob de Waghemakere who was living at a place and homestead that he had bought from him. He was very busy with this on January 13, the time that the service of vespers took place. Intending to hear the service of the vespers because it was a solemn religious day, the supplicant was coming along the Ghentstraat in Deinze when he met Rogier, who was angry and had a pike in his hand, and said to the supplicant: "Defend yourself, you hurt my daughter last night, don't you regret it?" making several stabbing gestures at the supplicant with his pike. When the supplicant saw this, he answered graciously and politely to Rogier: "Rogier my friend, what do you have against me? You already forgave me once for hitting your daughter and it pains me that I did it since I didn't realize I had hurt her." But Rogier did not pay attention to the decent answer from the supplicant. He intended to seize the dagger the supplicant had on him but the supplicant blocked the pike to prevent the blow Rogier had thrust at him. With hot anger, and to defend himself, the supplicant took his dagger and gave Rogier two blows, one in his left arm, and the other down into his left breast, breaking his pike into two pieces. Thereafter he

---

81. On the the Antonius Sanderus map of 1641, the Saint George hostel appears just next to the town hall in the middle of the marketplace; see Prevenier, *Geschiedenis van Deinze,* 1:447. This inn is documented in local sources as early as 1441: Jan Moerman, "Over oude Deinse herbergen," *Bijdragen tot de geschiedenis van Deinze* 64 (1997): 286–87.

82. This Romanesque Church of Our Lady, rebuilt after the fire of 1328, is located at the corner of the marketplace. Illustrations in Prevenier, *Geschiedenis van Deinze,* vol.1, 2 and 443–446.

went to hear vespers at Deinze's church. Rogier persisted in his bad design to go specifically after the supplicant, and for a good while continued to try to harm him. He would have continued even further if several people did not manage to make him return to take care of his injuries. Because of the wound or because of the poor attentiveness of the surgeon Rogier died within eight days.

Because of these facts, and although Rogier before his death had forgiven the supplicant, admitting that he had been the aggressor, the supplicant, fearing the rigor of justice, absented himself in neighboring territories. Some time thereafter, friends and relatives of the aforesaid dead man[83] made efforts to have him arrested by Deinze's bailiff so as to bring him to the court's criminal justice unless our grace and favor is imparted, which, recognizing that he otherwise is of good name and reputation, he very humbly beseeches. After new reflection on the said facts, having compassion for the supplicant, preferring grace over the rigors of justice, and by advice and counsel of members of our family and with great reason and to expedite the affairs of our lands of Flanders in this case, we forgive and dismiss, forgiving and dismissing the facts above declared, including all penalties and all corporal and criminal fines, as far as he has made mistakes and wrong steps against us and our justice in the cause above described.

Having returned him to his good fame and name and having not confiscated his goods, if he had any, we impose perpetual silence on our procurator general and all our other officers with satisfaction done among the parties so that it is done not only as a civil action. We order that the supplicant be held to a civil penalty to us, by settlement and penalty from our beloved and faithful president and men of our Council of Flanders, in the matter of the case and after the assessment of his goods. We request and order the men of our Council of Flanders to summon those who must be summoned, to proceed well and virtuously in the verification and registration of this, and the settlement and penalty of the civil judgment, as is required of them.

With this done and the civil penalty assessed, assigned, and paid into the hands of our receiver as is required of him, they shall tally the account on our behalf, requiring furthermore our president and men of our same Council, our bailiff of Ghent, of Deinze, and all other of our officers or their subordinate officials, and each insofar as it concerns them, that on the basis of this our present grace and pardon in manner described they will allow Christiaen van der Naet, supplicant, to take profit and use, completely, in peace and forever, without doing or allowing to do anything, now and in the future, against this [pardon]. If someone would arrest him or take his not yet confiscated goods, they should be immediately released, as we wish it to be. Intending that this be certain and perpetual, we have fastened the seal of our aforesaid Chamber of the Council of Flanders to hang here in the absence of our seal, preserving our rights in this as in other cases.

Given in our city of Ghent, in June in the year of our Lord 1489. Thus signed by my lord the Archduke in his Council, together with Philips van Kleef,[84] the lord of

---

83. On the mechanism of this network, see above and chapter 3.

84. Philips van Kleef (1456–1528), lord of Ravenstein, son of Adolf van Kleef, member of the advisory council for Archduke Philip the Fair in 1485 (Cools, *Mannen met macht*, 240–42).

Gruuthuuse,[85] van Rassegem,[86] the President of Flanders,[87] and others. [Signature:] J. de Beert.

Letter no. 2

Pardon for Jan Rutghers, from Bruges (county of Flanders). Bruges, April (6–30), 1455. ADN, Lille, B, 1689, fol. 18 (Lancien, no. 631); Petit-Dutaillis, 157–58.

Philip, duke of Burgundy, etc. Let it be known to all those present and to come that we have received the humble supplication of Jan Rutghers van onder de Linde a citizen living in this our city of Bruges and a poor man charged with a wife and children, stating that about four months ago a certain conflict broke out between Jossequin Richart and the supplicant, on the one side, and Denis Deilz, keeper of the Paon [hostel] in the city, on the other side. In this conflict, Denis was injured by the supplicant and Jossequin without any mutilation.

Although, since that moment, the supplicant, Jossequin, and Denis Deilz agreed to the settlement and the compromise of their conflict [made] by Jan van Nieuwenhove, burgomaster of our city, and by Jan de Bonne and Jan de Lenque, and although a certain meeting on this point has been organized during which the supplicant and Jossequin authorized the said burgomaster [and] Jan de Bonne to offer to Denis Deilz, by way of reparation for the beating, and as payment of the expenses of the physician, the sum of ten pounds groat, Flemish currency, Denis was not satisfied. Instead, he demanded a greater sum of money, which was impossible for the supplicant and Jossequin to pay.

However, quite soon afterwards, no longer than last February, Denis, out of his indecent intentions, was going into town. So too were the supplicant with his servant and one other person in his company, running errands and doing business, without any malice on their minds. Denis approached them, as the fourth man [of a group], together with several companions, namely, Jan van Straten named Wiltfranc, Pierquin, Jan Yver's servant, and another that he did not know. They were armed and carrying cudgels with unreasonable and premeditated intentions despite the peace that had been set and granted by the *deelmannen* of Bruges.[88] They ran to the supplicant

---

85. Lodewijk van Brugge, lord of Gruuthuuse (ca. 1427–1492), knight of the Golden Fleece (1461), chamberlain, stadtholder for Holland (1462), member of the two regency councils of Archduke Philip (1483–85 and 1488–89) (ibid., 180–82; Mario Damen, *De staat van dienst: De gewestelijke ambtenaren van Holland en Zeeland in de Bourgondische periode* (Hilversum, 2000), 464.

86. Adriaan II Vilain van Gent, lord of Rassegem, member of the two regency councils of archduke Philip (1483–85 and 1488–89), murdered in 1490 (Cools, *Mannen met macht*, 300).

87. Paul de Baenst (1442–1497), councillor and president of the Council of Flanders (highest court in the county of Flanders) from 1479 to 1497; see Alida J. M. Kerckhoffs-De Heij, *De grote raad en zijn functionarissen 1477–1531: Biografieën van raadsheren,* vol. 2 (Amsterdam, 1980), 12, 15; Frederik Buylaert, *Eeuwen van ambitie: De adel in laatmiddeleeuws Vlaanderen* (Brussels, 2010), 104–5.

88. The *deelmannen* were public officials. There were about ten of them in each of the six districts (*zestendelen*) of Bruges. The *deelman* was subordinate to the *hoofdman* of his district, mostly a member of the patrician elite. See Jacques Mertens, "Bestuursinstellingen van de stad Brugge," in *De gewestelijke en locale overheidsinstellingen in Vlaanderen tot 1795,* ed. Walter Prevenier and Bea Augustijn (Brussels, 1997), 325.

and his servant and assailed them, shouting and striking them. The supplicant pleaded and begged with Denis and offered again to give him a larger amends than previously had been offered, and asking if he would leave him in peace. Denis ignored [this plea], and Wiltfranc immediately threw the supplicant's servant, named Coppin van Hoorne, to the ground and cut his throat. They next came after the supplicant, who had his hand cut below his arm. After this, with his servant killed, and to escape the danger he was in, he started to defend himself the best he could, such that he wounded the principal [aggressors,] Denis Deilz and Wiltfranc, so severely that, since then, both went from life to death. He also wounded Pierqin, Jan Yver's servant, in one of his feet, so that he remained crippled.

Because of this conflict the supplicant, fearing the rigors of justice, has since then sought immunity and indemnity in a church where he still stays, and dares not to leave or engage in his business or earn a living for himself and his wife and children. He was forced to absent himself from our territory and county of Flanders, in great poverty and misery, and go to foreign borderlands, abandoning his wife and children, unless our grace is imparted to him. . . .

Given in our city of Bruges, April 1455, after Easter.

Letter no. 3

Pardon for Jan Claeys, from Hainault, inhabitant of Middelburg (county of Zeeland). Mechelen, June 1489. ADN, Lille, B, 1706, fol. 14v–15v (Lancien, no. 1886).

Maximilian, etc. and Philip, etc. Let it be known to all those present and to come that we have received the humble supplication of Jan Claeys, a rebec player, native of our territory of Hainault, a poor married man, living in our city of Middelburg, stating how this past Sunday January 12, between eight and nine in the evening, the supplicant came with some jongleurs whom he brought into Middelburg, to play the rebeque before them on the Dam in front of the Ter Platte hostel. At this place, several Spanish merchants were holding a big festival among themselves where there were several burghers and ladies from the city.[89]

And as soon as the supplicant had walked in the merchants made him play a piece called the *Savoynne*, which he did. While Jan was playing his piece the late Gheerkin Jans, native of our city of Nivelles[90] and a tambour player, approached him with two companions. They had all played that night at the festival, and all of them, even the late Gheerkin, started to make fun of the supplicant, insulting and vilifying him with words, calling him a rascal, a truant, a ribald, a ruffian, and urging him to leave the house if he was the son of a good mother.

---

89. Middelburg (The Netherlands, prov. Zeeland, Walcheren) was, indeed, in the fifteenth century a cosmopolitan and international business center; see Willem Sybrand Unger, "Middelburg als handelsstad (XIIIe tot XVIe eeuw)," *Archief Zeeuwsch Genootschap der Wetenschappen* (1935): 1–177. A seventeenth-century engraving of the Dam by Gaspard Bouttats can be found in Johannes Peeters, *Thooneel der steden ende sterckten van t' Vereenight Nederlandt* (Antwerp, 1674); copper engravings of harbor and Dam by J. Meertens in Mattheus Smallegange, *Nieuwe Cronijk van Zeeland* (Middelburg, 1696), 410, 429, and 443.

90. Nivelles, Belgium, prov. Walloon Brabant, arr. Nivelles.

The late Gheerkin, seeing that the supplicant did not move but kept patient and continued to pay attention only to his performance despite the insults he pronounced against him, bumped and knocked Jan with his shoulders to make him falter in his performance, injuring him and saying that he ruled out already three or four, and that the supplicant would be the fifth [meaning is not quite clear: perhaps he earlier tried to attack other musicians]. Having finished his performance, and confused from the insults and villainies the late Gheerkin had said in the presence of the honorable people who were at the festival, the supplicant called him to come outside.

Gheerkin did not say a word. But one of Gheerkin's companions suddenly pulled a dagger, which Gheerkin did as well. They struck at the supplicant, who covered himself with his jacket the best that he could. Upon seeing this, Gheerkin's other companion came over and threw the supplicant down to the ground, beating him with two grievous blows and wounds. The late Gheerkin was shouting to his other companions that they should strike forcefully and that he would pay for them. And while they were striking at the supplicant, they hit and wounded one of the Spaniards, who placed himself between them. Seeing this, the other merchants took the late Gheerkin and struck him with fist blows. Even though the supplicant was badly wounded, he jumped outside the house, and when he came out into the open air, his heart felt weak and faltering, which lasted a short time. In order to revive himself, he sat down on a bench near the house. As he sat there, the merchants threw the late Gheerkin outside. Immediately upon seeing him, and still heated and moved with hot anger, feeling the pain of the injuries, the supplicant ran after him and gave him two blows with a dagger he had. Doing this, they left and went away, he one way, the other the other way.

From these blows Gheerkin passed away the next day. Because of this case, fearing the rigors of justice, the supplicant absented himself from our city of Middelburg, and would not dare to return nor live there, but confined himself to keep absent and to live in foreign territories and countries, in great poverty and misery if our grace and mercy was not imparted to him . . .

Letter no. 4

Pardon for Francesco Spinola, from the duchy of Genoa. Mechelen, October 1492. ADN, Lille, B, 1707, fol. 43r–44v (Lancien, no. 1989).

Maximilian, etc and Philip, etc, let it be known to all those present and to come that we have received the humble supplication of Francesco Spinola, a young Italian man from Genoa,[91] stating how the supplicant had previously been in a suit before the aldermen of our city of Antwerp against the deceased Jacques du Puis, a native of the city of Nice,[92] as agent on behalf of Jean de Saint Jean de Barondo, concerning the remainder of forty-two crates of Greek wine for which the aforesaid deceased

---

91. Genoa, one of the Italian city-states; see Steven A. Epstein, *Genoa and the Genoese, 958–1528* (Chapel Hill, NC, 1996).

92. Nice, France, dépt. Alpes-Maritimes, chef-lieu de dépt; in the fifteenth century Nice was part of the duchy of Savoy.

had made a claim, and which the supplicant, in the first instance, was declared absolved. But on the pretext of certain privileges that the aforesaid [aldermen] in Antwerp claim to have to change sentences within a six-week period after they are pronounced, they issued a contrary sentence against the supplicant. In order to revise the sentence that was wrong, he appealed this before the chambers and officers of our Council of Brabant.

But since then, he accepted the sentence and paid Jacques the sum he was ordered to pay, including expenses. Although he was never condemned or required by the sentence to pay damages or interest to Jacques, Jacques since then initiated another suit against him before Antwerp's aldermen in order to vex him. He asked for compensation for damages with interest and also three crates of Greek wine. The proceedings occurred in the absence of this supplicant. He was sentenced to the damages, interest, and three crates of wine, on condition that if the supplicant returned within fifteen days to give an opposing argument he would be heard and entirely rehabilitated. It came to the attention of some of [the supplicant's] friends in Antwerp that neither he nor anyone around him was notified of this sentence before the period of fifteen days ended. They appeared before the aldermen, requesting the supplicant's complete rehabilitation given the fact that he was absent in our land of Holland on the day of the judgment and was still there, occupied with a lawsuit that he had pending before the officers and men of our Council there. The aforesaid [aldermen] from Antwerp had failed to consider this, due to the fact that Jacques was absent. When this Jacques returned to Antwerp the friends [of his] made him appear before the aldermen, insisting that the supplicant be entirely rehabilitated.

After this the aldermen ordered the friends to show the inability of the supplicant to come within fifteen days. During this time, these friends and Jacques must choose and agree upon arbitrators to reach a solution of their dispute, though the arbitrators could only reach an agreement when the supplicant returned from Holland to Antwerp. The deceased and the supplicant went before the aldermen of Antwerp and were heard. They charged the arbitrators they had chosen to conclude a settlement within the next eight days, during the present fair days, that is, by Tuesday the eleventh day of this past month of September.

Jacques and the supplicant, returning from their second appearance before the arbitrators, found themselves together in the company of Alberto Spinola, also a Genoese merchant, on Antwerp's stock exchange and marketplace. Talking about their dispute there, the deceased Jacques said to the supplicant in front of Alberto Spinola—the only other one present—several injurious words, calling him in Italian "rubado, grosso, trayto" and "homo dapoche" which is in French, "ribald, ruffian, traitor, and bad man," and other such words in substance. The supplicant was so troubled and affected because of these words that in hot anger he pulled his dagger and struck Jacques du Puis in the chest with one blow, from which he died the following Thursday.

Because of this case, which greatly upset the supplicant, he fled our city of Antwerp, and was since banished by the aldermen of this city, who made great efforts to proceed with the confiscation of his goods. Because of this he would not dare return nor cross our lands and territories unless our grace and mercy be imparted to him . . .

Given in our city of Mechelen in the month of October in the year 1492.

Letter no. 5

Pardon for Jan van Gavere, lord of Heetvelde (county of Hainault). Brussels, July 1460. ADN, Lille, B, 1690, fol. 8v (Lancien, no. 896). Petit-Dutaillis, 194–95; Champion *CNN,* lxxxix.

Philip, duke of Burgundy, etc. Let it be known to all those present and to come that we have received the humble supplication of our beloved and loyal knight messire Jan van Gavere, lord of Heetvelde,[93] stating that about thirty one years ago or thereabouts [ca. 1429], the father of this supplicant, Jan van Gavere, was beaten and wounded by a person named Daniel van de Werde, Wouter van Bouchout, and several other accomplices and adherents, and some time later from this wound, as is said, Jan van Gavere ended his life and died. At that time, the supplicant was on pilgrimage to the Church of the Holy Sepulcher in Jerusalem.[94] The supplicant returned from this voyage, and the quarrel stirred a great war and conflict between the supplicant, his relatives and friends, on one side, and on the other side Daniel, Wouter van Bouchout, and their friends. The war lasted a long time during which the supplicant had to be accompanied daily by several servants and armed valets who carried cudgels to maintain this war.

Twenty-seven years ago or thereabouts [ca. 1433], the supplicant was at dinner in a room on a high floor at the Court of Tassigny[95] in the parish of Galmaarden[96] in our land of Hainault. His servants Gillis and Clais Vierendeel and Gillis de Croman were on the ground floor and started a fight with Chrestien Serye and Loys David, who were both so wounded that they died. The supplicant had not consented to this nor was guilty of it. And for that reason he was allowed to travel and sojourn in all of our land of Hainault, with permission and notice of all the courts, without disturbance or obstacle. And since then a peace settlement has been concluded by both parties. With this, about twenty-two years ago or thereabouts [ca. 1438], the supplicant was in the city of Ninove in our county of Flanders, accompanied by Master Jan van Boerem, a surgeon, Pieter van den Abeele, and Gillis Vierendeel. Pieter van den Abeele and Gillis Vierendeel found Heyne van Bouchout there, son of the aforesaid Wouter, the one who had beaten and wounded the supplicant's father, as was recounted. At once, they threw Heyne down and wounded him so severely that he died. During the quarrel, when the supplicant heard about Heyne's name, he came to his aid there, but he did not arrive soon enough and found Heyne dead. With this done, they all left together as it pleased them.

---

93. Heetvelde, seigneurie in a hamlet of Gooik, the village of Oetingen, Belgium, prov. Vlaams-Brabant; the castle still exists; see Frans Doperé and William Ubregts, *De donjon in Vlaanderen. Architectuur en wooncultuur* (Brussel, 1991), 205–206.

94. On the social status of a pilgrimage to Jerusalem, see Jan van Herwaarden, *Between Saint James and Erasmus: Studies in Late-Medieval Religious Life: Devotions and Pilgrimages in the Netherlands* (Leiden, 2003), 36–80, esp. 45–48.

95. Tassigny is certainly the extant Hof te Tasseniers, a manor located in the Damstraat in Galmaarden; Jan Lindemans, "Het Hof te Tasseniers," *Eigen Schoon en de Brabander* 17 (1934): 401–426.

96. Galmaarden (Gammerages), Belgium, prov. Brabant, arr. Brussels, cant. Sint-Kwintens-Lennik, belonged to the county of Hainault in the fifteenth century.

For this case and crime the supplicant and perpetrators were banished from our land and county of Flanders, but have since received a pardon from the deceased messire Colart de Comines,[97] who was sovereign bailiff of Flanders when alive, with the exception of Master Jan van Boerem. In addition to this, they made a peace settlement. As a consequence, they have always traveled and lived since then in our land of Flanders with permission and notice of all the courts, without anyone requiring anything of them. But during the last war in Flanders, most of them lost their pardon letter. Because of this they fear that in the future they could encounter disturbances and obstacles. What is more, since this time a person named Roelquin, bastard of Gavere, wounded the face of Danel Donckerberre, and on this matter a peace settlement was concluded by both parties. Because of these cases, homicides, blows, and woundings—for none of which the supplicant was guilty—the supplicant had paid compensation to the injured party. Since some of them had previously obtained grace and pardons that were lost during the last war in Flanders, as was said, this supplicant fears that henceforth he and his servants and accomplices could be wounded and assaulted given also that they do not have any pardon and remission letters for the mentioned cases, unless our grace and mercy is imparted to them . . .

Given in our city of Brussels in the month of July, 1460.

Letter no. 6

Pardon for Gilles Brayman, from Brussels (duchy of Brabant). Brussels, October 1466. ADN, Lille, B, 1691, fol. 96r (Lancien, no. 926). Petit-Dutaillis, 35–36.

Philip, duke of Burgundy, etc. Let it be known to all those present and to come that we have received the humble supplication of Gilles Brayman called Kesteveke, son of Gilles, native of this our city of Brussels, stating that around Assumption Day [August 15] in the year 1465, the supplicant and one of his companions with him left, on a certain day, our city of Mons to go to Soignies,[98] and as they passed through a village under the authority of the collegiate church of Sainte-Waudru of Mons, named Nimy,[99] they went into a tavern where they found a companion from the territory of Liège, named Herman Steexkens, and certain other companions who were known to the supplicant sitting and drinking at a table, whose table the supplicant and his companion joined to eat with them. After they had eaten and drunk together and their bill was tallied and paid, it happened that one from their company drew the sign of the cross of Saint Andrew on the spot where their bill had been signed, blotting out the symbol that had been on the bill. This made the aforesaid Herman unhappy, saying that he would want to take away the cross of Saint Andrew and replace it with that of Liège's Perron because he was Liégeois. The supplicant responded that it was not advisable to use such language because if the other companions there who

---

97. Colart de le Clite, Colart de Commines, knight, lord of Renescure and Watten, sovereign bailiff of Flanders from 1454 to 1472, see van Rompaey, *Het grafelijk baljuwsambt*, 76–78, 224–25, 615; Damen, *De staat van dienst,* 453; Jelle Haemers, *De Gentse Opstand, 1449–1453: De strijd tussen rivaliserende netwerken om het stedelijke kapitaal* (Kortrijk-Heule, 2004), 135–36.

98. Soignies, Belgium, prov. Hainaut, arr. and cant. Soignies.

99. Nimy, Belgium, prov. Hainaut, arr. and cant. Mons.

were our subjects [the duke of Burgundy] had heard him, they would have rebutted and condemned the words he had said in such a manner that he would not have been able to support them. To which the deceased Herman replied, and said for the second time continuing in his folly and error, that he would not take that in account because he was Liégeois and for that reason he wanted Liège's Perron to be put there and in fact he said that it would be placed there. He said also several other things, saying, in contempt and disrespect for the supplicant and his companions, that he did not care about the greatest Brabanters and Hainuyers [people from Hainault] there, even if there were two of them, so long as he could hold onto his weapon. The supplicant responded that he was the only one sitting at the table, and that he would assault him provided it was just the two of them. Upon these words, before having said more, the deceased Herman rose from the table and went out in the street with his knife drawn.

Seeing this, the supplicant followed him out to the street to fight because, for the sake of honor, he could not refuse to fight in the quarrel, which to him was reasonable and well founded. And they fought in such a way that the supplicant was able to seize him [Herman Steexkens] by the neck and given him a dagger blow from which he went from life to death. Because of this case, the supplicant, fearing the rigors of justice, absented himself from our lands and territories . . .

Given in our city of Brussels, in the month of October, in the year 1466.

Letter no. 7

Pardon for Clais van Reimerswaal and his servants, from Lodijk in Zuid-Beveland (county of Zeeland). Nijmegen, August 1473. ADN, Lille, B, 1695, fol. 6r–v (Lancien, no. 1222).

Charles, duke of Burgundy, etc. Let it be known to all those present and to come that we have received the humble supplication of our beloved and loyal knight, Clais van Reimerswaal, and of Aerne Spurinchk, Danckaert Henriczone and Josse de Palfrenier, called Auterive, his servants, stating that by our order and decree the nobles of our land of Zeeland had been summoned some time ago to assemble in our city of Middelburg in Zeeland. They did so around January 8 of this last year to find the ways and means of imposing and collecting certain gifts and taxes from the inhabitants of Zeeland for our profit. For this session messire Clais van Reimerswaal had appeared in person. And soon after arriving in Middelburg, accompanied by his servants, he found his cousin the knight messire Jan van Heenvliet[100] there, who asked him if he would like to join him for dinner with the lord of Veere,[101] to discuss how to handle the murder perpetrated and committed against the person of the late

---

100. Jan van Heenvliet (d. 1500), married Margaret, son of an aunt of Clais van Reimerswaal, lord of Stavenisse, alderman of Brussels (1476–1480): Gerda Ros–de Korte, "De geschiedenis van het geslacht van Heenvliet," *De Nederlandse Leeuw* 89 (1972): 261, 278, 282.

101. Hendrik II van Borselen (ca. 1404–March 1474), lord of Veere, knight of the Golden Fleece (1445), commander of the Burgundian fleet, called "le plus riche et plus puissant de ces pays de Hollandes et Zellandes." See Jacques Paviot, *La politique navale des ducs de Bourgogne, 1384–1482* (Lille, 1995), 161–70; Adriaan W. E. Dek, *Genealogie der heren van Borselen* (Zaltbommel, 1979), 20–22; Damen, *De staat van dienst,* 447–48.

Michiel van Heenvliet[102] by the populace of our city of Zierikzee.[103] He responded that he would gladly accompany him. In fact, they and many other noblemen and important men dined with the lord of Veere, who received them well and had an excellent meal with them. As a result it was late when they finished dinner and discussion of their business.

Just as this messire Clais had left to return to his lodging he passed along a small street where young prostitutes were. He called one named Jehenne Rassens to his hostel and amorously asked her if she was not available for some enjoyment with him. She responded that she could not do anything then because it was too late and he should go to the hostel of one named Grietkins Bier, where there were some servants of our good cousin the lord of Ravenstein, and there he would find some beautiful girls. Hearing this, and because he was close to our aforesaid cousin and because he desired the company of the servants, he sent one of his servants ahead to open the door of the hostel and soon after he followed him. Having arrived there, he found the hostess in front of the house and asked her who were those men of our cousin the lord of Ravenstein in her hostel. She responded that they were Adriaan van Gavere, Heyne Peck, and others. Hearing this and wanting to go to see them, he asked the hostess if she would light a candle because he desired only to join their entertainment without doing anything bad. With the candle lit, the hostess told him where to find the door of their room. When he knocked there Heyne Peck asked who he was.

Messire Clais responded, "I am Reimerswaal." At the same time, Adriaan spoke and said, "Cousin Reimerswaal, are you there?" While this was going on in front of the door, and knowing also that they should open the door, Adriaan and Heyne spoke to others reposing in another room to ask their advice. Close to him there was another door but messire Clais was not across from it. All of a sudden, it opened and he saw two men, one with a lance and the other with a sword. They asked him what he wanted. He responded politely that he sought nothing but good. But nevertheless they told him to leave or otherwise they would make him leave. But messire Clais, not thinking they meant harm and thinking they were joking, responded lightly, "Companions, take your time!" To these words they began to shout "Ravenstein!" Because he did not know if they knew him or not, messire Clais was not worried. He said, "I'm also at Ravenstein's, like you. Be content." Suddenly, one of these companions made a great effort to strike messire Clais with a lance and punctured his vest. Had he not dodged the blow, his whole body would have been in danger. The other also struck messire Clais with his sword. Because he put out his hand to deflect the blow, half of one of his fingers was cut off. Seeing this, he suddenly ducked to the ground. Then his servants asked him who this was and whether he was hurt. He told them, "Yes, these scoundrels have killed me here, so wicked are they, kill them all." Messire Clais further said to the companions that they hurt him, and that he would revenge himself if they would do worse than they already had done.

Messire Clais and his servants started to follow the companions. They managed to get to the room where the companions Adriaan van Gavere and Heynke Peck

---

102. Michiel van Heenvliet, receiver for the Estates of Zeeland (1472), murdered while in office on November 20, 1472 (Ros–de Korte, "De geschiedenis," 261 and 281).

103. Zierikzee, The Netherlands, prov. Zeeland, Schouwen-Duiveland.

were. They opened the door where messire Clais had first been, asking if he could bring the companions to their mercy. He responded, excited and agitated, that he wanted no such thing and that before the night was over he would do as much harm to them as they had done to him. With these words, he said to his servants that they should find these companions, and he set about with his servants to do just that. In so doing, they found one of the companions named Pierquin or Pierre Agit who had insulted messire Clais; Heyne struck him with a hammer blow to the head. Messire Clais struck his body with a small dagger and he fell beaten to the ground. From these blows and strokes, he [the servant] died.

Because of this incident, which made messire Clais very unhappy, he [and his servants] dare not stay in our land and they were ordered to remain away unless our grace and mercy would be imparted, which they very humbly requested of us. Having considered these things, and preferring mercy to the rigor of justice, [we granted pardon] . . . to messire Clais van Reimerswaal and Aerne Spierinc, Dankart Henricz, and Josse de Palfrenier above named.

Given in our city of Nijmegen in the month of August, 1473.

CHAPTER 2

Violence, Honor, and Sexuality

Gillekin Dubois was a poor young man from the small Flemish city of Bailleul who worked as the servant of a family in Bruges. He found himself in trouble in the fall of 1506 after a night out in a tavern in search of drink, sex, and gaming. Accused of the death of a brothel keeper, he appealed for a pardon with a story about an outing gone terribly wrong (letter no. 8). In its ordinariness, his narrative tells us much about the setting of the events behind many pardon requests and about the social profile of the supplicant, featuring three elements found in countless other pardon narratives: a male petitioner, a social setting of alcohol and conviviality, and the combination of verbal and physical violence. Dubois recounts an assault against him that was both startling and sudden. He and a fellow servant had decided to spend their night off at a bath house to bathe, have a pint of beer, and "play games," a typical activity, the pardon letter recounts, of young men. The bath house happened to double, as was typical, as a brothel. In the Low Countries, just as in most European cities, prostitution was largely tolerated. But it was especially active in Bruges[1] because of the

---

1. Guy Dupont, *Maagdenverleidsters, hoeren en speculanten: Prostitutie in Brugge tijdens de Bourgondische periode, 1385–1515* (Bruges, 1997), 120–27. Good introductions to late medieval Bruges are: Andrew Brown, *Civic Ceremony and Religion in Medieval Bruges, c. 1300–1520* (Cambridge, UK, 2011) and James Murray, *Bruges, Cradle of Capitalism, 1280–1390* (Cambridge, UK, 2005). On bath houses

Scene in a medieval brothel. Woodcut in Willem Vorsterman, *Der Scaepherders kalengier* (Antwerp, ca. 1514). Copy in the Library of Ghent University, BHSL Res. 1076. Courtesy of the University of Ghent.

presence of so many clergymen, and because of the large number of foreign male residents who worked in the city's international commercial sector, away from home and families. Since Bruges had no separate red light district, many brothels were part of taverns, gaming houses, or bath houses where, as in the story of this pardon letter, men socialized, drank, gambled, and paid for sex: "Going together down the street they happened upon a priest they knew who was also considering going out for a drink, and he led them to the house owned by Myne Sgeests, where some prostitutes were residing." This recommendation by a clergyman is not surprising, as clerics were regular customers in late medieval brothels.[2] In many European countries clergymen, even

---

and prostitution and their spatial dimension, see Diane Wolfthal, *In and Out of the Marital Bed: Seeing Sex in the Renaissance* (New Haven, CT, 2010), 86–87, 121–23.

2. Evidence for England: Ruth Mazo Karras, *Common Women: Prostitution and Sexuality in Medieval England* (New York, 1996), 30, 76–81; in Dijon in the fifteenth century, 20 percent of the

bishops, were actually involved in the sex business as owners and managers of brothels, though several cities had statutes that prohibited their patronage of such venues.[3]

Both men drank for two hours and Gillekin's companion apparently also paid for a room, then left the scene with a woman, while Gillekin stayed for another drink. The brothel keeper, herself drunk, gained his confidence by pretending that she often frequented his hometown of Bailleul and convinced him to stay longer. Trouble ensued when she then charged what Dubois considered an excessive bill:

> He said to her that he wanted to pay his bill and leave, to which she replied that he had had two beers and one jug. Hearing this, the supplicant said, "Really, I had only one pint of beer and one jug, which amounts to the price of one white penny," and he gave it to her saying "see, here's your money." She wasn't, however, satisfied with taking the money that she put in her purse, and said to the supplicant that he owed still for the rental of the room that he had taken with the prostitute which she wanted to be paid.

Dubois reluctantly paid, but expressed outrage. Suddenly, he claimed, the brothel keeper and one of her "whores," in the ribald language of his pardon, lunged at him. His letter recounts the attack on him by unhinged women who stole his dagger from his waist belt, yanked at his hair, and threatened his life. Dubois struck the dagger-wielding prostitute with a blow of his fist, knocking the weapon to the ground. But suddenly, he reports, another prostitute joined the other two assailants, brandishing a knife: "They treated him so rudely with their blows and hair pulling that he yelled, "Whores, you are going to kill me here!" His life was for some time in great danger because one of the prostitutes had pulled a knife and he feared she would slit his throat." As Dubois tells the tale, he barely managed to escape with his life, leaving behind his dagger and his overcoat, both of which he returned the next day to retrieve. That proved no easy matter as the brothel keeper had left on pilgrimage to the chapel of Saint Godeleva in Gistel, a few miles

---

customers of brothels were clerics: Jacques Rossiaud, "Prostitution, jeunesse et société dans les villes du sud-est au XVe siècle," *Annales: Économies, Sociétés, Civilisations* 31 (1976): 305–6.

3. England: Karras, *Common Women*, 45; Florence: Richard C. Trexler, "La prostitution florentine au XVe siècle," *Annales: Économies, Sociétés, Civilisations* 36 (1981): 991; Lyon: Leah L. Otis, *Prostitution in Medieval Society: The History of an Urban Institution in Languedoc* (Chicago, 1985), 210. The most spectacular case is the episcopal city of Cambrai in the fifteenth century: Walter Prevenier, "La tolérance cléricale envers la prostitution et le concubinage dans les anciens Pays-Bas du 15e siècle," in *Liber Amicorum Monique van Melkebeek,* ed. Michiel Decaluwé, Véronique Lambert, and Dirk Heirbaut (Brussels, 2011), 59–85.

away, forcing him to appeal to Bruges' aldermen for the recovery of his personal belongings.[4] He had a solid case but for the fact that the brothel keeper whom he had struck fell ill and died shortly thereafter. To make matters worse, her pimp spread the news that it was the attack by Dubois that had fatally wounded her.[5] Fearing charges of homicide, Dubois fled Flanders.

Dubois won his case with a story of innocence and self-defense. What really transpired in the bath house is impossible to know since we are left only with Dubois' self-justifications. Straightforward in narrative, Dubois' pardon letter strategically deploys core cultural and gender assumptions to bolster his case. He admits to a night of drink and sex, permissible forms of male sociability and privilege, with taverns, brothels, and gaming houses the venue for such pursuits.[6] The mention of his hometown, Bailleul, may be an attempt to portray Dubois as a gullible small-town client overwhelmed by the lures of the cosmopolitan city. At the same time, Gillekin suggests that the women found in such places were compromised because they were sexually available, irrational, and prone to violence. They had wrongfully accused him, unfairly attacked him, and nearly killed him. By contrast, he had acted responsibly, paying even more than he owed, so that the brothel keeper would not have cause to complain further. He threw a few punches, he claims, only to deflect blows aimed against him, and then retreated until the next day to retrieve his personal belongings. The brothel keeper might feign an upright appearance, departing on pilgrimage like a good, pious citizen. But she was corrupt, and her death, Dubois intimates, was more likely the result of a prior illness—the reason for her pilgrimage to the chapel to pray for her recovery—rather than any wound caused by the blow of his fist.

The Spontaneity of Violence

Within the topographical complexity of the Burgundian Low Countries, rich in urban life but also a landscape punctuated with small villages and

---

4. On pilgrimages to Saint Godeleva at Gistel: Nicolas Huyghebaert, "Abbaye de Sainte-Godelieve à Ghistelles," *Monasticon Belge* 3 (1960): 239–269; Paul Declerck, ed., "De H. Godelieve en haar tijd," *Sacris Erudiri* 20 (1971): 1–343.

5. Dupont, *Maagdenverleidsters*, 121–22, is convinced that the assistance to the brothel keeper by the pimp and one of the prostitutes is a sign of the effective solidarity and consciousness of common interests in a brothel community.

6. On the network of gaming houses and their relationship to taverns and brothels in the Low Countries, see Katelijne Geerts, *De spelende mens in de Boergondische Nederlanden* (Bruges, 1987), 61–75; on the moral statements on these forms of recreation by writers, philosophers, and legal officials, ibid., 101–22.

pasturelands populated with farmers and urban laborers, estate-holding noblemen, and urban patricians and merchants, violence erupted across the social spectrum. In chapter 1, we explored feuds, disputes, and vendettas among extended families, party and political factions, and professional groups. But violence was also triggered by sudden, unplanned confrontations, and pardons were awarded to resolve them where there had been no prehistory of conflict or moments of pause or failure in efforts to broker a prior peace agreement. In many cases in chapter 1, the conflicting parties often knew each other, sometimes quite well. In some of the cases we explore here, confrontations occur suddenly, unexpectedly, and by coincidence between persons who have often never met before.[7]

There is no common denominator for unplanned violence, but several of our examples of it are linked to male recreational time and space. The combustible mix of men, their social spaces, and drink and sex frame many pardon narratives whose accounts hinge on the spontaneity of things gone wrong. The setting can be street theater, public gatherings, and festivals, but it is mostly brothels and taverns, where drink and celebration loosen tongues and social restraints, and quarreling men come to violent blows. Young men, described in medieval Latin sources as *adolesencia* and *juventus,* were often the protagonists. In the premodern era, the terms were understood to cover a fairly wide age range, including both teenagers and men in their early twenties. Generally speaking they were not yet heads of households, not yet masters of either their profession or a family.[8] Not fully formed morally or politically as men, nor permitted adult men's independence, they comprised a fluid social bloc whose members were understood to have a high capacity for violence and sexual misdeeds.

In some instances, the violence that flowed from the world of younger men is as dramatic as its causes are obscure, as, for example, what befell

---

7. Spierenburg also makes a distinction between impulsive and planned violence, and argues there is a crucial link between violence and honor: Pieter Spierenburg, *A History of Murder: Personal Violence in Europe from the Middle Ages to the Present* (Cambridge, UK, 2008), 6–7.

8. Ruth Mazo Karras, *From Boys to Men: Formations of Masculinity in Late Medieval Europe* (Philadelphia, 2003), esp. 12–17; Konrad Eisenbichler, ed., *The Premodern Teenager: Youth in Society 1150–1650* (Toronto, 2002). For pioneering work on youth as a critical liminal group, see Richard C. Trexler, "Ritual in Florence: Adolescence and Salvation in the Renaissance," in *The Pursuit of Holiness in Late Medieval and Renaissance Religion,* ed. Charles Trinkaus and Heiko A. Oberman (Leiden, 1974), 200–264; Barbara A. Hanawalt, *Growing up in Medieval London* (New York, 1993), 109–28 ("Life on the Threshold of Adolescence"), 199–222 ("On Becoming Sad and Wise"); Robert Muchembled, *A History of Violence: From the End of the Middle Ages to the Present* (Cambridge, UK, 2012), 17: "Young men between 20 and 29 . . . developed bachelor gangs . . . , based on competition to enhance their value in the eyes of the girls, . . . to extoll a manliness which made them exist in the eyes of others."

Lieven de Zomer in the city of Ghent around October 2, 1471 (letter no. 9). Like Dubois, de Zomer was a young man, self-described as "poor," who was critically injured in a fight that involved two young women: "Around the feast day of Saint Remy in the year 1471 between eight and nine of the evening, the supplicant went for frolic and fun with two young girls outside the city." The term *esbatre* that the pardon letter uses to describe his activity means "having a good time," but the word *ébat* refers more specifically to a "love game," one with sexual connotations.[9] Indeed, the fact that whatever happened took place outside Ghent's walls probably is because since 1350 Ghent's aldermen had ordered prostitutes to operate there.[10]

After their "joyful" encounter, de Zomer and the young women reentered Ghent. Upon their arrival at a place called the Twelve Rooms two men suddenly caught up to them. One, Joskin van Temse, abruptly demanded to know more about the women with de Zomer. When de Zomer replied that they were cheap prostitutes, and additionally, as the pardon letter enigmatically puts it, that he had spoken to a woman earlier about them, van Temse and his friend were upset, hectoring de Zomer further. Without explanation, they brutally attacked de Zomer: "the late Joskin inflicted three wounds on the supplicant, namely, one under his right arm, the other on his left arm, and the third on his head, so that six bones came out of it. . . . For a long time he was confined to his bed with his life in great peril, so injured and wounded that he never again could be the man he previously had been." Van Temse fared even worse, as de Zomer managed to fatally wound him in the skirmish. Given de Zomer's stricken state, and his terse account of a mysterious attack against him, he earned a pardon for homicide. It must have been the gravity of his wounds that convinced the duke, who, as a normal procedure in pardon cases, ordered his high bailiff of Ghent to verify the truth behind de Zomer's injuries.

Like Dubois' pardon concerning a night out at a brothel, de Zomer's setting involves young men, recreation, hired sex, and violence. Its fuller meaning is opaque, even more so than Dubois' narrative, since it is entirely unclear what provoked the fury of van Temse. The pardon letter itself gives no hint,

---

9. Froissart, *Chroniques. Livre 1. Le manuscrit d'Amiens*, vol. 5, ed. George T. Diller (Geneva, 1998), 145; Frédéric Godefroy, *Lexique de l'ancien français* (Paris, 1901), 188. Geerts, *De spelende mens,* 43, mentions a pardon letter from France of 1406, in which we learn that young people enjoyed unorganized leisure in "common places" ("au dehors de la ville en une place commune ou se jouent et esbatent communement les habitants") just outside the walls (as de Zomer did).

10. Mariann Naessens, "Seksuele delicten in het laat-middeleeuwse Gent," in *Violence, conciliation et répression,* ed. Aude Musin, Xavier Rousseaux, and Frédéric Vesentini (Louvain-la-Neuve, 2008), 164.

probably for reasons of either economy or legal strategy—the less said the better. Still the letter allows us room for some guesses. One thing seems certain: van Temse was upset that de Zomer was keeping company with the two young women. Perhaps de Zomer was their pimp and the fight was a competition between rivals looking to work with the same brothel keeper, who might be the mysterious woman mentioned in the pardon letter. It's even possible that van Temse may have been the lover of one of the women, or a family member, or a sympathetic neighbor charged to protect them, and thus was shocked and angered by de Zomer's behavior. De Zomer's letter is a reminder that pardon narratives often feature carefully doctored scripts that closely resemble the little white lies people tell their neighbors and friends

Pardons like those accorded to de Zomer and Dubois do not provide the exact social context of the vendetta narratives, but they do expose another feature of the place and time: how easily young men resorted to violence to address wrongs and how often the supposed wrongs involved rivalry over women. Young adults like Dubois and de Zomer figure prominently in Burgundian pardon letters; less common, though not absent, are teenagers, as we saw with the case of Parcheval van de Woestine in Ypres. A case from July 1493 in Cadzand,[11] for example, features another teenage boy, a fourteen-year-old schoolboy named Jan Melnairs, under the supervision and governance of trustees and guardians, who was attacked by a gang of boys in their schoolyard:[12]

> Someone who was there shouted in Dutch "Pull him Down!" which in French is "Tirez le Oultre." The children at the school, among others one named Willekin Janszoon Moer, age twelve or thirteen or thereabouts, ran over to the supplicant and threw him to the ground. In the pulling, scuffling, and pushing among them, the supplicant became so infuriated and enraged that in hot anger he took a small knife that he had and struck Willem Janszoon in his side; from this blow he went from life to death.

Older men were routinely guilty of violence, of course, but the stories that recount killing are more often embedded in social networks of work, kin, family, and neighborhood, the social relations themselves serving, in some sense, as the excuse for the violence or at least its cause. Younger men were

---

11. Cadzand, now The Netherlands, prov. Zeeland, Zeeuws-Vlaanderen; in the fifteenth century, county of Flanders, castellany of Bruges.

12. Pardon for Jan Jans Jacobsz Melnairs, Mechelen, July 1493. ADN, Lille, B, 1708, fols. 24v–25r (Lancien, no. 2021).

not free from such affiliations, but their tales seem more often to recount violence that erupts when social boundaries and social norms are weakened or completely in abeyance, often in a brothel or during a time of festival. As Natalie Davis has observed for early modern France, festive times and venues set the stage for many spontaneous eruptions of unplanned violence.[13]

One such example occurred during a charivari—a ritual in which young men were given festive license to badger newlyweds with often lewd and taunting songs and exclamations—at a wedding feast in the village of Baulay in Franche-Comté in 1437.[14] At a tavern with other revelers, the "poor journeyman" Vuillemin Grillot killed Jehan Loys, a man from the same village, who had violently threatened him, saying that Vuillemin was meddling too heavily in the charivari, and that the victims of the charivari should have had a chance to pay off the group ridiculing them—a gesture that was in fact commonplace at this ritual.[15] Typical too is the deadly confrontation Robin Bonenfant and his friends had when they went out for an evening to "have some fun" at the Cranenburg House in Bruges on the Sunday before Ash Wednesday in 1456.[16] They paused to watch some itinerant actors performing on the street, and one of Bonenfant's friends joined them in jest. That occasioned a scuffle between them; the actor shoved Bonenfant, Bonenfant shoved back, and the aggravated actor then pulled a dagger. In the ensuing fight, Bonenfant killed the actor, then fled to a local church for asylum.[17] In his pardon request, Bonenfant presents a straightforward case for self-defense, adding that he had tried after the confrontation to arrange compensation for the accidental killing. He also characterized the street actor who attacked him as a man of bad reputation, a foreigner from Brabant rumored to be a

---

13. Natalie Zemon Davis, *Fiction in the Archives: Pardon Tales and Their Tellers in Sixteenth-Century France* (Stanford, CA, 1987), 29; see also Claude Gauvard, *"De grace espécial": Crime, état et société en France à la fin du moyen âge,* vol. 2 (Paris, 1991), 504 on ritual space. In late medieval France, Gauvard found, men under third were 67.5 percent of the petitioners seeking pardons for crimes: ibid., 348.

14. On charivari: Joseph Guy and Natalie Z. Davis, "Le charivari entre l'historien et l'ethnologie," in *Le Charivari: Actes de la table ronde organisée à Paris, 25–27 avril 1977,* ed. Jacques Le Goff and Jean-Claude Schmitt (Paris, 1981), 391–96. Baulay: France, dépt. Haute-Saône, arr. Vesoul.

15. ADN, Lille, B, 1682, fol. 1r–v (Lancien, no. 184); pardon letter of April 1438 by Duke Philip the Good.

16. Pardon for Robin Bonenfant, from Bruges. The Hague, June 1456. ADN, Lille, B, 1686, fol. 72v (Lancien, no. 693); Petit-Dutaillis, 165–166; Champion *CNN,* lxxix. Cranenburg was the house at the corner of the Grote Markt of Bruges and the Sint-Amandstraat, where Maximilian of Austria was imprisoned during the Bruges revolt of 1488: Robert Wellens, "La révolte brugeoise de 1488," *Handelingen van het Genootschap Société d'Emulation te Bruges* 102 (1965): 5–52, esp. 26–27.

17. Jean-Loup Lemaître, "Asylum, Right of," in *Encyclopedia of the Middle Ages,* ed. André Vauchez, Barrie Dobson, and Michael Lapidge (Chicago, 2000), 126; Pierre Timbal, *Le droit d'asile* (Paris, 1939).

pimp. Bonenfant easily won his pardon. His letter cited his previous soldiering for the Burgundian duke, though because of his martial skills, Bonenfant was instructed to enlist in Philip the Good's planned crusade against the Turks—a much-ballyhooed event that never got off the ground.[18]

One case that exemplifies how small-town sociability and cheer, lubricated by alcohol, could quicken into violence happened in the hamlet of Guiesten in the village of Bondues, outside Lille, in August 1459.[19] A warm summer night of dancing and recreation turned confrontational when Willot Bouche recognized an older man, Alart Roussel. Sometime previously, Roussel's son had been beaten by Bouche's cousin Huchon le Maistre after being caught sneaking into Le Maistre's sister's bedroom one night. Since Le Maistre and Roussel were both at the dance, Bouche tried to steer the two men away from quarreling; for the sake of "honor," he asked his cousin Le Maistre to leave the party: "Huchon Le Maistre answered that he agreed with that suggestion, and indeed quickly left and went to dance at another party that was being held nearby." Le Maistre, Bouche, and some other friends then relaxed away from Roussel. But Alart Roussel and several associates weren't satisfied; they followed Le Maistre and Bouche, eager to settle an old score. Both sides drew weapons to defend themselves. A series of confrontations ensued during which Alart Roussel was fatally wounded. In social dynamic, the case is unremarkable, turning into a typical vendetta. But its setting is one of late evening dancing in a festive context, where drink and celebration commingle younger and older men. Bouche strained in his letter to present his party's behavior in a positive light. He also noted that his accomplices had already secured pardons at the processional entry of the furtive duke Charles the Bold into the small town of Wervik in 1460, where the ritual forgiveness of prisoners was part of the customary celebrations.

The Obligations of Honor

If younger men often figured prominently in incidents of spontaneous violence, another characteristic of such cases is how they were powerfully associated with concepts of honor. We have seen honor codes at work already

---

18. Philip the Good's ambitious crusade against the Ottomans was the inspiration for his great Feast of the Pheasant banquet in February 1454, during which vows were taken to go on the crusade. See Richard Vaughan, *Philip the Good: The Apogee of Burgundy* (London, 1970), 358–72; Agathe Lafortune-Martel, *Fête noble en Bourgogne au XVe siècle: Le banquet du Faisan (1454)* (Montreal, 1984); Marie-Thérèse Caron, *Les vœux du faisan, noblesse en fe^te, esprit de croisade* (Turnhout, 2003).

19. Pardon for Willot Bouche, from the castellany of Lille (county of Flanders). Brussels, September 6, 1460. ADN, Lille, B, 1690, fol. 12r–v (Lancien, no. 899); Petit-Dutaillis, 196–98; Champion *CNN*, xciii–xciv. Guiesten: a hamlet of Bondues, France, dépt. Nord, arr. Lille, cant. Tourcoing.

in chapter 1, especially with Christiaen van der Naet in Deinze, shamed by the contents of a chamber pot that landed on his head, and Gilles Brayman, compelled to defend Burgundian honor against his adversary from Liège who had insulted the ducal cross of Saint Andrew. Honor and honor codes reverberated powerfully in late medieval society. The notion of male honor shapes and informs many of the cases in this chapter and we consider how honor bound men in scripted ways and how it served also as a rhetorical device to invoke strategically in emergencies. Honor's compelling nature as a social value was repeatedly proclaimed by late medieval and early modern authors, who knew enough about its potency to covet its possession while admitting its complexity. The Florentine humanist Leon Battista Alberti famously argued that "life without honor was a living death."[20] Shakespeare knew honor's social importance but also its intractable demands. As Mark Antony tells Octavia in *Antony and Cleopatra,* "if I lose my honor, I lose myself." But Falstaff in *Henry IV, Part 1* isn't so certain of honor's social purchase; as he readies himself for the battle of Shrewsbury, Falstaff ponders:

> Can honor set to a leg? No. Or an arm? No. Or take away the grief of a wound? No. Honor hath no skill in surgery, then? No. What is honor? A word. What is in that word honor? What is that honor? Air. A trim reckoning! Who hath it? He that died o' Wednesday. Doth he feel it? No. Doth he hear it? No. 'Tis insensible, then? Yea, to the dead. But will it not live with the living? No. Why? Detraction will not suffer it. Therefore I'll none of it. Honor is a mere scutcheon. And so ends my catechism.[21]

Shakespeare's Antony and Falstaff capture both the insubstantiality of honor and its concrete power. Although nothing but the result of how one is seen and judged by the public to whom one addresses oneself, honor secures self-worth and guarantees social place; to lose it is a psychological and social demotion, or worse, a social death. It thus has to be constantly performed, sustained, and nurtured; and it has to be vigorously defended against the slightest threat. It is both a reason to kill and a reason to die. A mere turn of phrase or an insulting gesture, a disparaging look, even no look at all if an acknowledgment of one's presence is expected, any such small slight can oblige retaliation, compelling a man to take risks that may end in physical injury,

---

20. Quoted in James R. Farr, "Honor, Law, and Custom in the Renaissance," in *Blackwell Companion to the Renaissance,* ed. Guido Ruggiero (Oxford, 2002), 126.

21. *Antony and Cleopatra,* 3.4.23–24; *1 Henry IV,* 5.1.131–42.

even death, loss of property, imprisonment, harm to family and friends. So deeply felt and socially girded is honor that it has been a favorite topic of cultural anthropology. Scholars have studied honor as a universal concept, diverse in its particular configuration, but always firmly lodged in the social realm.[22] For some anthropologists, honor in the public realm is a male attribute, with sexual control over women its principal element. Pierre Bourdieu and others have expanded honor's social wellspring, arguing that the larger world of male sociability, of professional competence in craft or office, of creditworthiness and debt relations are equally important. Historians also study the diverse expressions honor can take, how its particular meaning is dependent upon any given society's and era's social makeup, be it in the urban world of Golden Age Spain or the rural world of the nineteenth-century American south.[23] Honor's social application is wide-ranging, including the important arena of work. Our cases, however, confirm honor's heaviest footprint in disputes centered on male sexual worth and status, as a term invoked to justify revenge or self-defense after an episode of male humiliation. The cases studied here show that despite Falstaff's skepticism about honor's value, in late medieval and early modern times it repeatedly compelled men to act to retaliate against slights to their persons, resorting to violence that could consume them or their families. In this chapter's cases, just like those studied in chapter 1, a petitioner's appeal to self-defense is always his main argument, tightly joined to conceptions of honor.

Honor, Work, and Male Self Worth

Honor might be seen as an individual attribute, but it was also woven into professional identities, especially in the bustling world of late medieval artisans and workers. Honor figured in work disputes that guild deans adjudicated, and all rank-and-file guild members were required, in the language of a 1426 ordinance in Ghent, to refrain from saying "ungracious

---

22. Jean G. Péristiany, ed., *Honour and Shame: The Values of a Mediterranean Society* (London, 1965). See also Pierre Bourdieu's celebrated model of social honor in Pierre Bourdieu, "From the 'Rules' of Honour to the Sense of Honour," in Pierre Bourdieu, *Outline of a Theory of Practice,* trans. Richard Nice (Cambridge, 1977), 10–15.

23. Scott K. Taylor, *Honor and Violence in Golden Age Spain* (New Haven, CT, 2008); Richard G. Nisbett and Dov Cohen, *Culture of Honor: The Psychology of Violence in the South* (Boulder, CO, 1996). For a review of this literature in relationship to the Burgundian Netherlands, see Walter Prevenier, "The Notions of Honor and Adultery in the Fifteenth-Century Burgundian Netherlands," in *Comparative Perspectives on History and Historians: Essays in Memory of Bryce Lyon,* ed. David Nicholas, Bernard S. Bachrach, and Jim Murray (Kalamazoo, MI, 2012), 259–78.

words" about guild regulations for "[the honor of] the whole community of deans."[24] In 1457, for example, Jacob de Paermentier was banished by Bruges' aldermen for publicly insulting the city's guild deans while in a public marketplace, though he later received a pardon for his misdeed from the duke of Burgundy.[25] For the sake of professional honor, guild deans also closely regulated the ranks of membership, passing judgments against concubines and illegitimate sons of guildsmen. In 1402, the dean of Ghent's fruit sellers forbade a young woman from bringing fruit to the marketplace to sell because she cohabited with a guildsman. In 1450, the city's dean of the grocers opposed Beatrice de Wilde's membership, even though she was the daughter of a grocer, because she cohabited with another man against the wishes of her family. She was allowed to matriculate only after agreeing to marry her lover.[26] The concern of guild deans over honor predicated professional integrity upon patriarchal authority and upright behavior. The guild ethos valued reliability, the notion that a product's goodness required that it be an honest piece of work, offered at a fair price by blameless and morally upright professionals. Their worries about concubinage, illegitimacy, and cohabitation also had practical implications, linked to the need to ensure that the property holding and lineage of their memberships remained undiluted.

Pardon cases about honor covered a varied terrain, detailing something so small as a slight provocation and as emotionally charged as a son usurping a father's authority, as the following two cases prove. What usually binds the diversity of honor cases together is the importance for men of public self-worth and its upholding before others. In 1452, to take an otherwise obscure case, the "poor man" Pasquier van Wetsteen of Wervik filed for a pardon after killing Jan de Clerc in a scuffle that followed an earlier fight between members of their two families. In his pardon request, Wetsteen claims he only confronted de Clerc—who apparently had earlier fled the area after he had injured Wetsteen's cousin—after he found out from his fellow townspeople that de Clerc had returned. Wetsteen immediately chased down and killed his cousin's attacker, no doubt because he wanted to maintain his social

---

24. Marc Boone, "Les gens de métiers à l'époque corporative à Gand et les litiges professionnels (1350–1450)," in *Individual, Corporative and Judicial Status in European Cities, Late Middle Ages and Early Modern Period,* ed. Marc Boone and Maarten Prak (Louvain, 1996), 23–47; for the Ghent ordinance, see Stadsarchief Gent, Ser. 156, no. 1, fol. 79r.

25. ADN, Lille, B, 1687, fol. 19r. (Lancien, no. 732) (pardon of April 25, 1457).

26. Prevenier, "The Notions of Honor and Adultery," 266.

worth and prove his manhood in defense of his family honor in front of others:[27]

> During the season of Carnival, in 1452, words were exchanged between Vincent de Man, Pasquier van Wetsteen's cousin, and Medart de Vliet in the presence of Jan de Clerc, which grew into a conflict between Vincent de Man and Medart. It led to Jan de Clerc giving a push and wounding Vincent de Man and imperiling his life. A certain time later, while Wetsteen was hearing mass in Wervik's church, some people told him that Jan de Clerc was in Wervik. When Wetsteen had heard mass and was leaving the church, they told him, "There is the person who put your cousin's life in peril." Hearing this, the supplicant right away went after Jan de Clerc. Hearing people murmuring and hearing that some people were coming after him, Jan de Clerc turned and pulled his dagger against Wetsteen, who moved to defend himself. A conflict broke out between them, during which Jan de Clerc was wounded, and from the wounds, as they say, he went from life to death within a few days.

The case of Guillaume Nollet, an innkeeper from Neuville-en-Ferrain in Flanders, shows how social perception of male worth, by contrast, could unravel a family and turn deadly (letter no. 10). On Good Friday (March 29) 1499, the Burgundian archduke pardoned Nollet for killing his son Hacquinot, the holy day of Christ's crucifixion both the appropriate occasion for forgiveness and a jarring comment on a son's sacrificial death. Guillaume Nollet was certainly guilty of the crime, egged on, so he reports, both by visiting merchants and by his own wife, each in their different ways registering disapproval of the disrespect Nollet's twenty-year-old son had shown him. On December 8, 1498, Nollet had lodged visiting French merchants in his inn:

> The supplicant kept company with them for dinner at the table, while Hacquinot Nollet, his son, age twenty, served them. This supplicant said to the merchants, "Did you see my son? I will make him jump up to the ceiling." Hearing this Hacquinot replied to the supplicant, "You are a real joker." This reply seemed very rude to the merchants, who said to the supplicant, "How do you suffer your son to speak thus to you. We can't believe he is your son." The supplicant was greatly angered.

---

27. Pardon for Pasquier van Wetsteen, from Wervik (county of Flanders). Lille, September 4, 1455. ADN, Lille, B, 1686, fol. 48r (Lancien, no. 654); Petit-Dutaillis, 161–62.

The supplicant shrugged off the retort, traveling with another merchant out of the village on errands the next day. When Nollet returned home, he experienced a double slight to his patriarchal authority. First, his wife had failed to prepare a meal for him, and second, his son Hacquinot was sitting before the hearth in his favorite chair, even though it was Nollet who had gone to the barn to fetch kindling to burn:

> The supplicant put the bundle into the fire, and sat low down on a small footstool opposite his chair. His wife came and, seeing him sitting low down, said to him "go sit in your chair." He replied, "How shall I sit there when my master is seated there already?" At that moment the merchant from Flanders came forward and encouraged the supplicant, who was greatly angered, reminding him that Hacquenot had called him a joker the night before.

With his reply to his wife Nollet angrily registered the injury to his status, and the remarks of the visiting merchant further provoked him. This inversion of male authority before his wife and the merchant was the straw that broke the camel's back. Though Hacquinot got out of the chair when his father accused him of usurping his position, it was too late. Nollet assailed his son with a knife, only to beg Hacquinot's forgiveness as he bled profusely, slipped out of consciousness, then died in his mother's arms.

Adultery and Honor

As the case of Nollet shows, concerns over honor might reverberate loudest in the intimate world of the family. The threat to the fragile domestic order and male authority posed by sexual transgressions was the subject of countless moral treatises, literary works, and legal cases, pardons especially. Adultery, particularly committed between a susceptible or lascivious wife and a scheming man, was among the most common tropes in late medieval literature, from Chaucer to Boccaccio, from comic theater to ballads. True, in the high Middle Ages, certain literary forms, like the poetry of the troubadours of southern France, might extol the ennobling power of the love of a married aristocratic woman, but these texts often reflected not so much social reality as a social game and literary conceit among the leisured elite.[28]

---

28. Christiane Marchello-Nizia, "Amour courtois, société masculine et figures de pouvoir," *Annales, Economies, Sociétés, Civilisations* 36 (1981): 969–82; William D. Paden, "The Troubadour's Lady through Thick History," *Exemplaria* 11 (1999): 221–44.

The late medieval bawdy tales of duped husbands and cunning, adulterous women likewise were literary artifice, stories spiced up for comic effect. At the same time, they also served the more serious purpose of warning what a world upside down—a family subverted and male authority traduced—threatened. The Burgundian *Cent Nouvelles Nouvelles* features repeated up-endings of husbands, starting with its very first tale, that of a man who sleeps with his neighbor's wife while he is away. When the husband returns earlier than expected from his trip, he catches his neighbor bathing together with a woman in a candle-lit and food-laden bedroom when he goes next door to say hello. But he is only allowed to see the woman from behind, and exclaims to his neighbor that she looks a lot like his wife, failing to recognize that it was in fact his wife's body he was admiring.[29] The story's *frisson* is not just the adultery, but the craftiness of the male seducer—a "notable citizen of Valenciennes"—the bawdiness of the sexual imagery, and the duping of the husband, who doesn't recognize his own wife's naked backside. This particular configuration of a crafty male seducer and gullible husband is repeatedly found in the *Cent Nouvelles Nouvelles*, as in the tale of young English clerk who feigned to his employer, an older lawyer, that he had been castrated, so he could secretly become a lover to the man's pretty young wife.[30] The lawyer entrusted his wife's fidelity to the clerk, relieved, or so he thought, that the young man's injury protected him against any possibility of being "dishonored" by adultery.

In these Burgundian tales, a husband's cowardliness as much as his stupidity provokes sexual scandal. In the fourth tale, a Scottish archer becomes infatuated with the wife of a mercer in the French city of Tours, and the mercer decides to settle the matter by setting a trap. He instructs his wife to allow the archer to make his way to her bed, and hides himself armed in the room, planning to kill the seducer.[31] When the brawny archer arrives also armed, however, the husband shrinks in fear. Two times the archer and the mercer's wife have sex, the mercer outraged but frozen by fear, forced to be a secret witness. When the mercer later confronts his wife, she upbraids him for his lack of courage and for his dishonoring himself by allowing another man into her bed without acting to prevent it. The tale's focus is not on the sexual violation of the woman, nor on her victimhood, but instead on the husband's weakness and lack of honor—how the plan he sets in motion ends up shaming him.

---

29. Champion *CNN*, tale no. 1, 15–18.
30. Ibid., tale no. 13, 45–58.
31. Ibid., tale no. 4, 26–29.

In the *Cent Nouvelles Nouvelles,* there are plenty of untrustworthy men—townspeople, noblemen, and clergy especially—but there are even craftier women, more brutally deceptive, and, in the gender imaginary of the era, overly sexualized. One example, story no. 91, which recounts the tale of a Flemish man's wife whose adultery is so commonplace that her husband threatens to make her pregnant with four children to rein her in, and lambasts her as no better than a pack of dogs in heat, might be regarded as extreme in its misogyny.[32] But it has in common with other tales the assumption that women are guileless or deceptive, but in either case sexually available. A husband at the mercy of either his wife or a male seducer was a source of spoof and amusement, especially when embellished with playful sexual language and metaphors. But it also spoke to cultural anxieties in a social landscape where adultery was commonplace, and marriage a social ballast whose foundations could easily be cracked by all sorts of wrongdoings.

If the *Cent Nouvelles Nouvelles* made honor adultery's victim, the social world of the Burgundian Low Countries legally penalized extramarital sex. Nevertheless, civic officials tolerated its practice, not just through networks of active brothels whose business thrived, but by criminalizing adultery without any commitment to strict enforcement. Because it concerned marriage, adultery was the legal responsibility of the church, though some civic statutes also levied penalties against its practice. While adultery was prohibited in canon law, the church, out of concern for the indissolubility of marriage, cautioned against the easy repudiation of a spouse because of a sexual transgression.[33] Urban authorities also monitored sexual transgressions. The aldermen in Aardenburg in the fourteenth century, Ghent at the end of the fifteenth century, and Ypres in the sixteenth century made adultery a crime subject to imprisonment or banishment.[34] But since so many ordinary people, from townsfolk to villagers, from guildsmen to priests, committed

---

32. Ibid., tale no. 91, 239–40 : " Pour quoy la laissa courre comme une lisse entre deux douzaines de chiens, et accomplir tous ses vouloirs et desordonnez desirs."

33. Leah Otis-Cour, "'De jure novo: Dealing with Adultery in the Fifteenth-Century Toulousain," *Speculum* 84 (2009): 347–92, esp. 349–52; James A. Brundage, "Sex and Canon Law," in *Handbook of Medieval Sexuality,* ed. Vern L. Bullough and James A. Brundage (New York, 1996), 33–50, esp. 42.

34. Aardenburg penalized adultery with a fine of ten pounds and one year of banishment: George Auguste Vorsterman van Oyen, *Rechtsbronnen der stad Aardenburg* (The Hague, 1892) no. 121, 110. Ghent decreed in 1491 that adultery was punishable by two weeks' imprisonment on bread and water: Albert-Eugène Gheldolf, ed., *Coutumes de la ville de Gand,* vol. 1 (Brussels, 1868), 672. Ypres in 1535 penalized with banishment any man who did not repudiate his adulterous wife: Louis Gilliodts–Van Severen, ed., *Coutume de la ville d'Ypres* (Brussels, 1908) no. 1, 489.

adultery with married and unmarried people alike, enforcement was uneven. Typically, someone was caught if they were denounced before the ecclesiastical court, whose episcopal "official" (the judge) would then impose penance and a small fine for the transgression.[35] In ten villages outside of Deinze between 1446 and 1481, there were an average of 5.2 such convictions a year in each village, though the number of accusations to the local courts was certainly higher. The percentage of inhabitants convicted of sexual offenses varied from village to village in this area, between 1.6 to 7.1 percent annually, so that in some villages 40 percent of the population had come before the episcopal court at least once in a lifetime. In the whole bishopric of Tournai in one fiscal year 1474–75, there were 227 "moral" transgressions in its 157 towns and villages, all of which were settled with minor financial sanctions registered in the episcopal ledgers.[36] We should keep in mind that these eye-opening figures were only the tip of the iceberg. Most "sinners" probably escaped punishment entirely because an accusation against them fell on deaf ears. The perception of late medieval society as under the thumb of rigid hierarchical institutions, guild regulations, municipal ordinances, and canon law masks a messier reality in which all sorts of passions convulsed the fragile edifice of law and order.

Since male adultery was commonplace, urban magistrates' main concern was less sexual straying, so long as homosexuality wasn't practiced, than preserving the social cohesion of family, kin, and property. In Ghent in 1450, for example, the aldermen intervened in the case of Lysbette Scheerms and Pieter de Wilde and their two children. Scheerms had confessed to the local priest that neither of the couple's children was her husband's, but instead the offspring of two sexual liaisons, the first with a Franciscan friar and the second with another townsman, Berthelmeeus Valke. The aldermen might have railed against the brazen adultery, but instead tackled the practical issues Scheerms's relationships had created. They ruled that Valke should pay a fine

---

35. On the role of the "official" (episcopal judge) in excommunications, see Anne Lefebvre-Teillard, *Les officialités à la veille du Concile de Trente* (Paris, 1973), 115, 235. On the function of the "official," see Richard H. Helmholz, *The Canon Law and Ecclesiastical Jurisdiction from 597 to the 1640s* (Oxford, 2004).

36. Walter Prevenier, Paul Huys, and Guy Dupont, "Misdaad en straf," in *Geschiedenis van Deinze*, vol. 3, ed. Walter Prevenier et al. (Deinze, 2007), 225–48, esp. 238–239; ADN, Lille, 14 G 96 (accounts of the episcopal court for 1474–75); Monique van Melkebeek, "Het parochiale leven in het oude bisdom Doornik tijdens de late middeleeuwen," in *Ter overwinning van een historische drempelvrees: De historicus en juridische bronnen,* ed. Serge Dauchy (Brussels, 1994), 31–59. A perfect analysis of the repression of moral transgressions by episcopal courts in France and the Burgundian Netherlands is Véronique Beaulande, *Le malheur d'être exclu? Excommunication, réconciliation et société à la fin du Moyen Âge* (Paris, 2006), 107–28.

to de Wilde and cover his biological child's clothing and school expenses.[37] In 1422 in Bruges, the aldermen ordered Pieter Menin, the father of children he had with a single mother, to pay for their support "as a good father ought to do," even though they did not live with him.[38] In 1435 the Court of Flanders instructed Jan de Heere of Waasmunster, already married, to buy a house and set up an annuity for a woman and two illegitimate children he had with her.[39] The three rulings are typical of the regular work of town aldermen whose legal interventions on matters of adultery and illegitimacy centered on the protection of widows, orphans, and above all children. If a harsher punishment was inflicted, it was typically against adulterous women with no offspring involved. In 1413, to take one example, the bailiff of Beveren, with the support of the aldermen of the small Flemish village of Kieldrecht, banished Eleinne, the wife of Jacques Martin, for a year because of an affair with Clais Lammyn. The aldermen condemned her de facto "repudiation" of her husband while restoring her husband to honor, at the request of "several good people" in the village.[40]

In the legal domain, adultery's main consequence was the potential risk to the family's social reproduction and its property. Adultery itself was less consequential since it was widely practiced, among men above all. For the Burgundian elite, sexual libertinism was woven into the world of masculine privilege and prerogatives. The longest serving Burgundian duke, Philip the Good, boasted twenty-six bastards and thirty-three mistresses. The illegitimate son of John the Fearless, bishop of Cambrai, had twenty-two illegitimate children of his own. And Jean de Heinsberg, the bishop of Liège, had no fewer than sixty-five children, two more than John II, duke of Clèves, a prominent nobleman. Outsiders commented on the respect shown to such offspring at the Burgundian court, a point made both by the Czech Leo von Rozmital in 1465–67 and the Spanish visitor Pero Tafur in 1438.[41]

---

37. Stadsarchief Gent, Reg. 301, 41, vol. 1, fol. 8r–v, dated September 10, 1450.

38. Stadarchief Brugge, 208, O.L.V Zestendeel, 3, fol. 215, dated March 13, 1422.

39. Rijksarchief Gent, Raad van Vlaanderen, no. 7510, fol. 89v–90r.

40. Algemeen Rijksarchief, Brussel, Rekenkamers, no. 6886, accounts of the bailiff of Beveren.

41. Marcel Bergé, "Les bâtards de la maison de Bourgogne," *L'intermédiaire des généalogistes* 60 (1955): 316–408. For the broader social world, see Myriam Carlier, *Kinderen van de minne? Bastaarden in het vijftiende-eeuwse Vlaanderen* (Brussels, 2001), esp. 251–54. For the outsiders' observations, see Malcolm H. I. Letts, ed., *The Travels of Leo of Rozmital through Germany, Flanders, England, Spain, Portugal and Italy, 1465–1467* (Cambridge, UK, 1957), 39–40, and Malcolm H. I. Letts, *Bruges and Its Past* (London, 1924), 202.

If adultery was a common currency of social life, and if clergy themselves could be morally compromised or downright corrupt, certain sexual scandals nevertheless had enough sting to sometimes provoke a legal remedy if public honor was at stake. Affronts to male honor by an adulterous wife and a seducer are the most commonplace crimes recounted in Burgundian pardon letters. Four sexual scandals typify the fallout from adultery and the use of violence to defend a husband's sense of male honor—a stain that unlike vendetta killings could not be erased by financial settlements or compromises. In the 1438 case of Ywain Voet of Nieuwpoort in Flanders, a messenger of the ducal equerry, the betrayal of adultery was all the more poignant because his wife's seducer was none other than a close friend, named Jan, messenger of the city of Nieuwpoort, but a superior who bore the title Master.[42] They had great affection for each other:

> The supplicant had love, acquaintance, and great affection for one named Master Jan, then a messenger from Nieuwpoort, in whom the supplicant put much trust; they often drank and ate together. With him he [Ywain] had fraternal company as if they were brothers. But during their companionship and company Master Jan, moved by a wicked and damnable will, and whom the supplicant did not expect to cause him sorrow or harm, acquainted himself with the supplicant's wife, such that he could have his way with her.

Jan thus used his friendship with Voet to get close to his wife, and for four years he was her lover, eventually convincing her to elope with him, taking much of the conjugal property along with her;

> However, it happened that the supplicant accidently encountered Master Jan. Moved by sentiments and remembering the good love and fraternal companionship that he had and exhibited toward Master Jan, and the great disloyalty, shame, reproach, damage, and dishonor that Master Jan, turning good into bad, did toward him, [Ywain Voet] beat and wounded Master Jan such that he died from these wounds.

Voet fled the area, but handily won a pardon with his tale of revenge motivated by his blemished honor and the treason of a personal friend.

---

42. Pardon for Ywain Voet. Brussels, December 1438. ADN, Lille, B, 1682, fol. 34r (Lancien, no. 224); Petit-Dutaillis, 14–15. On the functions of the ducal equerry, see Edward A. Tabri, *Political Culture in the Early Northern Renaissance: The Court of Charles the Bold, Duke of Burgundy, 1467–1477* (Lewiston, NY, 2004), 157–58; Vaughan, *Philip the Good*, 140.

In Voet's pardon, his wife's culpability is less the focus than Master Jan's trickery, especially his violation of a male friendship so close that it was described as fraternal. Not so with the case of Pierre Monié of Cuiseaux, in the county of Franche-Comté,[43] who in 1438 sought a pardon for his adulterous wife's murder.[44] Monié had married his wife Jehanette Boudot "thirty-six or thirty-seven" years earlier. His troubles began when, "seduced and tempted by the enemy [the devil]," his wife engaged in repeated adulterous affairs: "she began to converse day and night, in diverse and suspicious locations, with men of bad disposition and conduct, in adulterous relations with them to the extent that she had a bastard daughter with Messire Estienne Raton, knight. Jehanette continued in her bad and damnable life and her adultery went from bad to worse." This was without doubt a reference to prostitution. Jehanette plied her trade in one city after another, and finally settled in Avignon.[45] Her choice of location was hardly a coincidence. The city became famous as a center of prostitution as soon as the papal seat was moved there in the early fourteenth century.[46] The high density of clergymen offered a robust market for paid sex.[47] When Monié went years later to Avignon, he reported, a relative of his wife named Heliet Montaigner urged him to take Jehanette back with him. Monié reluctantly agreed; on their way out of Avignon, next to a bridge at Zoigne, several of Monié's friends ambushed her and killed her on the spot.

The pardon story reveals that Monié was content with his estranged wife's murder, "because of the great sorrow and extreme displeasure this woman and her behavior caused," implying, though the pardon request doesn't mention this, that the ambush was prearranged to kill Jehanette, probably with Monié's backing. For some reason, years later in 1438 Monié was charged with the murder by the bailiff of Chalon. While we'll never know the precise nature of his relationship to Jehanette, nor whether his characterization

43. Cuiseaux, France, dépt. Saône-et-Loire, arr. Louhans, chef-lieu canton.

44. Pardon for Pierre Monié. Brussels, August 1438. ADN, Lille, B, 1682, fols. 11v–12v (Lancien, no. 205).

45. Avignon, France, dépt. Vaucluse, chef-lieu dépt. From 1309 to 1378 Avignon was the formal seat of the papacy, afterward of antipopes; it was not attached to France until 1791; see Sylvain Gagnière et al., eds, *Histoire d'Avignon* (Aix-en-Provence,1979).

46. Vern L. Bullough, "Prostitution in the Later Middle Ages," in *Sexual Practices and the Medieval Church,* ed. Vern L. Bullough and James A. Brundage (New York, 1982), 180–81.

47. Jacques Rossiaud, *La prostitution médiévale* (Paris, 1988), 226, 314. Prostitution was so successful in this city that local proverbs made jokes about it. One suggested that it was impossible to cross the famous bridge of Avignon "without encountering two monks, two donkeys, and two whores." See Diane Cady, "Medieval Prostitution," in *Encyclopedia of Prostitution and Sex Work*, vol. 1, ed. Melissa Hope Ditmore (Westport, CT, 2006), 299–301.

of her was fair, Monié's portrait of his wife's serial adultery was enough to win him a pardon, especially since the men who had killed his wife were already themselves dead, and Monié himself had a new wife and four children.

The sting of dishonor that adultery inflicted was even sharper if the duped husband was the source of the public mockery or verbal taunts. This was the case with Jacot Barcueille, "a poor man and farmer" with a wife and six children in Morteau[48] in the bailiwick of Pontarlier[49] in Franche-Comté in 1455.[50] A neighbor, Estevenin d'Escoste, had courted his wife:

> the supplicant, perceiving that one Estevenin d'Escoste put great effort into getting to know his married wife, forbade the aforenamed Estevenin from approaching and frequenting his house and also from making advances to his wife, and otherwise, if he should do so, it would displease him. However, notwithstanding this, on the Monday of last Pentecost when he was returning home to his house in Morteau during the night he found Estevenin in his house and with his wife. He heard that they had agreed to sleep together.

Riled up with "hot anger," Barcueille stabbed and killed d'Escoste, fled Morteau, and had his property confiscated. He defended himself as a dishonored husband who had suffered additional public humiliation because "Estevenin was a man of bad conduct, a boaster about [his success with] women, a man of dissolute and bad life and behavior. He bragged many times and in many places that he had had sexual intercourse with the wife of the supplicant." In Barcueille's pardon, his wife is mentioned in passing, and not even named; the plea focuses instead on d'Escoste as the mocking, aggressive male whose obscene boasts and bad behavior caused his murder.

Barcueille's justification mirrors closely that of Pieter de Scelewe in Ypres in 1458, a man who also killed his wife's seducer (letter no. 12). A young innkeeper who ran a tavern, Scelewe reported that he had suffered the double humiliation of public rumors about his neighbor Christian de Cloot's adultery with his wife and de Cloot's own putdowns of him. Before he even could prove that a sexual relationship was taking place, "on the basis of many true presumptions and also by diverse reports by many and diverse people made to him that one named Christian de Cloot, his neighbor, pursued his

---

48. Morteau, France, dépt. Doubs, arr. Pontarlier, chef-lieu canton.

49. Pontarlier, France, dépt. Doubs, chef-lieu arr.

50. Pardon for Jacot Barcueille. Louvain, July 1455. ADN, Lille, B, 1686, fols. 39v–40r (Lancien, no. 643); Champion *CNN*, lxxviii.

wife to have carnal relations with her, and that rumor and public knowledge in the parish were that he knew her carnally . . . , he absorbed in his imagination and his conviction that the adultery of his wife was real." De Cloot's own domestic servants had apparently reproached their master's bad ways. But that failed to stop him, and one night de Cloot came to Scelewe's tavern. Christian "threw a glass of beer at his wife's face and said to some friends with whom he was drinking, and who reproached him for this, that the supplicant was a mongrel and had no balls and that he was hardly fit to be a man." The insults and taunts, added to the weight of public rumor and gossip, proved too burdensome an affront to Scelewe's masculinity. Scelewe attacked and beat de Cloot, who died from the wounds. As with Barcueille's pardon, Scelewe's narrative is entirely focused on his male adversary, his adulterous wife again described only in passing. The narrative frame of the pardon request turns on the legitimacy of defending honor blemished repeatedly by a verbally violent and aggressive male competitor intent on destroying both the family and its reputation.

Clergy, Sexuality, and Dishonor

In the Bruges case of Gillekin Dubois, it was a priest who had suggested that Dubois and his friend head to a brothel, a telling example that late medieval clergy were no strangers to the sexual world of prostitution and the larger domain of human sexual relations.

Before the Catholic reform movement and the Council of Trent of the mid sixteenth century, clerical celibacy was rarely enforced, although the celibacy rule had been decreed by Pope Nicholas II in 1059. From parish priests to promiscuous senior clergy like the bishops of Cambrai and Liège, Low Country churchmen were hardly models of chastity and moral probity. For clergymen two types of sanctions, ecclesiastical and civil, were applied to sexual transgressions, sometimes simultaneously, sometimes successively. The first was usually a fine paid to the bishop's court. In the civil procedure, urban authorities often required the sinning priest to pay alimony to his concubine if she had had offspring with him who needed financial support. Most sexual misdeeds by priests ended up at the bishop's court. In 1480, for example, the Ghent priest Andries Neut of Saint Michael's had sex with a nun in a brothel, provoking a public scandal.[51] That

---

51. ADN, Lille, 14 G 98, fol. 85v.

same year, Vincent Andries, the parish priest of Tielt, was accused of no less than four infractions. He had convinced several woman to oppose a marriage in the parish so he could split with them the fines collected for violations of canon law; he had blessed another marriage without publicizing the banns; he had had questionable contacts with a woman who had stolen part of her husband's property; and he had had sex with a nun who worked at a local hospital.[52] In fact, in 61 of the 157 villages under the jurisdiction of the bishop of Tournai, local parish priests were involved in transgressions that came before the episcopal court.[53] In some instances, a priest's sexual errors were of no concern to his patrons or parishioners, so long as he conducted parish life honorably in all other matters. In 1444, the local lord of Uutkerke, Joos van Halewijn, intervened to quash charges against the parish priest of the village of Blankenberge, Symoen de Grispeere, by arguing he was an honorable man, "of good repute and well loved by his parishioners." Van Halewijn did, however, add that "I trust that the deed is neither as serious nor as horrible as what you have been told."[54] Priests with illegitimate children mostly cared for them, just like other burghers. The entries in civic registers that list legacies are businesslike and without animus toward the priests concerned.

Concubines of clerics fared much worse, as they were regularly perceived as "priests' whores" and had diminished prospects for legal and valid marriages.[55] The common practice of local priests taking concubines, or having domestic partners, is the subject of a pardon awarded to the squire Antoon van Bavinchove of Saint-Omer in December 1459.[56] Bavinchove had been in an unexplained conflict that led to a violent confrontation in which a few horses were killed and his opponents wounded. For this misdeed, he had been banished from Saint-Omer. More interestingly, a few months later

---

52. Van Melkebeek, "Het parochiale leven," 51, 53.

53. ADN, Lille, 14 G 96; Van Melkebeek, "Het parochiale leven," 38–39, 46–47, 54–56.

54. Rijksarchief Gent, Fonds Bisdom, B 3295, fol. 22r.

55. On the expression "priest's whore" for a concubine: Ruth Mazo Karras, *Unmarriages: Women, Men, and Sexual Unions in the Middle Ages* (Philadelphia, 2012), 115–64; Emlyn Eisenach, *Husbands, Wives, and Concubines: Marriage, Family, and Social Order in Sixteenth-Century Verona* (Kirksville, MO, 2004), 147–58. In Catalunya, however, their reputation was not negative; see Michelle Armstrong-Partida, "Priestly Wives: The Role and Acceptance of Clerics' Concubines in the Parishes of Late Medieval Catalunya," *Speculum* 88 (2013): 184–85.

56. Pardon for squire Antoine van Bavinchove, from Saint-Omer (county of Artois). Brussels, December 1459. ADN, Lille, B, 1690, fol. 5v (Lancien, no. 874) ; Petit-Dutaillis, 32–33; Champion *CNN*, xcii.

en route in the area of Thérouanne, he encountered a young man named Omaer de Vos:

> the supplicant found a young companion on the road named Omaer de Vos, from a good social rank, who was coming from Thérouanne[57] with a woman who people said was a priest's concubine. Because he heard that Omaer intended to take this woman in marriage and go with her, he took pity on him. In order to preserve his honor and to prevent his alliance, he mounted his horse behind him while reproaching him for this marriage and led him to his aunt's house. Omaer spent around fifteen days there until his uncle came to find him. To bring an end to the love of the aforesaid woman, and in order that he would not take her in marriage, he led him to the castle of Hames in the land of Guines,[58] where he spent some time.

The details are murky, but it's obvious that Bavinchove had the backing of the young man's family, who were intent on preventing his foolish marriage to a priest's lover, with her low social status. Perhaps this was why Bavinchove, despite his earlier violent fight and his kidnapping of the love-sick young man, won a pardon for his misdeeds, though the pardon letter also commended his previous soldiering experience in the Burgundian military, "well and loyally in the company of our beloved and loyal knight, the councilor and chamberlain the bastard of Burgundy."[59]

Much more revealing is the case of Guillaume Doille, a priest from Thoisy in the duchy of Burgundy, an abusive cleric murdered in 1450 by three men from the village of Soussey fed up with his flagrant abuses and his "dissolute, bad, and dishonest life" (letter no. 13). If the pardon letter submitted by Ogier de Soussey and Perrenin and Pierre Rebel is credible, Doille was the epitome of the corrupt priest, guilty of both sexual misconduct and abuse of his pastoral duties. The three pardon seekers opened their appeal with an

---

57. Thérouanne, France, dépt. Pas-de-Calais, arr. Saint-Omer.

58. Hames-Boucre, France, dépt. Pas-de-Calais, arr. Boulogne, cant. Guines. Guines was a county for itself until 1350, after which it was attached to the French crown. It became administratively part of Artois, and therefore also of the Burgundian territory.

59. A reference to Anthony, the so called "great bastard of Burgundy" (1421–1504), illegitimate son of duke Philip the Good and Jehannette de Presles, chamberlain of Charles the Bold, knight of the Golden Fleece, and patron of the arts; see Vaughan, *Philip the Good,* 134–35; Hans Cools, *Mannen met macht: Edellieden en de moderne staat in de Bourgondisch-Habsburgse landen (1475–1530)* (Zutphen, 2001), 165–66.

assault that had occurred three or four years earlier: Doille's attempted rape of Soussey's sister:[60]

> Guillaume Doille, then a priest from Thoisy, one night, knowing that Jehan Maillet, who lived in Soussey, was out of town, secretly entered his house. He went to the bed where Claude, the wife of Jehan Maillet, full sister of the named Ogier, and relative of Perrenin and Pierre Rebel, lay down and was sleeping. Guillaume Doille, feigning to impersonate Jehan Maillet, Claude's husband, approached her and was on the verge of knowing her carnally. Claude woke up with a start and recognized him, realizing that this was not her husband but instead messire Guillaume Doille. Very afraid, angry, and bewildered, she immediately got out of bed, not wanting to consent to the bad wishes of the late messire Guillaume Doille. At this very late hour she ran, fleeing down into town, hurrying and crying as much as she could.

Claude's flight into the street, provoking public attention, "greatly displeased" the supplicants. Soussey reproached Doille for his sexual violence; in return, the priest verbally harassed and pursued him, summoning him before the episcopal court of Besançon for trumped-up misdeeds, where the "official" excommunicated him.[61] He did the same to Perrenin and Pierre Rebel's father Jehan, a prominent merchant, who had earlier confronted Doille and beseeched him to mend his unethical ways. Because Jehan Rebel had also testified on behalf of Claude Maillet's husband Jehan Maillet in a suit he had brought against Doille, he earned extra ire from the vengeful priest. Doille instigated Jehan Rebel's excommunication, and caused other problems, lawsuits included, for him. He harassed Perrenin Rebel for working on a feast day, and in general used excommunication and the threat of

---

60. Events from real life, including adultery during the absence of a husband and his unexpected return, as in this story of Doille, are also very common in the *Cent nouvelles nouvelles,* which lends support to the thesis of Champion that the authors of this literary work were involved in the ducal administration and were familiar with pardons. Boccaccio, a century earlier, offered similar stories. On Boccaccio's adulterous plots: Leigh Ann Craig, *Wandering Women and Holy Matrons: Women as Pilgrims in the Later Middle Ages* (Leiden, 2009), 56–60.

61. Besançon, France, capital of dépt. Doubs; in the fifteenth century it was the capital of the county of Franche-Comté. On ecclesiastical life and institutions in Besançon: Claude Fohlen, *Histoire de Besançon,* vol. 1 (Paris, 1964); Roland Fietier, "Notes sur la vie religieuse à Besançon au XVe siècle," *Miscellanea Historiae Ecclesiasticae* (Louvain) 44 (1967): 37–57.

prosecution before the episcopal court as a weapon to threaten and silence adversaries.[62]

Doille finally confronted the Rebel brothers and Soussey when the three men were playing a ball game on a feast day. Apart from a cryptic exchange of threats, nothing else occurred. A second dispute among the men on March 22, 1450, however, turned violent; Doille wounded Perrenin Rebel on the head with a blow of his sword, and Pierre Rebel and Ogier de Soussey reacted by beating the priest so severely that he died. In a startling conclusion to the violent tale, the men took away a large box containing all documents—excommunications included—Doille had collected on the Rebel family and others and had wielded to intimidate his parishioners. These they burned, fearing the vengeance of Doille if he had survived their beating. Murdering a priest and destroying legal paperwork were no small matter, and the men hastily fled Burgundy fearing arrest and punishment. In June 1450, they earned a pardon, the ducal official undoubtedly being convinced they had acted honorably against a corrupt priest who bullied his parishioners as a petty tyrant.

Women in Pardons

In the calculus of honor blemished and defended, women are the crux of disputes, but only as objects of male interest. The honor cases we have explored involve men as petitioners who have turned violent after affronts to their masculinity. Women are rarely the protagonists, much less the bringers of legal cases involving sexual dishonor. Two exceptions are a pair of cases from Bruges concerning sodomy, or male homosexuality, a crime that was punishable by death in the Burgundian Netherlands.[63] In 1473, Jehanne Sey accused her husband of sodomy, but was punished for two days, tied to a large wooden wheel and exposed publicly for a false accusation motivated by her

---

62. On the use of excommunication as a political and ideological instrument: Beaulande, *Le malheur d'être exclu?* 23–29 (typology), 48–52 (social backgrounds); Elisabeth Vodola, *Excommunication in the Middle Ages* (Berkeley, 1986).

63. Marc Boone, "State power and Illicit Sexuality: the Persecution of Sodomy in Late Medieval Bruges," *Journal of Medieval History* 22, no. 2 (1996): 135–53. The best-documented city for the persecution of male homosexuality is fifteenth-century Florence, which set up a special court, the Office of the Night, to pursue men who engaged in same-sex relations. See Michael Rocke, *Forbidden Friendships: Homosexuality and Male Friendship in Renaissance Florence* (Oxford, 1998). Guido Ruggiero, *The Boundaries of Eros: Sex, Crime, and Sexuality in Renaissance Venice* (New York—Oxford, 1985), 109–145, explores aggressive repression in Venice, and underscores that "sodomy" was not limited to homosexuality, but included anal intercourse with women.

"immense hatred."[64] She had "Accused her husband of the crime of sodomy because of her immense hatred of him, thinking that by doing so through dishonest legal means she could end her husband's life." Bruges' aldermen chastised Sey for trying to "dishonor" her husband, an echo of another case that same year in which they had punished Katerine van der Leene, who also had accused her husband Jean of sodomy. The aldermen imprisoned Jean, but after an investigation, they found out that the charge was fabricated. Katerine admitted to concocting it to rid herself of a husband who abused her with "harmful words." In fact, Jean had earlier proclaimed that his wife should be burned at the stake:[65]

> [Katherine, wife of Jan van der Leene] suspected her husband of the sin and very important case of sodomy. She proclaimed that he deserved to burn at the stake. And after she had been heard extensively before the court against her husband, on these words and grievances, she started to weaken her charges, confessing that everything on which she charged her husband was said because of her great rage, not thinking and not knowing the huge harm her statement contained, [confessing] that for this reason she could not live in peace with him, and that he himself had said in the past that she deserved to burn at the stake, that she had spoken these words in the heat of anger because of the harmful words that the aforesaid husband was hurling daily at her, as is commonly known . . . through malice and great hatred and envy that she had against her husband, and in order to destroy the husband completely.

The accusations of Sey and van der Leene were declared spurious, and neither legal suit went beyond its original municipal jurisdiction.

Claude Gauvard and Natalie Davis have found that women were rare as petitioners for royal or princely pardons, accounting for only between 1 and 4 percent of the total number of requests in late medieval and early modern France.[66] These figures dovetail with the fifteenth-century Burgundian pardons and repeals of banishments, where women are petitioners in only 16 pardon letters and 4 repeals out of a total of 2,339 legal remissions between 1386 and 1500. This is less than 1 percent of all cases, and in six of them, the female petitioner acted in concert with someone else, namely a husband, and

---

64. Algemeen Rijksarchief, Brussel, Rekenkamers, no. 13780, fol. 20r.

65. Ibid., fol. 40r.

66. Davis, *Fiction in the Archives*, 85; Gauvard, "*De grace espécial*," 300, whose sample has women as 4 percent of the supplicants for pardons.

in one instance a sister. In two other cases, the women are deemed "simple" or "not rational," that is, mentally impaired. Two different cases concern a wife poisoning her husband, and a third relates the efforts of a wife to help free her husband from a local prison.[67] This is a very small harvest, too meager to draw any wider conclusions about gender and pardon save that women were the rarest of petitioners, even if they were routinely present in the crimes pardon letters recount.

Perhaps the most dramatic pardon of women in the Burgundian records are three cases that concern infanticide, a crime punishable by death in fifteenth-century Europe, and one that was rarely pardoned.[68] Women found guilty of infanticide were regularly executed by drowning or burning, a crueler method of death than the hanging or beheading employed for regular capital offenses. The crime was considered so heinous and beyond the pale that it became associated with the witch hunts and its victims—an act of sorcery.[69] Prosecutions of infanticide in the Low Countries are hardly documented, with only seven cases found in the extensive records of bailiffs in the whole late medieval period, and six cases that are noted in the fifteenth-century Audience records of the court.[70] This small number reflects infanticide prosecutions elsewhere in medieval Europe.[71] This makes the trio of infanticide cases in the Burgundian pardon records of special interest, rare both in the detail they offer and the clemency they exhibit.[72] The opposite

---

67. For the twenty cases, see Lancien, nos. 28, 50, 59, 238, 239, 634, 675, 753, 780, 837, 843, 869, 979, 1041, 1264, 1322, 1734, 2014, 2212, and 2292. In 1565–66, only two women received royal pardons in France: Michel Nassiet, ed., *Les lettres de pardon du voyage de Charles IX (1565–1566)* (Paris, 2010), xxi.

68. On infanticide in Flanders: Pablo Fernandez, "Het verschijnsel kindermoord in de Nederlanden (XIVde–XVde eeuw)" in *Structures sociales et topographie de la pauvreté et de la richesse aux 14e et 15e siècles,* ed. Walter Prevenier, Raymond van Uytven, and Eddy van Cauwenberghe (Ghent, 1986), 111–33. For a consideration of fifteenth-century Florence: Richard C. Trexler, "Infanticide in Florence: New Sources and First Results," *History of Childhood Quarterly* 1 (1973): 98–116. See also Joanne Ferraro, *Nefarious Crimes, Contested Justice: Illicit Sex and Infanticide in the Republic of Venice, 1557–1789* (Baltimore, 2008); Marilyn Sandidge, "Changing Contexts of Infanticide in Medieval English Texts," in *Childhood in the Middle Ages and the Renaissance,* ed. Albrecht Classen (Berlin, 2005), 291–306.

69. Margaret King, *Women of the Renaissance* (Chicago, 1991), 10.

70. Fernandez, "Het verschijnsel," 131–32.

71. John M. Riddle, *Contraception and Abortion from the Ancient World to the Renaissance* (Cambridge, MA, 1992), 10–15; in the pardon letters of the Poitou eleven cases have been discovered for the fourteenth and fifteenth centuries: Yves B. Brissaud, "L'infanticide à la fin du moyen-âge," *Revue historique de droit français et étranger* 50 (1972): 229–56.

72. We examine two of these three cases. The third concerns the twenty-four-year-old Mariette de Marquette of Valenciennes (ADN, Lille, B, 1692, fol. 53r-v; Lancien, no. 979) who in 1467 drowned her newborn because the baby was born out of wedlock. Scared and repentant, she was held

social status of two young women pardoned for infanticide, the poor Marguerite de la Croix and the young aristocrat Antonie van Claerhout, make for an instructive contrast. However different the two women, in both cases they are characterized as young, unknowing, and scared, guilty of their crime, but with mitigating circumstances, none more important than the vulnerability of their sex. Of the two, de la Croix's case is the legally easier one; not only was she just eighteen years old, but she was a poor country girl from the small French village of Marcilly in the duchy of Burgundy near the city of Charolles, probably illiterate, who accidently got pregnant in 1459.[73] She secretly had carnal relations without being married. She concealed the pregnancy, understanding almost nothing about her condition:

> Around the end of last July she left the château of Terzé[74] in the morning after having milked the cows that belong to the lord of this château, as she had been doing for the last six weeks or thereabouts by the order of this lord and with the consent of her father and mother, who lived far from the château. After a quarter of a league or thereabouts she felt very sick and became bodily indisposed, as she already had been for some interval of time. Not knowing exactly what was happening, she went all alone into some bushes near to the gate of the château and after several pains she lay down on the ground and gave birth to a stillborn child. The baby was very small, not having been carried to term, and showed no sign of life. The supplicant was very frightened and sorrowful. She had such great and extreme sadness that she did not know what to do, because she was alone and without the comfort or help of any person. So she took the stillborn child and threw the corpse from the bushes into a water-filled ditch at the foot of the big tower of this château of Terzé. The child sank into the water, and the supplicant left [the corpse] there, hoping that no one would ever learn about her sorrowful case. Shortly thereafter, with much difficulty, she returned home to her father and mother, very sick, though dissimulating her

---

in the prison of the nunnery of Denaing. Although she escaped, she voluntarily returned and took perpetual vows. The terms of the pardon, like the case of Claerhout we explore below, required her to remain in the nunnery in perpetuity.

73. Pardon for Marguerite, daughter of Guillaume de la Croix. Autun, October 1459. ADN, Lille, B, 1687, fols. 73v–74v (Lancien, no. 869); Champion *CNN*, lxxiii. Marcilly-la-Gueurce, France, dépt. Saône-et-Loire, arr. and cant. Charolles; Charolles, France, dépt. Saône-et-Loire, chef-lieu arr.

74. Terzé, château located in Marcilly-la-Gueurce; in the middle of the fifteenth century the château was the property of Adrien de la Garde: Françoise Vignier, *Bourgogne: Nivernais* (Paris, 1980), 192.

sickness as best she could. It happened that three weeks later the supplicant was accused of this case, arrested, and taken into closed prison
in our castle of Charolles. There she was interrogated and questioned
about the crime, to which she confessed that what has been recounted
is the truth.

As the procedural section of de la Croix's pardon award reveals she was
thoroughly and repeatedly deposed by the procurator of Charolais, who determined that the premature birth was also a stillborn one. The characterization of de la Croix as a victim of her "youth and ignorance" but otherwise
"of good reputation and character" was certainly important in the clemency
she received. But equally relevant was the careful examination of Charolais'
procurator, whose determination of a stillborn miscarriage made offering the
pardon less controversial, easing the sting of the charge of infanticide.

More complicated was the pardon offered in 1455 to the young aristocrat
Antonie van Claerhout, living at the castle in Esquelbecq with the wife of
the lord of Esquelbecq, her relative. The complexity resulted not only from
her better-educated status and the fact that at twenty four she was somewhat
older, but also from the fact that her baby was born healthy—the offspring
of an affair she had had with a young man that had been born of "love" (letter no. 13). Claerhout kept the pregnancy quiet, but was reaching her term
when she traveled with her uncle the lord of Lichtervelde, a ducal councilor
and chamberlain, on family business.[75] While away and staying at a hostel in
the village of Lichtervelde, she went into labor and secretly bore the child,
which she wrapped up in a shirt:

> Then, determined to keep what happened a secret, and fearing the
> wrath and indignation of her uncle the lord of Lichtervelde, and
> tempted by the enemy [the devil], she took a knife and cut the throat
> of the child. She hung the child from the neck with one of her gar-
> ters, and threw the corpse, in the same state as it had been born, into
> a ditch filled with water in the hostel's garden, staying there a little to

---

75. The uncle was from a prominent family of ducal officials, among them Jacob van Lichtervelde, sovereign bailiff of Flanders in 1396–1402; the nobleman in this story is probably Lodewijk
van Lichtervelde, mentioned in a list of Flemish nobility of 1437 as lord of Staden, a seigneury in
the castellany of Bruges (Brugse Vrije); see F. Buylaert et al., "De adel ingelijst: Adelslijsten voor
het graafschap Vlaanderen in de veertiende en vijftiende eeuw," in *Bulletin de la Commission royale
d'histoire*, 173 (2007): 139, no. 1429. As such he was very often a representative of this castellany at the
meetings of the Four Members of Flanders and the Estates of Flanders from 1428 to 1456: Willem
P. Blockmans, *Handelingen van de Leden en van de Staten van Vlaanderen, Regering van Filips de Goede*,
vol. 1 (Brussels, 1990), 397, vol. 2 (Brussels, 1995), 1322.

The château of Terzé in Burgundy. Photo by Walter Prevenier.

watch if it would sink. When she saw that it had sunk to the bottom, she returned to her room and pretended to be sick and menstruating, so that no one would pay attention to her.

The next day she got up and appeared well, and a few days later she returned home to Esquelbecque. Weeks later, the corpse was discovered in the water-filled ditch where she had thrown it, and Claerhout was arrested. She immediately confessed, both to having lost her virginity to her secret lover, but also to her desperate efforts to terminate the pregnancy, all to no avail:[76] "Before these councilors she confessed to the things described above and also that, after she was deflowered and not knowing that she was pregnant, she often consumed mustard seed on her own initiative to avoid pregnancy." Claerhout's pardon is rare for a crime that was among the most harshly punished in early modern Europe, especially since, unlike in de la Croix's case, she had had a healthy baby and admitted to killing it in a panic. It is remarkable that the pardon letter calls the killing *murdre* (murder), indicating a premeditated and intentional act in contrast to homicide.[77] Her pardon had something to

---

76. John M. Riddle has documented that women from ancient Egyptian times to the early modern period have relied on an extensive pharmacopoeia of herbal abortifacients and contraceptives to regulate fertility. See John M. Riddle, *Eve's Herbs: A History of Contraception and Abortion in the West* (Cambridge, MA, 1997).

77. We follow here, as in the introduction, the definition of Corien Glaudemans; see note 5 there.

do with the fact that she was young, a "lady of noble birth," and also had the protective support, as the letter explicitly points out, of powerful relatives with Burgundian political connections. But it is in the procedural section of her pardon that another motive for forgiveness can be found. As a noble-woman and relative of the lord of Esquelbecq and the more senior lord of Lichtervelde, Claerhout was both politically connected and rich. Her pardon was predicated on very specific conditions, especially the requirement that she take religious vows and spend the rest of her life in a closed nunnery as a form of extended penance for her crime. Equally important, she was ordered to forfeit her property to the Burgundian authorities, namely her seigneury of Beernem and all other fiefs and lands to which she held title. This transfer of lands, titles, tithes, and rents to Burgundian coffers was hardly a typical requirement of a pardon letter, and speaks to a financial interest that ducal officials had in exacting a tidy gain in property and income in exchange for sparing Claerhout from capital punishment. Her high-born status and her network of supporters won Claerhout her life, but unlike the case of Mar-guerite de la Croix, forgiveness came at a stiff price: deprivation of her lands and immurement in a nunnery where she would spend the rest of her years.[78]

Sexual Mores and the Ubiquity of Violence

The pardons centered on public violence, male aggression, honor, and sex-ual misdeeds are a diverse set of cases, often lacking explicit motives for the murderous actions recounted. They have neither the structure nor the predetermined course of the vendetta that we explored in chapter 1. The narratives themselves, while varied, are succinct, even clipped—perhaps stra-tegically so, for the less revealed, the stronger the case for a pardon. In all but the infanticide cases, self-defense against physical violence is the common denominator. The obligations of male honor bulk large, particularly in the cases of sexual scandal involving an adulterous wife and a Machiavellian male seducer. The narratives typically represent petitioners as victims who acted in defense of their lives and their honor. Arguments centered on male social and sexual self-worth served as justifications for vengeance and murder, the petitioner's success predicated upon a quick recitation of how these values

---

78. Frederik Buylaert, *Eeuwen van ambitie: De adel in laatmiddeleeuws Vlaanderen* (Brussels, 2010), 34, is convinced that Antonie's noble status ("gentil femme, partie de noble generacion") was the decisive factor in the pardon.

had been violated. That this was a male domain explains why so few women petitioned for pardons, though they featured in pardon petitions. The two infanticide cases cited here, concerning women of sharply different social position, are important exceptions, and in both instances, the pardon hinged on the young women's vulnerability and youth. All cases reveal the coercive power of sexual mores, while underscoring the ubiquity of violence that flared up in spaces and times not predetermined by the social umbrella of friends, family, and community.

THE PARDON LETTERS

Letter no. 8

Pardon for Gillekin Dubois from Bailleul (castellany of Bailleul, county of Flanders). November 1506. ADN, Lille, B, 1718, fol. 1 r–v (Lancien, no 2905).

Let it be known to all those present and to come that we have received the humble supplication of Gillekin Dubois, son of Guillemin, a poor young man, native of our city of Bailleul[79] in Flanders, servant of and living in the house of Jan de Witte in Bruges. This supplicant has conducted and governed himself well and honestly without doing anything worthy of reproach. But some months ago on a Wednesday, the supplicant was asked by another companion, a servant in his master's house in Bruges, to come with him after dinner to go to the stews [public baths] to bathe, play games, or drink a pint of beer as young people are used to do. With his master absent, this supplicant got permission from his [the master's] wife to take the night off.

Going together down the street they happened upon a priest they knew who was also considering going out for a drink, and he led them to the house owned by Myne Sgeests, where some prostitutes were residing. They drank there for around two hours and each spent a *braspennick*,[80] which the companion of the supplicant paid because of a prostitute who arrived, and thereafter they left together.

At the moment of their departure from the premises, the brothel keeper learned that the supplicant came from Baillieul, and said to him that she often had frequented this quarter in the past,[81] and that they should really drink another pint of beer together to get to know each other better. The supplicant was rather wary about this, because he perceived that she was drunk. Nonetheless, he consented and while he was drinking he saw her conduct herself dishonestly, going from one place to another, both outside the house and in the neighborhood and back. He said to her that he

---

79. Bailleul, France, dépt. Nord, arr. Dunkerque.

80. A small silver coin, worth ten pennies illustrated in Chris Derboven, *Van muntslag tot muntschat: Twintig eeuwen geldgeschiedenis in het Land van Waas* (Brussels, 1985), 81, plate 7, comments on 72–73.

81. Guy Dupont discovered a prostitute from Bailleul in his sample of fifteenth-century prostitutes from Bruges (Dupont, *Maagdenverleidsters*, 203). She might well have been the brothel keeper of this story.

wanted to pay his bill and leave, to which she replied that he had had two beers and one jug. Hearing this, the supplicant said, "Really, I had only one pint of beer and one jug, which amounts to the price of one white penny," and he gave it to her saying "see, here's your money." She wasn't, however, satisfied with taking the money that she put in her purse, and said to the supplicant that he owed still for the rental of the room that he had taken with the prostitute which she wanted to be paid. The supplicant said, "You want to make me outraged by paying what I don't owe?" The brothel keeper loudly and very proudly responded, "You won't take away what is mine."

Suddenly a whore who was there moved forward to seize and take away a small dagger hanging at the supplicant's waistbelt, though he had not intended to do anything wrong. Then the brothel keeper seized the supplicant's hair from behind; with the help of the whore they threw him violently against a chair and pulled his dagger on him. Seeing the danger he was in, he avoided their hands the best he could and he escaped in his jerkin. Seeing that this whore had a dagger in her hand, he struck her with such a blow of his fist that this dagger fell to the ground. While he wanted to retrieve it, he couldn't. Again these two women assaulted and seized him by the hair, with a third helping them. They treated him so rudely with their blows and hair pulling that he yelled, "Whores, you are going to kill me here!" His life was for some time in great danger because one of the prostitutes had pulled a knife and he feared she would slit his throat. With a few maneuvers he found a way to free his hands and struck the face, and nothing more, of both the brothel keeper and the whore who had his dagger in his attempt to escape from them. When the one who had his dagger ran out of the house this supplicant went after her to retrieve his dagger. When he was outside he realized that he had left his cloak behind, so he returned but he found the door closed; he left the cloak and dagger there without any fuss or complaint.

The next day he went back to the brothel keeper to get his cloak and dagger, but was told she had left on pilgrimage to Gistel[82] and he would be told when she returned. The supplicant issued a complaint to the burgomasters of our city of Bruges who summoned the brothel keeper, interrogated the other persons involved, and ordered her to return the robe and dagger to this supplicant. Because this brothel keeper had complained about the bill even though the supplicant had paid more than he had owed, and so that she would not have cause to complain further, he paid her the balance.

Now it happened that four or five days after this case had occurred, the brothel keeper fell very sick. Her pimp let it be known to her neighbors that the brothel keeper's illness was the result of the supplicant's beating and that if she died she would want him to be killed, even though it was known that for at least a half of the last year she had been laid up sick in bed. Because of her illness and her bad life, she shortly thereafter died.

Because the supplicant had only struck her once with his fist after the abovementioned blows he had received, he cannot be considered guilty. This is also because the next day after the incident she had gone away on pilgrimage. Nevertheless, fearing the rigors of the law and having been assaulted because of this incident, he dared not

---

82. Gistel, Belgium, prov. West-Flanders, arr. Oostende.

remain in our lands and territories. He would keep himself away unless our grace and pardon could be imparted . . .

Letter no. 9

Pardon for Lieven de Zomer, from Ghent. Mechelen, August 1473. ADN, Lille, B, 1695, fols. 9v–10r. (Lancien, no. 1217).

Charles, duke of Burgundy, etc. Let it be known to all those present and to come that we have received the humble supplication of Lieven de Zomer, a poor man and native of our city of Ghent, stating that around the feast day of Saint Remy [October 2] in the year 1471 between eight and nine in the evening, the supplicant went for frolic and fun with two young girls outside the city.

As soon as he arrived at a place called the Twelve Rooms[83] the late Joskin van Temse and someone called Gillekin Busterman followed him. Immediately they caught up to him, Joskin demanded to whom belonged the girls he had with him. The supplicant, who had never before exchanged words with Joskin and Gillekin Busterman, replied that they were prostitutes of a small price, saying to the late Joskin that two or three days earlier he had spoken with a woman, which displeased Joskin.

Not satisfied with this response, the late Joskin and Gillekin continued to follow the supplicant until the end of the Twelve Rooms, where the late Joskin pulled his dagger and the supplicant his. They struck one another such that the late Joskin inflicted three wounds on the supplicant, namely, one under his right arm, the other on his left arm, and the third on his head, so that six bones came out of it, which also resulted from the blows that Gillekin, the late Joskin's accomplice, gave him. For a long time he was confined to his bed with his life in great peril, so injured and wounded that he never could be again the man he previously had been.

Seeing himself so wounded, the supplicant defended himself and gave the late Joskin not more than one blow to the chest, near the nipple, from which Joskin died after four days. Because of this case the supplicant, fearing the rigors of justice, no longer dared to be, live, go, or travel in our lands and territories. It seemed recommendable to him to absent himself and live in foreign borderlands and countries in great poverty and misery, unless it pleases us to pardon him of this case and impart our grace, which he very humbly requests of us.

Considering this case, and having pity and compassion for this poor supplicant, wishing in this instance to prefer grace and compassion to the rigors of justice, and on the advice of our high bailiff of Ghent, who by our ordinance confirmed the truth of this case, we dismiss, remit and pardon, . . . , pardoning the murder committed, ordering that it be proceeded well and diligently with the verification and registering of this letter, the fine being determined, negotiated, and paid to the receiver who is in charge of this receipt and account to our profit.

Given in our city of Mechelen in the month of August, 1473.

---

83. A place located near the city limits, also called Molenaarsstraat; see Maurits Gysseling, *Gent's vroegste geschiedenis in de Spiegel van zijn plaatsnamen* (Antwerp, 1954), 61, no. 284.

Letter no. 10

Pardon for Guillaume Nollet, from the village of Neuville-en-Ferrain (county of Flanders). Brussels, March 29, 1499. ADN, Lille, B, 1710, fols. 27–28 (Lancien, no. 2244).

Philip, etc. Let it be known to all those present and to come that we have received the humble supplication of Guillaume Nollet, aged fifty or thereabouts, who runs an inn named *Au Dronckairt* located on the high road between our cities of Kortrijk and Lille in the parish of Neuville-en-Ferrain,[84] stating that on the feast day of the Immaculate Conception [December 8] in 1498, some merchants from France lodged in his inn. The supplicant kept company with them for dinner at the table, while Hacquinot Nollet, his son, age twenty, served them.

This supplicant said to the merchants, "Did you see my son? I will make him jump up to the ceiling." Hearing this Hacquinot replied to the supplicant, "You are a real joker." This reply seemed very rude to the merchants, who said to the supplicant, "How do you suffer your son to speak thus to you. We can't believe he is your son." The supplicant was greatly angered.

Nevertheless, everyone went to sleep that night without anything else happening. The next day, a Sunday, the supplicant went together with another merchant from Hulst, in our land of Flanders, who had also spent the night at his inn and headed toward Halluin,[85] where they stayed until night, after which they returned back to lodge at the inn. Upon arriving there, the supplicant asked his wife if she had prepared a meal for them, and she responded no, because they had never asked or ordered her to do so. The supplicant went to sit in his chair, and a little time later he got up and went to get a bundle of kindling from his barn. When he returned, his son Hacquinot, who had come to the inn, sat in his chair. The supplicant put the bundle into the fire, and sat low down on a small footstool opposite his chair. His wife came and, seeing him sitting low down, said to him "go sit in your chair." He replied, "How shall I sit there when my master is seated there already?" He then got up when he said this. Hacquinot, seeing his father getting up, left the chair. The supplicant went forward to sit in the chair, with a small knife in his hand, and gave Hacquinot a blow to his leg, beneath the knee. Feeling the blow, Hacquenot said very loudly, "my father, you have mutilated me."

At that moment the merchant from Flanders came forward and encouraged the supplicant, who was greatly angered, reminding him that Hacquenot had called him a joker the night before. Shortly thereafter Hacquenot, who was bleeding heavily, began to succumb, and his mother supported him by taking him in her apron.

In seeing that he had so cruelly and mortally wounded his son, the supplicant got on his knees before him and begged him mercy to pardon him for his death. Hacquinot answered neither yes or no, but instead gave up his spirit and died.

Because of what occurred in this case the supplicant feared the rigors of justice, even though he was very sorry and had made satisfaction for the victim [by some

---

84. Dronkaart is a hamlet on the French-Belgian border, on the old road from Lille to Kortrijk, located in the village of Neuville-en-Ferrain, France, dépt. Nord, arr. Lille, cant. Tourcoing.

85. Halluin, France, dépt. Nord, arr. Lille, cant. Tourcoing.

payment]. He absented himself from our lands and seigneuries, and dare not ever return or to cross them, but is forced instead to keep away and live in poverty and misery in foreign borderlands and countries, unless our grace and mercy be imparted to him.

Considering that in all other things the supplicant until now has been a man of good life, fame, renown, and honest morals, without having committed or been named in another villainous case, nor incurred blame or reproach, he very humbly requests (pardon) of us . . .

Given in our city of Brussels, Good Friday [March 29] in the year 1499.

Letter no. 11

Pardon for Pieter de Scelewe, from Langemark (castellany of Ypres, county of Flanders). Bruges, January 8, 1458. ADN, Lille, B, 1688, fol. 3v (Lancien, no. 759bis); Petit-Dutaillis, 23–25.

Philip, by the grace of God, duke of Burgundy [etc.], let it be known to all those present and to come that we have received the humble supplication of Pieter de Scelewe, our poor subject, living in the parish of Langemark[86] in our castellany of Ypres, stating that two years or more ago, on the basis of many true presumptions and also by diverse reports by many and diverse people made to him that one named Christian de Cloot, his neighbor, pursued his wife to have carnal relations with her, and that rumor and public knowledge in the parish were that he knew her carnally. [The supplicant also stated that] by Christian's behavior and manner toward his wife, he absorbed in his imagination and his conviction that the adultery of his wife was real. He was also alerted that Christian's domestic servants had reproached him many times, saying that he was wrong to pursue this supplicant's wife and that only bad would come from it. But [Christian] would mock them, saying he knew the supplicant well, and that he would never do him [Pieter] wrong.

But more and more, he continued to come to the house of the supplicant, who was running a tavern and selling beer. The supplicant feared therefore that a conflict would come about between them, especially because [Christian] threw a glass of beer at his wife's face and said to some friends with whom he was drinking, and who reproached him for this, that the supplicant was a mongrel and had no balls[87] and that he was hardly fit to be a man. The supplicant had some of his good friends tell [Christian] that he was not happy with all this and that he was displeased with his pursuit of his wife and about the displeasure caused him, and with the insulting words he had said about him, and that he wanted him to refrain from coming to his tavern, and if he came again, it would displease him. Christian replied that he would come so long as beer was sold there and that he would stop those who would be displeased. Following this, on this past feast day of Saint Clement [November 23], Christian

---

86. Langemark, Belgium, prov. West-Flanders, arr. Ypres.

87. Mongrel: the original French text uses the word "gooc," a term of abuse identified as "gos" or "gous," meaning a mongrel or a bastard dog; see *Trésor de la Langue française informatisé* (http://atilf.atilf.fr), s.v. "gos." "Had no balls": "piffre," a term of abuse identified by the *Trésor*, on the basis of this document, as "homme dont les testicules sont restés dans le ventre."

came to drink in the supplicant's tavern, which displeased him. Because he did not want a conflict in his house, he went out to his garden and took a cudgel. It was only a short time later that he came across Christian, who likewise had a cudgel on him. Christian told him to defend himself and assaulted him, beating him between his legs with the cudgel and all over his body so that the supplicant fell down on the ground. He got up and beat Christian so that he fell down on the ground, and a short time thereafter, six or eight days later, Christian died. As soon as this had happened, Pieter brought it to the notice of several of his neighbors, who had come to his aid and led him to his tavern.

Now, it is true that the bailiffs of the count of Saint Pol, in the land and seigneury of Conchy, and in the seigneury of Dentergem,[88] which belonged to the son of the late Lodewijk van Lichtervelde, seized his movable and immovable goods. The bailiff of Conchy publicized this case in order to banish him for murder, because it had occurred in the seigneury of the aforesaid Conchy, and because it occurred during the night, and to declare his goods confiscated. This would result in his total ruin, given that he is a poor young man and all that he has is not worth one hundred francs, and that what happened would force him to absent himself from our county of Flanders to finish his days miserably in poverty unless our grace is imparted to him . . .

Given in our city of Bruges, January 8, 1458.

Letter no. 12

Pardon for demoiselle Antonie van Claerhout, from Esquelbecq (castellany of Bergues, county of Flanders). Bruges, May 1455. ADN, Lille, B, 1686, fol. 27v (Lancien, no. 634); Petit-Dutaillis, 19–22.

Philip, by the grace of God duke of Burgundy, etc. Let it be known to all those present and come that we have received the humble supplication of demoiselle Antonie van Claerhout, daughter of Euleat van Claerhout, twenty-four years old or thereabouts, stating that about a year ago she was living at the castle in Esquelbecq[89] with the wife of the lord of Esquelbecq, her relative, and fell in love with a young man named George Perche living also in Esquelbecq. They were so acquainted with one another that from their meetings she became pregnant with a child. The beloved and faithful knight, councilor, and chamberlain, the lord of Lichtervelde, her uncle, ordered her to go with him while she was pregnant to the aforesaid Lichtervelde to an appointment with lord Adriaan van Claerhout, knight, her brother,[90] concerning a certain inheritance to which they were both party, which she did. She arrived there on the eve of the feast day of Saint Andrew [November 29], 1453.

---

88. Conchy-sur-Canche, France, dépt. Pas-de-Calais, arr. Saint-Pol, cant. Auxi-le-Château ; Dentergem, Belgium, prov. West-Flanders, arr. Tielt.

89. Esquelbecq, France, dépt. Nord, arr. Dunkerque, cant. Wormhoudt. Euleat (or Eulaard) van Claerhout was lord of Koolskamp and Assebroek: Frederik Buylaert, *Repertorium van de Vlaamse adel, ca. 1350–ca. 1500*, Historische monografieën Vlaanderen, no. 1 (Ghent, 2011), 164.

90. Lichtervelde, Belgium, prov. West-Flanders, arr. Roeselare. Adriaan van Claerhout is mentioned in a list of nobility: Buylaert, et al., "De adel ingelijst," 147, no. 1645.

It happened that the supplicant was at the aforesaid Lichtervelde in a hostel named the Court de Bousbecque[91] on December 16 of that year—which was a Sunday—when, sometime before noon, she gave birth to a child. She quickly wrapped the child up, naked as he was born from her womb, in one of her shirts and at this point held the child close to her, covered with a robe until the next day, a Monday [December 17]. Then, around ten in the morning,[92] determined to keep what happened a secret, and fearing the wrath and indignation of her uncle the aforesaid lord of Lichtervelde, and tempted by the enemy [the devil], she took a knife and cut the throat of the aforesaid child. She hung the child from the neck with one of her garters, and threw the corpse, in the same state as it had been born, into a ditch filled with water in the hostel's garden, staying there a little to watch if it would sink. When she saw that it had sunk to the bottom, she returned to her room and pretended to be sick and menstruating, so that no one would pay attention to her.

On the following Tuesday, she arose as if normal, and went on foot to the castle of the aforesaid Lichtervelde, about a half-quarter of a league away. On the following Thursday, she went on foot to Torhout,[93] a full league away from the aforesaid Lichtervelde, and on the following Saturday, she arrived back at Esquelbecque without making any reference to anybody about the case. The case was still concealed until the following January 24, when the child was discovered and Antonie, supplicant, was suspected.

When the lord of Lichtervelde informed the lord of Esquelbecque about this, he quickly seized Antonie and imprisoned her. When this news came to our attention, we sent some from our council to examine and interrogate the supplicant. Before these councilors she confessed to the things described above and also that, after she was deflowered and not knowing that she was pregnant, she often consumed mustard seed on her own initiative to avoid pregnancy. Because of what happened, this supplicant was arrested and taken into custody by our attorneys and has been continuously detained since then as a prisoner under great duress. She would have been bound to miserably finish her days there unless our grace and mercy were imparted to her, as she said; which, given what has been recounted, she very humbly did implore and request.

Given the aforesaid actions, given the youth and the great fear the supplicant had of being found out, having compassion and pity for her, and wishing in this case to prefer compassion and pity to the rigors of justice, we incline toward the pardon request of this supplicant, who is a gentlewoman of noble birth, and also in favor of some lords and others of her relatives and friends who had humbly implored and requested [a pardon]. In this case, we have dismissed, remitted, and pardoned, and by

---

91. Bousbecque, France, dépt. Nord, arr. Lille, cant. Tourcoing; in the fifteenth century the village was the seat of the seigneurie de la Lys and had a court: Jean Dalle, *Histoire de Bousbecque* (Wervicq, 1880), 131 and 427.

92. The tenth hour of the morning must reflect the so-called "modern hour," the equivalent of our contemporary time, because in the older system (of unequal hours), the tenth hour ran from 1:30 to 2 PM. See Egied Strubbe and Léon Voet, *Chronologie van de middeleeuwen en de moderne tijden* (Antwerp, 1960), 15.

93. Torhout, Belgium, prov. West-Flanders, arr. Bruges.

our certain knowledge, authority, power and special grace, by this letter we dismiss, remit, and pardon the facts, the actions, and the murder that have been described above, including all penalties, amends, and criminal and civil offenses, in which she has and may have misbehaved against us and our justice, for the cause and the circumstances of the above-described events.

We impose perpetual silence upon our procurator and all our officers on condition that the supplicant Antonie will legally transfer to us, before the bailiff and the men of the fief to which that belongs, her seigneury of Beernem[94] and its appurtenances, together with all her other fiefs, lands, farmed-out fisheries, tithes, houses, woods, and other goods and revenues, wherever they may be located and whatever their size and by whatever title or means she holds them. All these she must renounce entirely to our profit. And provided also that the supplicant will be required, by next Christmas, to join a closed monastery, becoming and living as a nun for all the days of her life, without leaving. For her keep there, we have consented, by special grace, that from one tithe that she will transfer to us she will take an annual pension of six Flemish pounds groat for her entire life . . .

Given in our city of Bruges, in May 1455.

Letter no. 13

Pardon for Ogier de Soussey, Perrenin Rebel, and Pierre Rebel, from Soussey (duchy of Burgundy). Beaune, July 1450. ADN, Lille, B, 1684, fols. 142–143v (Lancien, no. 533).

Philip, duke of Burgundy, etc. Let it be known to all those present and to come that we have received the humble supplication of Ogier de Soussey, around thirty-seven years old, charged with a wife and small children, Perrenin Rebel, around twenty-two years old, and Pierre Rebel, around eighteen years old, sons of Jehan Rebel from Soussey, stating that about three or four years ago the late messire Guillaume Doille, then a priest from Thoisy,[95] one night, knowing that Jehan Maillet, who lived in Soussey, was out of town, secretly entered his house. He went to the bed where Claude, the wife of Jehan Maillet, full sister of the named Ogier, and relative of Perrenin and Pierre Rebel, lay and was sleeping. Guillaume Doille, feigning to impersonate Jehan Maillet, Claude's husband, approached her and was on the verge of knowing her carnally. Claude woke up with a start and recognized him, realizing that this was not her husband but instead messire Guillaume Doille. Very afraid, angry, and bewildered, she immediately got out of bed, not wanting to consent to the bad wishes of the late messire Guillaume Doille. At this very late hour she ran, fleeing down into town, hurrying and crying as much as she could. This greatly displeased the supplicants.

It happened that messire Guillaume Doille since then said many great villainous and injurious words about Ogier because he was upset about what the supplicant Ogier had related about the actions that messire Guillaume had done. He menaced

---

94. Beernem, Belgium, prov. West-Flanders, arr. Bruges.

95. Soussey-sur-Brionne, France, dept. Côte d'Or, arr. Montbard, canton Vitteaux ; Thoisy-la-Berchère, France, dépt. Côte-d'Or, arr. Montbard, cant. Saulieu.

Ogier, and menaced him very strongly, ordering him before the [episcopal] court of Besançon without cause, without Ogier owing him anything or being obliged to him in any way. [Guillaume] oppressed Ogier with excommunication and extortion, levying many expenses and putting costs on him before he could be absolved.

Jehan Rebel, father of Perrenin and Pierre, a good and notable merchant, had at one time warned Guillaume Doille, accusing him about his faults and dissolute life and pleading with him and admonishing him to make amends and correct his behavior. Jehan Rebel had also introduced an inquest in a certain case that was then pending before the court of the official of Besançon between the procurator of the very reverend father in the Lord, the archbishop of Besançon, concerning a complaint against Jehan Maillet, plaintiff of the one part, and messire Guillaume Doille, of the other part. Messire Guillaume developed such hatred and malevolence against Jehan Rebel and his children that he maliciously said to Rebel, both in his presence and in his absence, many villainous, injurious, and defamatory things. Doille instigated Jehan Rebel's excommunication, troubled him, and provoked problems with lawsuits and other things, all wrongly and without any reasonable cause.

It is true that messire Guillaume was a quarrelsome man of a dissolute, bad, and dishonest life, accustomed to wrangle with many people who were under our protection and security and in opposition to him. This and other things can be proven by inquests and information made and taken against him by public notaries, reliable witnesses (*preudommes*) worthy of trust.

It so happened that since the last beginning of Lent [February 18, 1450] the supplicant Perrenin Rebel did or said something to displease messire Guillaume. Messire Guillaume had Perrenin excommunicated for having been at work, as Doille said, during a feast day. And messire Guillaume Doille received one franc before he would absolve him, and several times he menaced the supplicant Pierre Rebel with excommunication. Whenever messire Guillaume wanted to do harm to someone, even to ordinary people, he would immediately have them excommunicated. He continuously followed and frequented the Court of Besançon and of Gray,[96] as did the messengers of the Court.

It happened that a certain day after this past beginning of Lent these supplicants were at Thoisy, playing and amusing themselves with a ball game, when messire Guillaume, who always wanted to quarrel and cause problems, suddenly turned up and told them that the game was prohibited, and that he would stop [the game], and that it would cost them; he said many injurious and villainous things to them, defying them and saying, "We are three brothers who defy the three sons of Jehan Rebel and want to combat them."

After these words of defiance and on the Sunday when *Iudica Me* [March 22, 1450] is sung by the [Roman Catholic] Church, between nightfall and daybreak, the supplicants accidentally found messire Guillaume Doille in a place commonly called Sur Verrea,[97] carrying a large sword (*braquemart*) at his belt. He began to vilify and say injurious things to these supplicants, and he gave Perrenin a blow to the head with

---

96. Gray, France, dépt. Haute-Saône, arr. Vesoul, chef-lieu canton.

97. Sur Verrea can probably be identified as Verrey-sous-Salmaise, France, dépt. Côte d'Or, arr. Montbard, canton Vénarey-les-Laumes.

his sword, which caused the spilling of blood and a large wound. The supplicants, moved by this and the aforesaid things, struck messire Guillaume, one with a club of wood on the head and the other with a knife in the leg at the back of the knee.

Although they had neither the desire nor the intention to kill him, nevertheless death followed to the person of messire Guillaume. This messire Guillaume carried [at the time of the murder] a large file full of documents of excommunications and summonses of [the bishop of] Besançon. The supplicants took the file with the excommunications and summonses, because messire Guillaume had boasted that he would have many people excommunicated from the parish of Soussey before Easter. They shredded the file, the excommunications, and the summonses into pieces, and threw them in the fire out of fear that Guillaume would not be dead and would not have died from the blows. They did this with the intention that Guillaume would not be in a position to have executed those excommunications and summonses against the people for whom they were written.

Because of this case, the supplicants, fearing the rigor of justice, absented themselves from our territories of Burgundy, and dare not ever return nor live [there]. It would require them to live miserably and in great poverty in foreign borderlands and countries, unless our grace and mercy be imparted to them. Considering what has been said and that these supplicants always have been men of good fame, reputation, and irreproachable conduct in life without ever having been admonished or convicted of any other villainous case, reprimand, or reproach, as they say, they very humbly request and beg [our pardon] . . . and we have in this case quitted, remitted, and pardoned.

Given in our city of Beaune in the month of July 1450.

CHAPTER 3

Marital Conflict

A Widow Kidnapped

Like many women in the fifteenth century, Antoinette de Rambures, a new resident of Mechelen, found herself widowed while still in her mid-thirties. Widows were an ordinary part of the social landscape in premodern Europe; in Florence, perhaps the best-documented case, they made up 9.9 percent of heads of household in 1427.[1] Younger widows like de Rambures typically reentered the marriage marketplace, especially in parts of northern Europe in which they held rights to succeed to significant marital property. In one sample of marriage contracts from fifteenth-century Douai, for example, widows figured in 30 percent of the cases; during the same period they typically wrote two-thirds of the wills.[2] In the dotal systems of southern Europe, in particular Italy, widows remarried less often than they did in the Low Countries, though marital property regimes and the numbers of remarriages differed from city to city.[3] What distinguished de Rambures' widowhood was

---

1. Christiane Klapisch-Zuber and David Herlihy, *Tuscans and Their Families: A Study of the Florentine Catasto of 1427* (New Haven, CT, 1985), 301.

2. Martha Howell, *The Marriage Exchange: Property, Social Place, and Gender in Cities of the Low Countries, 1300–1550* (Chicago, 1998), 152–56.

3. For Florence, with its strict dotal regime, see Klapisch-Zuber and Herlihy, *Tuscans and their Families,* 214–222; Christiane Klapisch-Zuber, *Women, Family, and Ritual in Renaissance Italy,* trans.

not her age but rather her level of social prestige, the singular prominence of her husband, and the circumstances surrounding his death in 1477.

In 1463, Antoinette de Rambures had married Guy de Brimeu, lord of Humbercourt, a Picardian nobleman who had risen to the most senior ranks of the confidants of Burgundian Duke Charles the Bold.[4] Guy de Brimeu served the Burgundian administration faithfully, earning the coveted honor of knighthood in the Order of the Golden Fleece in 1473—the elite badge of Burgundian prestige.[5] Among his many titles was that of lieutenant general of Liège. In 1467 and 1468, he oversaw the ruthless repression of the city following a protracted revolt, including the destruction of much of the urban center, as punishment for its campaigns against the Burgundian duke. For this and other services to the Burgundian cause, Brimeu grew rich from titles, gifts, and favors. Between 1473 and 1476, his annual income was an astonishing 23,000 pounds tournois, a sum only exceeded by the most senior Burgundian official, the chancellor Nicolas Rolin, who collected 25,000 pounds tournois a year.[6] Yet shortly after Charles the Bold died in battle against the Swiss on January 5, 1477, de Brimeu's luck turned. Urban protests against the deceased duke's heavy hand and in favor of restoring traditional rights and privileges swept through Brabant, Flanders, and elsewhere. With a young and inexperienced heiress, Mary of Burgundy, at the helm, de Brimeu and the ducal chancellor at the time, Guillaume Hugonet, rode to Ghent to staunch

---

Lydia G. Cochrane (Chicago, 1985), 117–31. In Venice widows had many material advantages so long as they did not remarry; see Stanley Chojnacki, *Women and Men in Renaissance Venice: Twelve Essays on Patrician Society* (Baltimore, 2000), 99–100, 124–25, 172–73. If a widow in Siena remarried "she would lose all claims to those properties beyond her dowry": Samuel K. Cohn Jr., *Women in the Streets: Essays on Sex and Power in Renaissance Italy* (Baltimore, 1996), 65–66.

4. See the comprehensive study of Brimeu in Werner Paravicini, *Guy de Brimeu: Der burgundische Staat und seine adlige Führungsschicht unter Karl dem Kühnen* (Bonn, 1975), esp. 502–4 on de Rambures' kidnapping. Antoinette de Rambures was married to de Brimeu in 1463 and died in 1517. While her age is not explicitly documented, it would have been typical for her to be around twenty at marriage. On these dates, see ibid., 513 n. 68, 557. A full analysis of the case is in Walter Prevenier, "Geforceerde huwelijken en politieke clans in de Nederlanden: De ontvoering van de weduwe van Guy van Humbercourt door Adriaan Vilain in 1477," in *Beleid en bestuur in de oude Nederlanden: Liber Amicorum Prof. Dr. M. Baelde*, ed. Hugo Soly and René Vermeir (Ghent, 1993), 299–307.

5. On the order, see D'Arcy Jonathan Dacre Boulton, "The Order of the Golden Fleece," in *The Knights of the Crown: the Monarchical Orders of Knighthood in Later Medieval Europe, 1325–1520,* ed. D'Arcy Jonathan Dacre Boulton (New York, 2000), 356–96; on Guy Brimeu's membership: Raphael de Smedt, *Les chevaliers de l'Ordre de la Toison d'or au XVe siècle: Notices bio-bibliographiques* (Frankfurt am Main, 1994), 152.

6. Paravicini, *Guy de Brimeu,* 409–449, esp. 423. Herta-Florence Pridat, *Nicolas Rolin: Chancelier de Bourgogne* (Dijon, 1996); Hermann Kamp, *Memoria und Selbstdarstellung: Die Stiftungen des burgundischen Kanzlers Rolin* (Sigmaringen, 1993).

the rebellion. In a city known for its pugnacious radicalism, urban rebels seized the two men along with former aldermen they suspected of complicity with Charles the Bold's administration. De Brimeu and Hugonet were tried and tortured for violations of the city's legal privileges and related transgressions, and then—despite a personal appeal for clemency from a stunned Mary of Burgundy—summarily executed on April 3 on Ghent's Vrijdagmarkt.[7]

Suddenly widowed, de Rambures settled in the city of Mechelen with her six young children. The city was an obvious choice. Home to the Parlement of Mechelen and a favored residence of the Burgundian court, the city was a hive of political activity and cultural life. In the months since de Brimeu's execution, on March 31 and April 24, the ducal administration, had intervened on de Rambures' behalf, requesting the city to give her financial support and issuing directives to preserve her late husband's estate from confiscation.[8] But as a widow, she was nonetheless vulnerable.

On December 13, 1477 de Rambures set out on pilgrimage to the church of Our Lady of Hanswijk on the outskirts of Mechelen. Once arrived, she offered her devotion, but as she stepped out of the church, she was seized by a group of men led by Adriaan Vilain, a squire of Gavere and Liedekerke. Forced into a horse-drawn wagon, de Rambures was transported to the small town of Rupelmonde, where in the house of a local marshal, and over a well-prepared meal, Vilain urged her to marry him (letters nos. 14 and 15). The testimony does not suggest that Vilain sexually assaulted de Rambures, although he did keep her sequestered against her will. After three terrifying days, de Rambures' luck turned when a search party located her, apprehended Vilain and his men, and promptly imprisoned them.

Vilain's seizure of de Rambures was a startling, confounding act: a kidnapping that served as a platform for a marriage proposal. Taken violently hostage by several armed men and transported against her will, de Rambures was then treated to a well-prepared meal and her kidnapper's entreaties that she wed him. For all the incongruity of a marriage proposal delivered by abduction, de Rambures' ordeal was not without precedent in the Burgundian Netherlands, as the case of Jan van Gavere's abduction of Maria van Schoonvorst that we considered in chapter 1 has already indicated. Its target

---

7. On the context of the 1477 urban rebellion, see Jelle Haemers, *For the Common Good: State Power and Urban Revolts in the Reign of Mary of Burgundy (1477–1482)* (Turnhout, 2009), 5–18. On the executions: Paravicini, *Guy de Brimeu*, 490; Polydore-Charles van der Meersch, ed., *Memorieboek der stadt Ghendt van 't jaar 1301 tot 1737*, vol. 1 (Ghent, 1852), 300–301.

8. Paravicini, *Guy de Brimeu*, 489–93; Christine Weightman, *Margaret of York, Duchess of Burgundy, 1446–1503* (New York, 1989), 114.

The church of Our Lady of Hanswijk just outside the walls of the city of Mechelen (visible in the background). Nineteenth-century drawing by Arnold van den Eynden, copy of an older drawing from before 1577. Stadsarchief Mechelen, Verzameling Schoeffer. Courtesy of and © Stadsarchief Mechelen, www.beeldbankmechelen.be.

was familiar: a well-to-do widow, propertied, marriageable, and despite money and assets, friends and family, easy prey to schemers and predators. More violent still was an earlier case in 1447 that involved Anna Willemszoon: a rich widow like de Rambures, near sixty years old, and twice married to well-to-do husbands who had predeceased her. Willemszoon was abducted in the middle of the night from her home—literally seized from her bed in her nightgown. A group of armed men forced her into a wagon, then threatened to rape and kill her if she refused the marital proposal of her kidnapper Cornelis Boudinszoon. Terrified, threatened, and coerced, she consented, but remarkably several months later, escaped her captors and registered a suit against her kidnapper and his accomplices (letter no. 16).[9]

Antoinette de Rambures and Anna Willemszoon suffered abduction as a means to effect coerced marriages. Like many other pardon cases, their cases allow us to peer into the urban social world and the political and social networks that framed them, nurtured their alliances, and provoked their

---

9. On this case, see Walter Prevenier, "Vrouwenroof als middel tot sociale mobiliteit in het 15de-eeuwse Zeeland," in *De Nederlanden in de late middeleeuwen,* ed. Dick E. H. de Boer and Jannis Willem Marsilje (Utrecht, 1987), 410–24.

considerable tensions. While the overwhelming majority of Burgundian pardon letters centered on appeals for clemency for homicide or murder, a small number were awarded for the crimes of abduction and seduction, two distinct yet overlapping legal actions against women that concerned urban magistrates and ducal courts. In what follows, we take up the stories of de Rambures, Willemszoon, and three others as recounted in pardons awarded to their abductors and seducers to delve into how marriage, marriage law, and familial networks linked public governance and private life, and to excavate the social world in which they were anchored. We will explore how tensions between official marriage law and customary social practice provoked regular domestic woes, and how the princely pardon became a tool employed to resolve or short-circuit such conflicts, sometimes at the expense of a victim of a violent crime. The utility of the pardon letter in settling voluntary elopements and violent kidnappings points to its importance on a broader social plane than that of just a single individual and his or her misdeed. As with family vendettas and work conflicts, the pardon could be used for wider social purposes, in these instances to settle crimes of kidnapping, abduction, and even rape, sometimes with an eye to protecting the victim and keeping the social peace, and sometimes to helping the violent perpetrator at the expense of the female victim. For the petitioner, a princely pardon was yet again a legal lifeline, and for the prince, pardons in cases involving abductions and marriage disputes were yet another way to exercise authority in the social world, whether to restore social harmony, affirm patriarchal authority, or recruit a new ally by intervening to forgive a violent abductor.

Medieval Marriage

Our cases of elopement, seduction, and abduction were the products of marriage customs and legal practices in which the Catholic Church's canonical rules for matrimony collided regularly with the conflicting interests of princes, urban authorities, extended families, and parents. Other cultural and social ingredients also mattered. Beyond marriage itself, late medieval authorities, both religious and secular, vigorously enforced gender and sexual norms, from actual sexual practice to legal rules of family property and inheritance.[10] Nowhere was such intervention more obvious than in domestic

---

10. The degree of such enforcement varied, depending on administrative structures, political circumstances, and interpretations of law, both secular and canon. For a comparative analysis of late medieval London and Paris, see Ruth Karras, "The Regulation of Sexuality in the Late Middle Ages: England and France," *Speculum* 86 (2011): 1010–39.

life itself, particularly in respect of the church's enforcement of the canon of marriage and municipal and state government regulation of marital contracts and family life.[11]

In the course of the twelfth century, especially in the writings of Hugh of Saint Victor, marriage was defined as a holy sacrament.[12] Thereafter, marriage existed in uneasy tension between ideal and practice. On the one hand, the church claimed legal and spiritual control of the institution of indissoluble marriage, based on free consent between bride and groom. The church insisted upon its exclusive authority to define, sanction, and occasionally annul a marriage. On the other hand, familial interests shaped marital practice, for families continued to oversee and approve, if not directly select, partners for marriageable children in an effort to control the future of both the kin group and its property.[13] Families, kin networks, and the world of work and social obligation thus shaped marriage choices and patterns. Among rich and poor alike, the church's ideal of free consent was subordinated to socially strategic concerns of parents and other relatives over the choice of spouses. The pattern in the north and south of western Europe favored family-brokered unions between men on the cusp of their economic and political adulthood, in their mid-twenties, and young women in their late teens to early twenties.[14]

Despite the enormous weight of the family and practical considerations in marriage, the role of choice in marriage partners was never entirely absent. The church's position was paramount. The canonist Gratian (circa 1140) considered marriage dependent on the consent of the partners, and the Fourth Lateran Council of 1215 confirmed the free will of groom and

---

11. See Stanley Chojnacki's discussion of Renaissance Italy: Chojnacki, *Women and Men*, 27–52, also Judith C. Brown and Robert C. David, eds., *Gender and Society in Renaissance Italy* (London, 1998). On the Low Countries, see Marc Boone, Thérèse de Hemptinne, and Walter Prevenier, "Gender and Early Emancipation in the Low Countries in the Late Middle Ages and Early Modern Period," in *Gender, Power, and Privilege in Early Modern Europe*, ed. Jessica Munns and Penny Richards (London, 2003), 21–39, 176–80.

12. Georges Duby, *The Knight, the Lady, and the Priest: The Making of Modern Marriage in Medieval France* (Chicago, 1993), 172–76, 183. The idea can be found, however, in works of theologians such as Augustine from the fourth century on: John Witte Jr., *From Sacrament to Contract: Marriage, Religion, and Law in the Western Tradition* (Louisville, KY, 1997), 19–22.

13. See Georges Duby, *Medieval Marriage: Two Models from Twelfth-Century France*, trans. Elborg Forster (Baltimore, 1991). Studies of medieval and early modern marriage as a tool of social alliance abound. For a rich urban case study, see Anthony Molho, *Marriage Alliance in Late Medieval Florence* (Cambridge, MA, 1994), and for a rural counterpart, see Barbara Hanawalt, *The Ties that Bound: Peasant Families in Medieval England* (Oxford, 1989).

14. Jack Goody, *The Development of the Family and Marriage in Europe* (Cambridge, UK, 1983), a cornerstone work, now widely contested for its portrait of premodern marriages as bereft of sentiment, and of companionate marriage as the innovation of the social elite.

bride as essential for a valid marriage.[15] In the literary realm, Chrétien de Troyes and other twelfth-century writers wrote about the transformative power of the emotions inspired by physical love.[16] That canonical stipulations about free will and literary expressions of love coincided was no accident.

The medieval church stipulated three elements for a legal marriage: the betrothal, that is the bride's and groom's consensual promise to marry (in the future tense, or *verba de futuro*); the publication of the banns three times at the door of a church, so that objections—over close degrees of kinship or involving a former marriage that was still valid, for example—might be aired; and the declaration in the present tense (*verba de presenti*) of vows before a priest, immediately followed by a nuptial mass. For most theologians the sexual consummation of a relationship (*copula*) was a final condition for a legal marriage. Of these criteria, consent was both crucial and inevitable. The marriage was deemed clandestine if any one of these requirements for a canonically legal marriage was not observed. Clandestine unions were marriage vows between a man and woman not solemnized by a priest or preceded by the publication of banns but still deemed valid because vows had been freely exchanged, not in a church, but at home, in a tavern, or anywhere else, with reliable witnesses.[17] Most parish priests were not particularly concerned by such couplings so long as vows had been exchanged and a relationship had been sexually consummated, but the ecclesiastical hierarchy obviously frowned upon such arrangements. Nevertheless the Lateran Council of 1215 and the later canonists declared these clandestine marriages acceptable and valid, even if not fully legal, much to the chagrin of secular authorities and families determined to manage the choice of marriage partners. In the late Middle Ages most extra-ecclesiastical marriages were socially recognized just like the canonically legal alliances.[18] In 1563, the Council of Trent finally invalidated clandestine marriages after centuries of criticism.[19]

---

15. Conor McCarthy, ed., *Love, Sex and Marriage in the Middle Ages: A Sourcebook* (London, 2004), 68–70.

16. Leslie Thomas Topsfield, *Chrétien de Troyes: A Study of the Arthurian Romances* (Cambridge, UK, 1981), 89–91.

17. Shannon McSheffrey, *Marriage, Sex, and Civic Culture in Late Medieval London* (Philadelphia, 2006), 29–30; marriage contracts discussed at home, in the street, in taverns, ibid., 122–34.

18. For fifteenth-century London, see ibid., 28.

19. On the distinction between valid and legal marriages: Richard H. Helmholz, *Marriage Litigation in Medieval England* (Cambridge, UK, 1974), 25–73; Jeremy Boulton, "Clandestine Marriages in London: Examination of a Neglected Urban Variable," *Urban History* 20, no. 2 (1993): 191–210; Monique Vleeschouwers–Van Melkebeek, "Bina matrimonia: Matrimonium praesumptum versus matrimonium manifestum," in *Auctoritates: Xenia R. C. Van Caenegem oblata,* ed. Serge Dauchy et al., Iuris

France refused, however, to follow this decree, and preferred to use French inheritance law in order to achieve the same goal.[20]

Consent and Free Choice in Marriage

If we judge by the provisions of canon law and ecclesiastical writings on marriage in late medieval society at large, we might assume that the principle of free choice of marital partners, so emphatically expressed by twelfth-century canon law, carried the day for most young couples. But despite law and theology, families continued to exert the authority of parents and kin in arranging marriage choices for sons and daughters, concerned as they were over social status and economic and familial livelihoods. Arranged marriages, therefore, were commonly practiced, and civic and state authorities often issued decrees that facilitated this type of union, as was the case in 1438 with legislation in the Burgundian Netherlands that we shall later explore.[21]

At the same time, we have cases of young people who attempted to evade paternal dictates about marriage, risking their place in their families and even their share of family inheritances to unions of their choice. In reality, however, for most young men and women marriage choices were poised somewhere between the arranged and the negotiated, as Shannon McSheffrey has observed for late medieval England.[22] It is impossible for the historian to know what blend of sentiment and strategy lay behind the decisions of young people to make choices of marriage partners that were different from those that their families might have desired. Purely material factors might be at play, from profession to level of income and ownership of goods and assets like landed properties, houses, and household goods. Pardon letters and other legal and literary documents that expose marriage conflicts between young people and parents and kin also uncover a range of emotional factors,

---

scripta historica, no. 13 (Brussels, 1997), 245–55; Monique Vleeschouwers–Van Melkebeek, "Aspects du lien matrimonial dans le Liber Sentenciarum de Bruxelles (1448–1459)," *Revue de l'Histoire du Droit* 53 (1985): 49–67; Monique Vleeschouwers–Van Melkebeek, "Classical Canon Law on Marriage: The Making and Breaking of Households," in *The Household in Late Medieval Cities: Italy and Northwestern Europe Compared,* ed. Myriam Carlier and Tim Soens (Louvain, 2001), 15–23; Walter Prevenier, "Les réseaux familiaux," in *Le prince et le peuple: Images de la société du temps des ducs de Bourgogne, 1384–1530,* ed. Walter Prevenier (Antwerp, 1998), 185–92.

20. Martha C. Howell, *Commerce Before Capitalism in Europe, 1300–1600* (New York, 2011), 121 n. 56.

21. Frans de Potter, *Petit cartulaire de Gand* (Ghent, 1885), 66–69.

22. McSheffrey, *Marriage,* 18: "balancing their own desires with the expectations of family, friends and society."

from physical attraction and looks to sexual desire, friendship, and the linked notions of "affection" and love.[23]

The emotional texture of late medieval marriage is an important consideration here because a few decades ago, most historians of the European family were still convinced that marital love was not a genuine experience for most premodern people. As recent as 1974 Edward Shorter declared that "in the Middle Ages only the elite were able to express tenderness and passion, and so love. Only around the middle of the eighteenth century did love really appear as an independent force bringing young people together."[24] In 1977 Lawrence Stone noted that "social relations from the fifteenth to the seventeenth centuries tended to be cool, even unfriendly," and concluded that before the eighteenth century spouses of all social backgrounds experienced "little love and low and widely diffused affect."[25] Stone's portrait of premodern marriages as bereft of sentiment in his cornerstone work is now widely contested.

Alan Macfarlane and Rudolf Lenz in the 1980s were among the first scholars to detect sentiment and attraction in medieval marriage, followed by Stanley Chojnacki for Renaissance Venetian patricians.[26] The debate over whether affection and love were felt in medieval marriage continues even after several decades of scholarship, in part because of the lack of medieval records that address the issue. Even the term "love" is slippery because it was widely applied in the late Middle Ages; married men and women might "love" each other, but they also "loved" their neighbors, lords, friends, their

---

23. Pierre J. Payer, *The Bridling of Desire: Views of Sex in the Later Middle Ages* (Toronto, 1993), 68–83; Albrecht Classen and Marilyn Sandidge, eds, *Friendship in the Middle Ages and Early Modern Age: Explorations of a Fundamental Ethical Discourse* (Berlin, 2010). Jean Leclercq, "L'amour et le mariage vus par des clercs et des religieux, spécialement au XIIe siècle," in *Love and Marriage in the Twelfth Century,* ed. Willy Van Hoecke and Andries Welkenhuysen (Louvain, 1981), 102–15, esp. 105, reveals contemporary definitions of the concept "affection" linked to the notion "love" in the Middle Ages: "amoureux état d'esprit" and "attachement profond et efficace."

24. Edward Shorter, "Différences de classe et sentiment depuis 1750: L'exemple de la France," *Annales : Économies, Sociétés, Civilisations* 29 (1974): 1039.

25. Lawrence Stone, *The Family, Sex and Marriage in England, 1500–1800* (London, 1979), 814 and 93.

26. Alan Macfarlane, *Marriage and Love in England: Modes of Reproduction, 1300–1840* (Oxford, 1986); Rudolf Lenz, "Emotion und Affektion in der Familie der Frühen Neuzeit," in *Die Familie als Sozialer und Historischer Verband,* ed. Peter Johannes Schuler (Sigmaringen, 1987), 121–46; Chojnacki, *Women and Men,* 151–68, esp. 156. For medieval England, see Peter Fleming, *Family and Household in Medieval England* (Houndmills, UK, 2001), 23–31, 53–59. See also Albrecht Classen, *Sexuality in the Middle Ages and Early Modern Times: New Approaches to a Fundamental Cultural-Historical and Literary-Anthropological Theme* (Berlin, 2008). Classen argues that medieval people "acknowledged the positive and constructive value of marriage as an institution where sexuality could be lived out," 8.

magen en vrienden (extended families), and their business associates. Over the whole of the Middle Ages, there is a body of work—from Saint Augustine's theology to Andreas Capellanus' writings to late medieval household advice manuals—that extols the virtues of love and marriage.[27] And yet the language of conjugal love could also be seen as a strategic tool to strengthen marriage in an era of shifting and unstable property relations. That said, there is no reason to deny that the "love" medieval people expressed for a spouse was a feeling of special attachment and devotion.

If medieval marriages were not bereft of affection, it's another matter whether they were "companionate," a term used to describe unions based on mutual affection and shared responsibilities rather than those driven purely by strategic and material interests.[28] Martha Howell's empirical consideration of marriage in late medieval Douai, a city with a preponderance of small family businesses and nuclear households, reveals that couples' common responsibilities were considerable and greater than in most other cities.[29] Yet Douai's households were also patriarchical and hierarchical—the essential difference from companionate marriages in many societies today.[30]

Medieval sources that can shed light on the affective dimension of medieval marriages are not numerous. A thirteenth-century schoolbook of Ghent's Saint Peter's Abbey, with pedagogical models of letters intended for well-to-do children, offers us some insight despite its fictional nature. In one letter, a burgher of Saint-Omer in the county of Artois inquires about a young woman whom a business partner in Ghent has proposed to him as a potential bride. The man specifies the qualities of this young women about which he seeks information: her physical and psychological particularities (*tam corporis quam animi circonstancias*), her moral behavior (*cum moribus et vita*), and the amount of her estate and how the properties have been acquired (*ac bonorum suorum summam, etiam qualiter acquisita fuerint*).[31] Chojnacki found

---

27. Roy J. Deferrari, ed., *Treatises on Marriage and Other Subjects,* trans. Charles T. Wilcox (1955; reprint, New York, 1999), 211. On Capellanus and other late medieval writers: Neil Cartlidge, *Medieval Marriage: Literary Approaches, 1100–1300* (Cambridge, UK, 1997), 24–32; on his treatise *De Amore,* influenced by Countess Marie de Champagne: Hildegard Baumgart, *Jealousy: Experiences and Solutions* (Chicago, 1990), 114–18; McSheffrey, *Marriage,* 18.

28. For a contemporary sociological definition, see Judith S. Wallerstein and Sandra Blakeslee, *The Good Marriage: How and Why Love Lasts* (New York, 1995), 155.

29. Howell, *The Marriage Exchange,* 169–75, 233–39; on the specific legislation on marriage, succession, and inheritance in Douai: Robert Jacob, *Les époux, le seigneur et la cité: Coutumes et pratiques matrimoniales des bourgeois et paysans de France du Nord au moyen âge* (Brussels, 1990), 174–240.

30. Howell, *Commerce before Capitalism,* 93–144.

31. Napoleon de Pauw, *La vie intime en Flandre au Moyen Âge* (Brussels, 1913), 46–48, no. 25.

similar concerns in late medieval Venice, where the "well-being of daughters also had its place in marriage strategies," and "mothers, fathers, and brothers acted out of both affection and practical interest."[32] Or consider the Valentine letters the Englishwoman Margery Brews sent to her future husband, John III Paston, in February 1477. As English gentry, she and her family were interested in issues of property and other assets. But here, Margery expresses—whether genuine or formulaic—affection, especially in her utterance to her husband-to-be that "I will do all my myght yowe to love," and "if that ye hade not halfe the lyvelode that ye hafe . . . I wold not forsake yowe."[33]

In the legal arena, affection and compatibility factored in the adjudication of marriage and other familial disputes. In fifteenth-century decisions, the episcopal courts of Cambrai and Brussels routinely accepted incompatibility of character (*morum discrepantia*) as a justification for separation from bed and board.[34] The same held for civil courts; in 1383 Jean Pastoure, from a small village near Troyes in Champagne, invoked the same justification during his trial before the Parlement of Paris. Pastoure was accused of the abduction of the married woman Jehannette Coleau, but countered that she had come to him of her own accord. Jehannette herself explained her actions by an appeal to emotion—"for the affinity that she had for him greater than for anyone else"—and as a means to flee a husband "who had caused her great injury" (*avoit fait et faisoit plusieurs grans durtez a icelle*).[35]

The arrangement of marriages and the choice of partners of course varied across the social spectrum, from peasants to noble families, although calculations about status and material wellbeing mattered to all. In a 1478 letter John Paston observed that London, a marketplace for the intermarriages of merchants and gentry, was an ideal location for news about potential spouses and their social status.[36] But even marriages arranged by parents between boys and girls who had hardly met—a pattern not practiced by ordinary people—had the potential to become affectionate, with bonds of appreciation between husband and wife. Pragmatism was not necessarily in conflict

---

32. Chojnacki, *Women and Men*, 12.

33. James Gairdner, ed., *The Paston Letters, 1422–1509*, vol. 3 (Edinburgh, 1910), 170–72.

34. Vleeschouwers-Van Melkebeek, "Aspects du lien matrimonial," 67–74.

35. Archives Nationales, Paris, X 2A, 10, fol. 162r; Walter Prevenier, "Methodological and Historiographical Footnotes on Emotions in the Middle Ages and the Early Modern Period," in *Emotions in the Heart of the City (14th–16th Century)*, ed. Elodie Lecuppre-Desjardin and Anne-Laure Van Bruaene (Turnhout, 2005), 283–84.

36. Fleming, *Family and Household*, 34.

with emotion; in the short term, the value of a dowry might be essential, but in the long term affectionate companionship was a stronger anchor.[37] Several of our pardon letters point to that affective domain, and the importance of sentiment and affection in courtship and marriage.

Civic Authorities

In the cities of the Low Countries, rich in commerce, artisanal life, trade, and manufacturing, propertied families pursued marriage with socially exacting care.[38] Even without official political rights, women had genuine areas of social and legal latitude. As children, daughters could attend city schools to acquire literacy and numeracy; as adults, women were active in commerce, trade, and shopkeeping, not just in the household, but in the public arena: the workshop and the marketplace. As wives and mothers, women wrote wills, managed property, and could file legal briefs in their own names. If married, they were entitled to a sizable part of the marital estate because of the community property law that governed most cities of the Low Countries.[39] In most Flemish towns succession laws were egalitarian: daughters inherited automatically from their parents and in the same amount as sons, and did not need dowries as a condition of marriage. As a widow, a woman received the succession of half of the community property of the couple, including movable goods, and retained exclusive ownership of all immovable property she had brought to the marriage or inherited from her own family.[40] She was also entitled to a *bijlevinge,* a lifetime right to the usufruct of that part of the community property of the couple she did not inherit, a stipulation that secured the rights of the children and other family members after her death.[41] If active in the artisanal trades, a widow could assume responsibility for the family workshop or managerial tasks of the family business.[42] The property and inheritance

---

37. Ibid., 53–59.

38. Eric Bousmar, "Des alliances liées à la procréation: Les fonctions du mariage dans les Pays-Bas bourguignons," *Mediaevistik* 7 (1994): 11–69.

39. Philippe Godding, *Le droit privé dans les Pays-Bas méridionaux du 12e au 18e siècle* (Brussels, 1987), 268–73.

40. On the technical difference between succession (by widows) and inheritance (by other heirs): Jacob, *Les époux,* 359.

41. Marianne Danneel, "Gender and the Life Course in the Late Medieval Flemish Towns," in *Secretum scriptorum: Liber alumnorum Walter Prevenier,* ed. Wim Blockmans, Marc Boone, and Thérèse de Hemptinne (Louvain, 1999), 225–33, esp. 230–32; Godding, *Le droit privé,* 272–73.

42. Peter Stabel, "Women at the Market: Gender and Retail in the Towns of Late-Medieval Flanders," ibid., 259–76; Walter Prevenier, "Les réseaux familiaux," 194–96.

laws that operated in the different territories and cities of the Low Countries were not uniform, and complicated distinctions were made between strictly conjugal property and the property of the broader lineage, also called common property, with rights to these differently apportioned. Cities whose economic engine was small-scale production like Douai placed a premium on the married household and preserving its patrimony whereas larger cities with bigger textile enterprises such as Ghent and Ypres were less specifically focused on the conjugal unit because wider groups, guilds and confraternities for example, provided a more secure social safety net for widows and orphans. But on the whole, women fared better in the northern cities of the Low Countries than in southern Europe, where the rules of marital inheritance favored the lineage over the conjugal unit, with women having rights only to their dowries (which their fathers or brothers often controlled when they were widowed) and to some predetermined yield rather than an actual portion of the assets of the community property of the married couple.[43] Sons in Florence, for example, inherited from mothers to the exclusion of daughters.[44] In thirteenth-century Genoa daughters were excluded from further inheritance claims after they had received their dowries.[45] But if a widow lived in the parts of northern Europe with laws that privileged the community property of the couple, she had rights she had not possessed as a wife since during a marriage the husband had the authority to manage and dispose of conjugal property, even if such an action required her approval. As a widow, a woman gained independent legal rights over the marital assets she inherited.[46]

The rights of widows in the Low Countries served larger social purposes than women's individual wellbeing. Although never uniform, marital

43. Howell, *Marriage Exchange*, 27–46, 205–10. For comparisons with the south, see Elisabeth Crouzet-Pavan and Elodie Lecuppre-Desjardin, eds., *Villes de Flandre et d'Italie (XIIIe–XVIe siècle): Les enseignements d'une comparaison* (Turnhout, 2008); Myriam Carlier, "The Household: An Introduction," in *The Household in Late Medieval Cities: Italy and Northwestern Europe Compared*, ed. Myriam Carlier and Tim Soens (Louvain, 2001), 1–11. On Italy, see Christiane Klapisch-Zuber, "La mère cruelle: Maternité, veuvage et le dot dans la Florence des XIVe–XVe siècles," *Annales: Economies, Sociétés, Civilisations* 38 (1983): 1097–1109; Anna Bellavitis, *Famille, genre, transmission à Venise au XVIe siècle* (Rome, 2008), 35–54, 55–72.

44. Thomas Kuehn, *Heirs, Kin, and Creditors in Renaissance Florence* (Cambridge, UK, 2008), 58–61.

45. Steven Epstein, *Wills and Wealth in Medieval Genoa, 1150–1250* (Cambridge, MA, 1984), 82–83.

46. Jacob, *Les époux*, 345–362. Margaret Labarge, for example, has argued that widowhood "freed women to act as individuals, and they had the ability to adapt to their own desires. . . . They retained a considerable amount of the influence and power to which they were accustomed." Margaret Wade Labarge, *A Medieval Miscellany* (Ottawa, 1997), 75.

property systems there favored the conjugal unit and the rights of the sur-viving partner. A widow with underage children, for example, had rights on the yield of the portion of the inheritance reserved for the minors.[47] As a result of such marital property regimes, widows were especially attractive marriage partners, especially in the Low Countries, where their rights to half of the community property of the couple and the assets, investments, and goods they had brought to the marriage could be considerable.[48] Noble-women usually had the greatest worth, not only in the form of dowries and legacies bequeathed by their husbands, but also of succession rights to mov-able and real common property such as domains, houses, and land.[49] The social and political order of the city depended upon the smooth functioning of marriage and inheritance laws, the routine acquisition and dispersal of property and other assets, and observance of gender norms in political and social life. Abductions like those of the widows Antoinette de Rambures and Anna Willemszoon with which we began this chapter were, therefore, not just random instances of sexual violence with little social impact, but more broadly disruptive of the social compact that knit together political and domestic life.

Seduction and Abduction

While exceptional events, abductions of marriageable women were hardly isolated incidents, and for centuries, town fathers and ducal officials had grappled with the kidnapping of women of all ages and social backgrounds for the expressed purpose of forced marriage. Law was both an essential tool and a hindrance in efforts to punish male abductors. On the one hand, late medieval customary law acknowledged a distinction between *abductio* and *raptus,* abduction and rape. And yet, the meaning of each was elastic, and confusingly overlapped; *abductio* could signify both a forced kidnapping and a seizure without force (a seduction) whereas *raptus* defined the sexual vio-lence of rape but also the physical act of abduction.[50] The Middle Dutch

---

47. On widows and orphans in Flanders, see Marianne Danneel, *Weduwen en wezen in het laat-middeleeuwse Gent* (Louvain, 1995), 132–242, 264–292.

48. McSheffrey, *Marriage,* 54–58; Danneel, "Gender and the Life Course," 232.

49. Godding, *Le droit privé.* 264–65, 268; Jacob, *Les époux,* 316–19.

50. Jan Frederik Niermeyer, *Mediae Latinatis Lexicon Minus* (Leiden, 1954), 4; Godding, *Le droit privé,* 540–60; Raoul C. Van Caenegem, *Geschiedenis van het strafrecht in Vlaanderen van de XIe tot de XIVe eeuw* (Brussels, 1954), 372–94. For a comparison with England, see Caroline Dunn, "The Language of Ravishment in Medieval England," *Speculum* 86 (2011): 79–116.

equivalent of abduction, *ontscaken,* likewise carried this double meaning.[51] As a concept, abduction therefore had no precise legal referent but assumed its meaning based on the level of coercion the perpetrator exerted. If a woman was taken against her will and by force, abduction was indisputable and rape likely. But if she went voluntarily, the crime was considered a seduction, an act just as threatening to domestic social order but less severe in terms of criminal intent. Any seizure of a woman for the purpose of a marriage, whether violent or consensual, was a fundamental breech of the social world of family and kin within whose purview marriage alliances fell.

Because of lack of documentation it is impossible to quantify how regularly abductions occurred in Low Countries' cities and villages, still less how many were voluntary elopements as opposed to forced kidnappings. Legislation by princely officials and urban magistrates against the classificatory trio of abduction, rape, and seduction clearly indicates, however, that officials considered these serious social problems. As early as 1191, the count of Flanders prescribed the death penalty or lifelong banishment for abductors of women. The impression that many of these abductions were actually elopements later officialized by a priest and validated as clandestine marriages is reinforced by a law issued by Count Guy of Dampierre in 1297. It restated the penalty for abduction set forth in the 1191 decree, singled out seduction as punishable by a three-year banishment for both elopers, but also stipulated the loss of the woman's inheritance if she had married her seducer. However, if the two natal families reached mutual agreement over the match, the marriage gained post facto approval and the wife was reinstated in her inheritance rights.[52] By depriving the woman of her inheritance and predicating its restoration upon approval of the couple's families, the 1297 decree was clearly motivated by concern in the social world of propertied families that both abductions and seductions threatened to destabilize the rites and protocols of the marriage marketplace. Although there is a world of difference between abduction and seduction, to families concerned about their patrimony, they were the same threat against which they must fight. Yet the

---

51. Van Caenegem, *Geschiedenis van het strafrecht,* 104, and in general, Walter Prevenier, "Les multiples vérités dans les discours sur les offenses criminelles envers les femmes dans les Pays-Bas méridionaux (XIV–XVe siècles)," in *Retour aux sources: Textes, études et documents d'histoire médiévale offerts à Michel Parisse,* ed. Sylvain Gouguenheim (Paris, 2004), 955–64.

52. For a discussion of this legislation, see Boone, de Hemptinne and Prevenier, "Gender and Early Emancipation," 30. The 1297 decree is in Albert-Eugène Gheldolf, ed., *Coutumes de la ville de Gand,* vol. 1 (Brussels, 1868), 450. From the 1297 text on there is a clear distinction between the definitions of abduction (against the will of the woman) and seduction (with the consent of the woman).

problem apparently persisted, and in 1438 there was another decree, this time by the Burgundian Duke Phillip the Good, heir to the office of count of Flanders. As its preamble makes clear, the impetus behind the law came from the urban magistrates and the wealthy families of Ghent, Flanders's largest city. The timing was pertinent; the county had a fragile social landscape after social upheavals among the guilds, economic woes, and a large-scale rebellion against Burgundian policies in neighboring Bruges.[53] Philip's law reinforced the penalty against violent abductions and voluntary elopements, "since for some time many abductions, rapes, and violence against virgins and other women have occurred under the appearance of marriage . . . by some men eager for their patrimony."[54] Philip's decree might have been timed to curry favor with Ghent's elites so as to blunt any alliance with rebellious Bruges, but no matter what its immediate political motive, it strove, as the previous efforts also had done, to renew efforts to tamp down on violent abductions that so disrupted marriage customs and laws. As in the earlier comital decrees, the 1438 law also stipulated the loss of the woman's family inheritance in the starkest terms—"as if she were dead"—and all future inheritance if she remained in a clandestine marriage that fell under the blanket classification of abduction and rape. At the same time, the law offered inducements for her to recover her inheritance, but only if she left her seducer and had not consummated the marriage. If her abductor-turned-husband died, the woman could also reclaim her inheritance rights.

The Burgundian dukes and the urban aldermen were both active in the political and social arenas of regulating marriage, sometimes acting in concert, but other times acting separately. Often such interventions were made in the interests of social elites or political allies, but they could also be motivated out of broader concerns for social peace and even social fairness. The 1438 legislation against abductions is a prime example of a shared consensus between prince and civic rulers to protect the patrimonies of urban elites, and therefore to stabilize social relations, while addressing some very immediately political matters in a dangerous time of plague and famine. The archives are full of examples of efforts to ensure a stable familial order as the bedrock of a well-functioning and properly ordered civic life. Typical is the 1451 case of Gherem Borluut, a scion of one of Ghent's patrician families. Borluut had gotten the working-class Lysbeth van der Steene pregnant, but when

---

53. On Bruges' revolt, see Jan Dumolyn, *De Brugse Opstand van 1436–1438* (Kortrijk-Heule, 1997), esp. 189–266.

54. For the 1438 text, see de Potter, *Petit cartulaire de Gand*, 66–69.

pressed to marry her, he showed no desire to do so because she was his social inferior. The city aldermen intervened, not to force a marriage, which was not their prerogative, but instead to order Borluut to pay a lifelong annuity of ten schillings groat to van der Steene, a sum transferable to the natural child of their union should the mother be deemed irresponsible.[55] The aldermen's ruling displays a subtle compromise between their desire to cater to urban elites and their concern to care for the needs of the vulnerable in society as a measure to prevent social troubles. In the Borluut case the aldermen chose a practical solution that offered some basic assistance to the mother yet gave a green light to Borluut to move on as a privileged patrician. The aldermen favored social care and the upholding of family structure over rigid moralism.

The Burgundian dukes also exercised occasional flexibility when dealing with marriage woes. Their legal officials could readily dismiss charges of seduction and abduction by parents if the young partners had proof of the canonical validity of a union—especially when the social stakes mattered little. Such was the case when Alard Stouten of the village of Lembeke complained in 1425 to the bailiff of Ghent that his daughter had been abducted by Peter de Wulf. The daughter testified that she had freely married de Wulf the day after the elopement in defiance of her father. The bailiff dismissed the complaint, knowing that the couple was liable for a fine only, that the daughter would have to forgo her inheritance, that the families involved had no great social significance, and that the union, even if it was clandestine, was canonically valid.[56]

At the same time, both elite families and the Burgundian dukes could approach marriage disputes or use marriage itself as a means of navigating a world animated by alliances, clientism, and networks. In 1455 in Bruges, the Metteneye family—rich merchants with ties to the Burgundian court—brought considerable pressure to bear on the aldermen of the city to have a young man banished who was close to convincing a daughter "to marry him without the consent of either the father or mother." This was one of probably countless such requests to which well-connected families resorted if circumstances forced them.[57] A similar abuse is visible in many cases of political pressure by the dukes and the duchesses, who felt no hesitation about

---

55. Stadsarchief Gent, Ser. 301, section 41, vol. 1, fol. 99r.

56. Algemeen Rijksarchief Brussels, Rekenkamers, Rolrekeningen, no. 1293.

57. ADN, Lille, B, 1686, fols. 40v–41r, dated July 11, 1455. For a discussion, see Walter Prevenier, "La stratégie et le discours politique des ducs de Bourgogne concernant les rapts et les enlèvements de femmes parmi les élites des Pays-Bas au XVe siècle," in *Das Frauenzimmer: Die Frau bei Hofe in Spätmittelalter und früher Neuzeit,* ed. Jan Hirschbiegel and Werner Paravicini (Stuttgart, 2000), 431.

forcing marriages upon their subjects with the same goal of building social and clientage networks. The case of Bonne Herbaumez shows this dark face of ducal policy. She filed a complaint with Duke Philip the Good in 1440 after her husband, Jan van Uutkerke, son of the ducal councilor Roland van Uutkerke, had been executed for sodomy. She complained not about his homosexuality, for which he had lost his life, though this was surely a social stigma for her, but rather that he had squandered the family patrimony, particularly her part of the common property, leaving her destitute.[58] Herbaumez had been subjected by the duke himself to an arranged marriage at the age of only eight, and her case exemplifies a ducal policy of forced marriages as a way of making alliances among peers and subjects, using threats, gifts, and payouts to broker and arrange them.[59]

The Case of Antoinette de Rambures

The kidnapping of Antoinette de Rambures in 1477 by Adriaan Vilain with which we began this chapter vividly illustrates the ways in which officials' position on marital quarrels and abductions followed political exigencies. What we know of the case comes from two ducal pardons—one for Vilain, and the other for his accomplices—as well as from four letters in which the duchess Mary of Burgundy, her husband Archduke Maximilian of Austria, and the dowager duchess Margaret of York intervene in the days following de Rambures' kidnapping to locate her and bring her back home to safety (letters nos. 14, 15). The two pardons and these court-directed missives comprise a lot of information, but they also lack internal coherence and a well-ordered chronology. The date of Vilain's original pardon is unknown and its copy lost; his accomplices' pardon bears the date August 1481, four years after the event. Vilain fled beyond the boundaries of ducal territory and never registered his original pardon, though in 1491 he requested its legal certification and renewal before the Council of Flanders.[60] Despite

---

58. Marc Boone, "Une famille au service de l'Etat bourguignon naissant: Roland et Jean d'Uutkerke, nobles flamands dans l'entourage de Philippe le Bon," *Revue du Nord* 77 (1995): 252–54.

59. Werner Paravicini, "Invitations au mariage: Pratique sociale, abus du pouvoir, intérêt de l'état à la cour des ducs de Bourgogne au XVe siècle," *Comptes rendus, Académie des Inscriptions et Belles-Lettres* (Paris, 1995): 687–711.

60. For the two pardons, see letters nos. 14 and 15. Vilain's original pardon after the kidnapping is lost. Because he never registered it, he was forced to resubmit a new request more than a decade later. For the four court letters, see Stadsarchief Mechelen, Lettres Missives, nos. 307, 308, 309, and 311, dated December 13, 14, 15, and 16, 1477. Two are published in Bartholomeus Gyseleers-Thys, *Additions et corrections à la notice sur les archives de la ville de Malines*, vol. 3 (Mechelen, 1840), no. 2, 6–8.

such gaps and omissions, the six documents still reveal the determination of a man willing to resort to abduction to advance socially, the resolve of the new duchess and archduke and the experienced dowager duchess to rescue a high-status widow belonging to the ducal clan, and the reluctance of the aldermen of Mechelen to intervene. They also tell us how new political circumstances could yield a reversal of ducal policy. Finally, they demonstrate that the pardon letter could be invoked to request a remission of a penalty even if a razor-thin justification for the crime's occurrence was laid out.

Antoinette de Rambures' abduction caught the public's eye. It shocked the entire ducal family, who sent short, urgent missives to Mechelen's aldermen in the days following the kidnapping in their efforts to rescue her. Adriaan Vilain and his seven accomplices had forcibly kidnapped de Rambures and transported her to the house of a unnamed marshal outside of the small town of Rupelmonde, where the supposed entreaties—these at the hands of a group of armed men—began in earnest (letter no. 14). The accomplices' 1481 pardon constructs a narrative that softens the violent seizure of de Rambures with mention that a fine meal awaited her. Most important to their claim to innocence, they insisted that nothing was forced upon her other than pleas: "He [Adriaan] took the lady across cities and villages to the village of Rupelmonde in the house of a marshal, where Adriaan and the lady had a meal together, all the while hoping and meaning to make such an impression that the lady of Humbercourt would marry him and take him for her husband."

The pardon's opening paragraph is a narrative oxymoron: a kidnapping by a group of eight men metamorphosed into a marriage proposal over dinner. To be sure, the excuse offered is part of the exculpatory purpose of a pardon request; a plea must demonstrate either mitigating circumstances or misunderstood or false accusations. But the marriage angle as a defense for the kidnapping provides a poor justification for abduction. Indeed, the Burgundian court had originally refused to interpret Vilain's abduction as anything other than a straightforward act of aggression and violence, and as a result, the duke and duchess had immediately sprung into action. Writing from Brussels on the very day of Antoinette de Rambures' abduction, December 13, to Mechelen's aldermen, Archduke Maximilian of Austria demanded to know exactly what had happened and directed them to dispatch a search party to find the missing widow.[61] They transported her where they desired. Because we have taken this incident very gravely to heart, we desire to know the truth about this, namely, how and in what manner this matter occurred."

---

61. Ibid., 6–7.

What made the abduction particularly odious to the duke and duchess was Rambures' prestige as the widow of Guy de Brimeu, lord of Humbercourt, the former second-in-command to duke Charles the Bold. In the Archduke's letter, Rambures is referred to as "our very beloved and very dear niece," an indication of her close family ties to the Burgundian court.[62] The abductor's identity too was no less important. There were several Adriaan Vilains in Flanders at this time, and it would be easy to mistake him for the one who was lord of Rassegem and alderman of Ghent in 1479, except that this man died in 1490, the year before the second pardon was secured.[63] The correct Adriaan Vilain is revealed in Maximilian's letter of December 13, where he is more precisely identified as Adriaan van Gavere and van Liedekerke. We have encountered Vilain before, as one of the men in the lord of Ravenstein's party who attacked Clais van Reimerswaal at a brothel in 1473 when two noble factions clashed with one another. Van Gavere was a Flemish squire who was a nephew of the lord of Rassegem, and a member of a political faction in Ghent aligned with forces that opposed the new Archduke Maximilian's effort to clamp down on the rebellious city where Guy de Brimeu and the Burgundian chancellor Hugonet had been executed, previous aldermen banished or killed, and a host of political treaties revoked that had curtailed traditional rights and privileges.[64] Whether one reads Vilain's deed as a foolhardy wager or as shrewd financial calculation, the political irony that a man identified with oppositional forces in the very city that executed Guy de Brimeu thought it possible to kidnap and then marry his widow is as startling as the act itself.

Whatever we make of Vilain's motivations, his abduction of such a high-profile widow in a year of ongoing political turmoil was an enormous risk, and one that backfired. Three days after he seized de Rambures, a search party dispatched from Mechelen located the house in Rupelmonde where Vilain was holding her. She was immediately freed, having refused Vilain's supplications; her captor was put under arrest and imprisoned in a local castle. The three days leading up to de Rambures' rescue were busy ones for the ducal court, with three more letters sent to Mechelen's aldermen on the days after the abduction.

Revealing is the letter the Burgundian archduke fired off the day after his first letter, December 14, expressing dismay that the aldermen of Mechelen had apparently not yet acted to find de Rambures, even though, as he points

---

62. Ibid.

63. What follows is based on the prosopographical analysis in Prevenier, "Geforceerde Huwelijken," 303–6.

64. Haemers, *For the Common Good*, 125–126.

out, there were three specific roads out of the city that they could easily check:[65] "We are astonished by the lack of diligence shown by you in helping the lady and arresting those who have committed this offense against us and against our lordship." If the archduke's letter implies suspicion of a town government not fully aligned with the ducal agenda, even as a city that hosted the court of the ducal family, the one dated December 15 from Margaret of York, dowager duchess and widow of Charles the Bold, goes even further. Rumor has it, the dowager duchess writes, that: "you have placed the supervision of the goods of the children of the lady in the hands of people who are related to the criminal, and we are astonished by this, considering the great damage imposed on the lady and her children, a thing which is not tolerable." She demands an immediate transfer of legal authority over these goods to a neutral third-party administrator.[66]

A day later, Maximilian intensifies the court's efforts with a two-pronged set of actions. He specifies that four prominent Burgundian clients of his, including Philippe de Croy,[67] Thomas Malet, the lord of Berlettes,[68] Robert de Boulogne,[69] and Philippe de Brimeu, abbot of Saint-Amand, a brother of de Rambures' executed husband,[70] have been appointed guardians of the children's goods and names the members of a search party to find the captured widow that includes a nobleman and a ducal bailiff, backed up by an armed posse. In a final jab at the aldermen, he even details the kidnapper's location, the village of Bornem outside Rupelmonde. How he knows this is not clear, but the fact that he does know it is a stinging rebuke to townsmen whom he suspects are uncooperative.[71]

---

65. Stadsarchief Mechelen, Lettres missives, no. 308.

66. Gyseleers-Thys, *Additions et corrections*, 7–8.

67. Philippe de Croÿ, count of Chimay, lord of Sempy and Quiévrain, stadholder of Guelders, prominent captain in the army of Charles the Bold, knight of the Golden Fleece: Vaughan, *Charles the Bold*, 248–50, 327–28; Hans Cools, *Mannen met macht: Edellieden en de moderne staat in de Bourgondische-Habsburgische landen (1475–1530)* (Zutphen, 2001), 194–95.

68. Thomas Malet, lord of Savy-Berlettes, counselor at the Chamber of Accounts in Lille: Mireille Jean, *La Chambre des comptes de Lille (1477–1667): L'institution et les hommes* (Paris, 1992), 117, 145, 358; Jan Dumolyn, *Staatsvorming en vorstelijke ambtenaren in het graafschap Vlaanderen, 1419–1477* (Antwerp, 2003), 35, 83, 192.

69. Robert de Boulogne, counselor at the Chamber of Accounts in Lille; Dumolyn, *Staatsvorming*, 60–61; Jan van Rompaey, *De Grote Raad van de hertogen van Boergondië en het Parlement van Mechelen* (Brussels, 1973), 280; Paravicini, *Guy de Brimeu*, 432.

70. Philippe de Brimeu, protonotary at the Holy See, abbot of Saint-Amand (1486), canon of Cambrai (1487), counselor at the Parlement of Mechelen since 1473: Paravicini, *Guy de Brimeu*, 98, 508; Van Rompaey, *De Grote Raad*, 505.

71. Stadsarchief Mechelen, Lettres missives, no. 311. The four guardians remained in charge of the finances of the widow after the events of 1477: Paravicini, *Guy de Brimeu*, 512, no. 64.

Vilain and his accomplices lost their wager, and decisively so, with the heavily armed search party dispatching them to a dungeon. And yet we know this case principally from the legal fact they were all eventually pardoned. The kidnappers snatched a legal victory, despite Antoinette de Rambures' status as widow of one of Charles the Bold's right-hand men and regardless of the sheer determination Archduke Maximilian and Dowager duchess Margaret of York had shown in finding de Rambures, protecting her children's inheritance, and returning her to safety. As we do not have Vilain's original pardon, we must read his victory through a double lens: the 1481 pardon of his accomplices (letter no. 14), awarded after Vilain had been given his pardon at some earlier date, and the 1491 pardon submitted to the Council of Flanders as part of Vilain's later effort to recertify his original victory (letter no. 15).

The two pardons admit few mitigating circumstances and feature petitioners who freely admit to the crime, though taking care to point out that no sexual violence occurred. Only minor, partial explanations for the abduction are offered. In part, this has to do with the fact that Vilain's original pardon is lost, keeping us in the dark about how it recounted the abduction. In 1481, his accomplices make their case for a full remission of the charge of abduction because the chief culprit, Vilain, has already been pardoned. The 1491 renewed pardon of Vilain is constructed on technical terrain, more preoccupied with the registration process than with the finer points of what happened, because of the fact that the original pardon had expired.

Neither pardon letter explains why a group of men so doggedly pursued by the archduke and the two duchesses would win clemency. The court's original purpose is obvious: to rescue Antoinette de Rambures, to stir Mechelen's officials to action, and to secure the widow's estate for her children in case she is not found. As a court city, Mechelen was more conservative than most, and in 1477, its population had not openly rebelled against ducal authority.[72] The archduke Maximilian and the dowager duchess Margaret of York had accused its aldermen of foot dragging, and even, "as the rumor goes," of transferring the management of de Rambures' marital estate to guardians close to the Vilain family. There is no proof that either had actually happened. To the contrary, municipal records reveal that the aldermen had posted guards outside of de Rambures' house following her abduction, sent out a search party for four consecutive days, appointed local supervisors—but not necessarily relatives—for de Rambures' estate, and dispatched Mechelen's

---

72. Raymond Van Uytven, ed., *De geschiedenis van Mechelen* (Tielt, 1991), 95.

mayor, Hendrik van Coelem, and an alderman, Willem Trabukier, to the small town of Duffel between Mechelen and Lier to obtain information about her possible whereabouts.[73] It is clear from these entries that the aldermen took the abduction seriously, and even if there was some antiducal sentiment lurking, most likely the court's finger-wagging was merely tactical: to accuse in order to cajole. Mechelen's aldermen certainly didn't want to risk political relationships with the new ducal administration over a private affair that, while consequential, was not part of the normal routine of civic dealings with the court. The happy outcome—de Rambures rescued and Vilain and his men jailed—seemed to conclude the matter.

Antoinette de Rambures returned home, resurfacing in the records only years later when she declined to challenge Vilain's renewed appeal for a pardon (letter no. 15). The reasons for her reluctance to reengage with the case do not appear in the archival record. More than a decade had passed, and she had gone on with her life. She would have known that nine months after their imprisonment, her kidnappers had slipped out of prison, likely with tacit connivance of their jailers. Most telling, she would have known that in the intervening years Archduke Maximilian had reversed his position on the kidnapping, pardoning first Vilain and then his fellow kidnappers.

The court's shift from an unflinching commitment to rescue de Rambures to blanket pardons turned on brute political facts that trumped the legal case. The pardon letters offer no compelling narrative justification for the crime of abduction save for two points: for Vilain, the fact that the kidnapping was merely a marriage proposal conducted without physical harm or sexual violence, and for his accomplices, the fact that they were merely Vilain's servants and retainers. All the men had admitted to the crime of abduction, and all had escaped from prison after nine months. What followed thereafter for Vilain was consequential. He fled to Calais, an English enclave on the continent, then went on to various places within French jurisdiction. He ended up in the retinue of Jacques de Savoy, count of Romont,[74] who so helped Charles the Bold in 1477 with his campaigns against French incursions into Artois that when Maximilian became the Burgundian archduke

73. See the excerpts from the town's accounts in Paravicini, *Guy de Brimeu*, 502–3 n. 30, and on the dismissal of the original guardians of de Rambures' estate, see ibid., 512, n. 65.

74. Jacques de Savoy, count of Romont, born between 1447 and 1452, died in 1485. For his multiple services to the Burgundian dynasty, he became a member of the Order of the Golden Fleece (de Smedt, *Les chevaliers de l'Ordre de la Toison d'or*, 201–2). He became a ducal lieutenant for Artois and Picardy in 1473 and of the two Burgundies in 1475. In 1482 he became lieutenant general in the Burgundian Netherlands (Cools, *Mannen met macht*, 290–291).

he awarded him a knighthood in the order of the Golden Fleece. The two jousted politically in the years that followed, but the count remained a valuable enough player within the archduke's clientage networks that Maximilian simultaneously curried favor with him.[75] Burgundian politics was a congeries of such shifting alliances, antagonisms, and deals, and Vilain's two pardons were a minor product of these incessant realignments. The accomplices were bit players and their clemency was an easy gift without much consequence to the court. Their employer, Vilain, was an urban squire on the make, bold enough to try to marry up, incautious enough to try to force marriage upon an aristocratic widow, and shrewd enough when his ploy failed to seek refuge with a count with political ties to the Burgundian court. His strategy failed, and he suffered more than a decade attempting to repair his reputation.

Antoinette de Rambures' subsequent years are not well documented, though we know she died in 1517 in her mid-seventies.[76] Her person and her fortune had enough importance to have been the target of both Vilain's abduction and the Burgundian court's rescue. At the time of her husband's death in 1477, madame de Rambures was the prototype of a rich widow enfolded in a significant political network. Her patrimony of 1477 was the sum of several components. Her marriage contract with Guy de Brimeu, written at Montreuil-sur-Mer on March 19, 1463, confirms an important dowry to which the duke of Burgundy, Philip the Good, and then later his son Charles, added additional gifts.[77] In a testament of 1471, Guy de Brimeu awarded his wife and their future children the right of succession to several domains from the marital estate.[78] With her husband's untimely death in 1477, de Rambures also received the couple's movable and immovable community property, directly or as usufruct.[79]

As a wealthy widow, de Rambures was constrained by the gender boundaries and political circumstances of her society: marrying at the upper reaches of the Burgundian state, losing a husband in dramatic fashion, struggling to

75. For a fuller analysis, see Prevenier, "Geforceerde huwelijken," 305–6. On clientage and clientelism as systems in the late Middle Ages: Willem P. Blockmans, "Patronage, brokerage and corruption as symptoms of incipient state formation in the Burgundian-Habsburg Netherlands," in *Klientelsysteme im Europa der frühen Neuzeit*, ed. Antoni Mączak, (Munich, 1988), 117–26; Gunnar Lind, "Great Friends and Small Friends: Clientelism and the Power Elite," in *Power Elites and State Building*, ed. Wolfgang Reinhard (Oxford, 1996), 123–47.

76. Paravicini, *Guy de Brimeu*, 513 n. 68.

77. Ibid., 99–101.

78. Ibid., 240–43; text of the testament, 579–81.

79. Ibid., 509–13.

maintain her assets, and falling victim to a forced kidnapping while overseeing a household of six young children.[80] Archduke Maximilian and Mary of Burgundy intervened to secure her safe return and insisted that her properties remain intact. Besides the honor due to the widow of the executed lord of Humbercourt, the court surely had financial interests at stake, a point confirmed by the transfer of the extraordinary sum of thirty-one hundred lions d'or to the ducal receiver from the widow's estate in 1480, the equivalent of more than sixty years' wages of an unskilled worker.[81] The money was registered as a gift to the cash-strapped ducal administration, an indication of Antoinette de Rambures' level of wealth and the payback she felt obliged to offer in return for the court's earlier support. And yet for all that, Vilain and his men went free in an act of artful political juggling by Archduke Maximilian that allowed him to reclaim the widow of Humbercourt's honor, family, and patrimony, and to free those who had imperiled them to gain a political alliance. Everyone got a piece of this outcome: the rescued widow protected within the ducal network, the court with a client defended and a gift proffered, and Vilain and his men, with no capital penalty hanging over their heads. This outcome, however, flowed more from the political pulse of Burgundian life rather than from the logic of the pardon letter or the laws on abduction and rape.

The case of Antoinette de Rambures' abduction is riven with political and legal contradictions; as a high-profile event, it exposes the vulnerability of women to coerced marriage and indicates a shared concern among urban magistrates and the Burgundian administration both about the violence of the incident and the widow's property at stake. At the same time, it proves that political expediency could nevertheless triumph, with the pardon letter used as a vehicle for political favoritism and the crime against the abducted woman erased. Most important, in both outcomes—prosecution and pardon—considerations of property and politics are paramount; the crime lies in an assault on the existing order, not on a woman's person or status. The dramatic storyline is certainly unique, though its juridical contours, a pardon letter for abduction, and its social logic, a widow kidnapped to force a marriage, are more frequent. That Antoinette de Rambures three times failed

---

80. From Stammtafel 3 ibid., 656, we learn that de Rambures had six, perhaps seven, children at the time of the abduction. These children were born between 1471 and 1476, so were between one and six years old in 1477.

81. ADN, Lille, B, 2121, fol. 258v–259r.

to appear to challenge Vilain's tardy decision to register his pardon in 1491 may indicate that she saw no political hope now that he was within a client network of the archduke. Perhaps she simply wished to put the trauma of the kidnapping behind her. Perhaps she wished to preserve her family from further scandal, now that her children were grown and her property secured. Or perhaps her decision reflected a resigned awareness that even as a widow wealthy enough to float loans and present gifts to the Burgundian archduke, as a woman she could not trump political decisions among elite men.

The Abduction of Widow Anna Willemszoon

That the political calculus could blot out all other considerations in a high-profile case is amply proven by an earlier abduction of a widow that had strong parallels to what happened to Antoinette de Rambures. It concerns the seizure of a rich widow named Anna Willemszoon, but this time the abductor was a low-profile servant of a squire. The case takes on colors both more complicated and more violent than what befell de Rambures, since the victim was threatened with death and forced to marry under duress. Held against her will, Anna Willemszoon was able months later to slip back to her city of Hulst within the jurisdiction of Ghent, where she successfully registered the charge of abduction against her kidnappers. In the end, however, politics overturned her initial victory, and all her abductors were pardoned (letter no. 16).[82]

In 1449, Anna Willemszoon was a twice-widowed woman around sixty years old who lived in the city of Hulst in Flanders. By marriages to urban patricians, first to Hugo Crabbe, and after his death, to Christoffel de Winter, a wealthy and politically active burgher in Hulst, she had acquired a large estate which she managed in her widowhood. One of her sons was Abbot Jan Crabbe of the prestigious Cistercian monastery of Ten Duinen, a humanist, scholar, and well-known patron of the arts; another was a lesser-known parish priest, Pieter Crabbe, who had helped to arrange his mother's second marriage. Jan Crabbe belonged to the cultural and political high society of Flanders, and was familiar in the ducal court.[83] He is perhaps

---

82. See also Prevenier, "Vrouwenroof als middel tot sociale mobiliteit," 410–424.

83. See Noël Geirnaert, "Le triptyque de la Crucifixation de Hans Memling pour Jean Crabbe, abbé de l'abbaye des Dunes, 1457–1488," in *Memling Studies,* ed. Hélène Verougstraete and Roger Van Schoute (Louvain, 1997), 25–30; Noel Geirnaert, "Commentary: Some Experiences of an Archivist in Bruges," in *Early Netherlandish Painting at the Crossroads: A Critical Look at Current Methodologies,* ed. Maryan W. Ainsworth (New Haven, 2001), 40–45.

best remembered today for his portrait on the right wing of the devotional triptych he commissioned from Bruges' celebrated painter, Hans Memling. Since Jan Crabbe was a churchman, he placed his mother kneeling in prayer on the left wing of the triptych in lieu of the standard depiction of the dedicator's spouse.[84] Anna Willemszoon was clearly everything an urban patrician could hope to be: well off, with successful children, two of whom were in the church, and of enough social attainment to sit for Memling, Bruges' painter par excellence of the Burgundian and Flemish social elite.[85]

At a mature age and with grown children, Willemszoon enjoyed circumstances distinct from those of de Rambures, whose widowhood came unexpectedly and when she had six young children under her care. On the other hand, Willemszoon did not have the direct ear of the Burgundian court or the benefit of a famous deceased husband who was a knight of the Golden Fleece. And yet both shared the burden that the combination of widowhood with significant property and social vulnerability imposed on women who were at once people of consequence and without adequate social buffers. In the mid fifteenth century, sixty was considered old and hardly an age of marriage. It says something about the social menace of the abduction of widows and single women in general that the ruthless Cornelis Boudinzoon, a servant of a minor squire from Zeeland named Zweer van Kruiningen, would concoct a plan to kidnap and marry her, despite her age and the existence of a powerful son, the abbot of Ten Duinen.

Boudinszoon's gamble is recorded in an unusually lengthy pardon letter that excerpts parts of an earlier legal sentence pronounced by Ghent against both him and his fellow abductors, charging rape and abduction (letter no. 16). This unique quality gives the pardon request a double face, with the body of the text an attempt to address the condemnation of abduction by Ghent's officials that the letter incorporates. But it also stands apart because, like the pardon secured for Vilain and his men in 1481 and 1491, its justification is weak. True, the letter attempts to protect Boudinszoon's employer, the squire Zweer van Kruiningen, describing him as wary of the original plot to

---

84. Reproduction of the painting in Dirk de Vos, *Catalogus Hans Memling* (Bruges and Antwerp, 1994), 42–45. The pardon letter concerning Anna Willemszoon's abduction has led scholars to redate the Memling triptych to ca. 1467–70 from ca. 1480. The central panel is now at the Museo Civico in Vicenza, Italy; the outer panels are in New York's Pierpont Morgan Library.

85. Several art historians consider the Memling painting of Widow Willemszoon and her son an interesting familial and gender pairing. See Susan Broomhall and Jennifer Spinks, *Early Modern Women in the Low Countries: Feminizing Sources and Interpretations of the Past* (Burlington, VT, 2010), 33; Jeanne Nuechterlein, "The Mystery of Jan van Eyck: The Early Netherlandish Drawings and Paintings in Dresden and Memling's Portraits," *Renaissance Studies* 20 (2006): 408–19, esp. 415.

Outer panels of a triptych by Hans Memling, painted ca. 1467–70. Left: The widow Anna Willem-szoon with Saint Anne. Right: Her son Jan Crabbe, abbot of the abbey of Ten Duinen, Flanders. Courtesy of the Pierpont Morgan Library, New York.

kidnap the elderly widow and someone who tried to broker an agreement between the kidnapper and Willemszoon once she had been taken against his advice. But the crime is freely and cynically admitted in all its violent detail, and the text does not minimize the physical, sexual, and verbal violence as the two pardons in the de Rambures case did. In the Willemszoon case the crime is shamelessly presented in all its brutality.

What happened to Anna Willemszoon was terrifying. She was forced out of bed in the middle of the night in her house in Hulst by a group of eight heavily armed men, all servants of the squire of Kruiningen. In the words of the sentence pronounced by Ghent's aldermen and reproduced in the pardon letter,

> Cornelis Boudinszoon and his accomplices came into our city of Hulst in the Four Offices of our county of Flanders, and abducted the widow, aged sixty years old or thereabouts, in the night, where she was lying in her bed. They wrapped her in her nightgown, and while calling for help and crying forcefully she was taken against her will out of our county of Flanders to Zweer van Kruiningen's house and manor, which lies in our land of Zeeland.

The men whisked her out of Flanders and travelled overland and across the river Honte (later called Westerschelde) to the manor of Zweer van Kruiningen in the village of Kruiningen on the island of Zuid-Beveland in Zeeland.[86] After van Kruiningen expressed his probably insincere displeasure at the men's arrival,

> Cornelis and his accomplices took the widow on a boat at the waterfront [of the Honte] in the village of Hansweert, where they threatened the widow with words if she refused to marry Cornelis Boudinszoon. Some of the men threatened to cut the widow's throat, others said they would take her to Scotland, still others said they would take her to England, and other such things in various ways. Frightened by these threats, the widow asked to be brought back to Zweer's house, where she would do everything they asked of her.

When the men had brought her back to the squire van Kruiningen's residence, van Kruiningen once again turned them out. They fled to a tavern nearby, and three days later, van Kruiningen came with three other vassals

---

86. Engraving of 1696 of the manor of the squire of Kruiningen, in Mattheus Smallegange, *Nieuwe Cronijk van Zeeland* (Middelburg, 1696), 713.

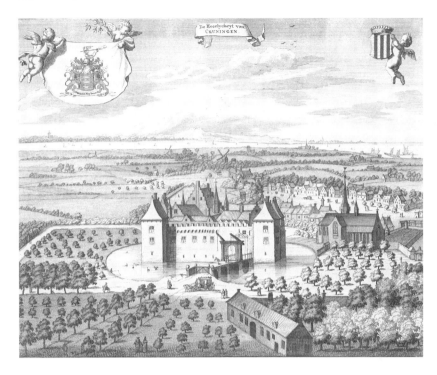

The castle of Kruiningen in Zeeland. Copper engraving from Mattheus Smallegange, *Nieuwe Cronijk van Zeeland* (Middelburg, 1696), p. 713. Copy in the Library of Ghent University, Acc. 002649. Courtesy of the University of Ghent.

from Zeeland, and in their presence, Anna Willemszoon publicly vowed to marry her kidnapper. Boudinszoon kept the widow with him at the tavern for fifteen days—presumably to garner public legitimacy for the forced union—after which Squire van Kruiningen led the couple to Hulst to certify their marriage before the aldermen. As the pardon letter recounts, the local aldermen consented, but they refused to produce written certification of this approval. Some months later Willemszoon, who was being kept at van Kruiningen's manor, snuck away. She returned to Hulst, where she lodged a formal complaint of abduction and rape against all the men, Squire van Kruiningen included, before Ghent's aldermen, since Hulst was in their jurisdiction and one of the kidnappers hailed from there. The aldermen issued a thumping denunciation of the crime, and railed against "the vile, horrible, and wicked deed plotted and carried out by them in the dead of night against an old woman within our castellany of this city [of Hulst]." The men, Squire van Kruiningen included, were banished for fifty years, and thereafter requested the grant of a pardon for their crime from Duke Philip the Good (letter no. 16).

The kidnappers were awarded their pardon on the tepid grounds that "the aforesaid persons have never previously been accused or condemned for any vile deeds or shameless crimes, but have always lived courteously and kept company with good fame and in good name."

This charitable act of mercy is standard fare in many pardon letters, but in this instance it is pure nonsense, not to mention a false argument. The letter itself, after all, mostly recounts a tale of violence, menace, and coercion against a widowed older woman who was taken in the middle of the night, threatened with death, forcibly married, and presumably sexually assaulted. Because of this internal contradiction, the pardon is clearly tilted toward an obvious person involved: not the assailant himself or his conspirators but rather his employer, the squire Zweer van Kruiningen.[87] The pardon letter suggests that in the absence of the squire, van Kruiningen's mother gave Cornelis Boudinszoon and his friends authorization to leave the house in order to kidnap Anna Willemszoon, after Cornelis led her to believe he had her son's support in this effort. Yet van Kruiningen himself is presented as the reluctant, accidental party to the abduction who eventually scrambles to broker a modus vivendi between Willemszoon and her abductor. He appears in the pardon letter as everywhere involved and nowhere responsible, except in his post facto role as a helpful mediator. And yet the cracks in his portrait as a mere bystander turned go-between are apparent, if nowhere else than in the attempt to distance himself from support for an abduction to which his own mother apparently lent her approval. He knows of the plot from the beginning, but conveniently goes away on business to Ghent before he can give his advice about it. When he returns home, the abduction has become a fait accompli and Willemszoon is lodged in his home, as he claims, "much to his disapproval." He orders all involved to leave, only to have to repeat the command a second time when they return. But once Willemszoon consents to marry her abductor, van Kruiningen shifts his role, a process he initiates when he arrives with three other vassals to witness the clandestine betrothal between the two at a tavern. Once vows are exchanged and the language of coercion conveniently disappears, van Kruiningen plays host to the new couple and facilitator of an officialization of their union. He works to "broker a peace" between the abductor and the victim, bringing both to Hulst,

---

87. Prevenier, "Vrouwenroof als middel tot sociale mobiliteit," 413–414. See also Adriaan Willem Eliza Dek, "Genealogie der Heren van Cruijningen," *Jaarboek van het Centraal Bureau voor Genealogie* XI (1957): 79–120. The family had important ties to Flemish nobility such as the Gruuthuuse and Gavere clans, the families Borselen, Renesse and Reimerswaal in Zeeland, and the all-important Heemstedes in Holland.

where he requests the aldermen certify the clandestine marriage. While the pardon claims that the aldermen did so, they curiously refused to document their decision in writing, raising questions about what actually transpired at Hulst's town hall.

Yet Willemszoon escaped from van Kruiningen's home after Hulst's aldermen recognized the existence of a valid clandestine marriage, though they had no right to declare it valid in canon law. She won her case against all her abductors and van Kruiningen himself in Ghent, whose aldermen condemned them with an unusually strong rebuke. The full success of the widow's complaint can be explained by blunt violence against her but also by her social position as a mother to a very high-ranking abbot. The inclusion of part of Ghent's sentence of banishment in the pardon letter has the effect of undermining the narrative's effort to smooth van Kruiningen's, and returns the focus squarely back to abduction and rape. Yet the men are summarily pardoned, despite the weakness of the arguments in the letter itself, and despite the affirmation of sexual and bodily violence against an aged woman two of whose adult sons were in the church, the one at a very senior rank. As with Antoinette de Rambures' case, basic yet compelling political reasons were certainly behind Philip the Good's decision to pardon van Kruiningen and his men. As it turns out, van Kruiningen was part of a noble faction in Zeeland that had thrown up roadblocks to the Burgundian administration.[88] Despite the gravity of the crime, and despite Willemszoon's high profile, the pardon was a means of peeling one person away from this anti-Burgundian coalition. In the hardball of late medieval politics, an abbot and a widow, no matter how high their rank, mattered less than an aristocratic opponent with land, money, and political and military resources.[89] In the case of the van Kruiningen pardon, the judicial procedure of issuing a pardon letter was a tool for a larger political purpose; whatever rigorous legal protocols the pardon typically required—fact checking, the interviewing of witnesses, the right to challenge its registration—were subordinated to this purpose. The pardon letter itself could not even muster an internal coherency. The shallowness and the twists and turns of its narrative are a strong reminder that the realm of law could play second fiddle to the demands of politics and its often brutal requirements.

---

88. On the social and political entanglement of the Kruiningen family with various noble families in Zeeland and Flanders, and on the marriage of Squire Zweer van Kruiningen with a woman from the Voorhoute clan, see Frederik Buylaert, *Eeuwen van ambitie: De adel in laatmiddeleeuws Vlaanderen* (Brussels, 2010), 164 and 202.

89. Prevenier, "Vrouwenroof als middel tot sociale mobiliteit," 413–14.

The pardon cases of the abductors of Antoinette de Rambures and Anna Willemszoon carry both social and legal lessons. Above all, they show just how easily a widow, of no matter what rank or age, could be the target of schemes and attacks, precisely because she had more rights but less security than an unmarried daughter or a married woman in a household. The two cases also show that the pardon letter, for all its legal intactness, varied considerably in form and quality. None of the pardon requests associated with these two cases offers a good exculpatory narrative of the crimes involved. They suggest that a pardon could be granted on weak evidence and without much princely reason except on grounds of mercy and grace—proof positive that a sovereign lord could do as he chose, as both Archduke Maximilian and Duke Philip the Good clearly did.

Abduction or Elopement? Dirk van Langerode and Katharina Meulenpas

The third case of a widow abducted eerily resembles what befell Antoinette de Rambures just a year later. In 1476, the wealthy and young Katharina Meulenpas was on her way to hear mass in Louvain with two of her servants when a group of nine armed men led by the patrician Dirk van Langerode seized her and fled town on a horse-drawn wagon. The similarity between the two incidents, however, stops there, since Meulenpas knew her abductor well. The kidnapping apparently morphed into an elopement—the precise nature of Meulenpas's prior knowledge about her seizure an open question—with the young couple privately wed by a priest awaiting them in the woods near Wezemaal (letter no. 17).[90] If the violent abduction of widows by strangers stirred enough social controversy to end up as pardonable crimes, many were clouded with questions of complicity and consent. Such concerns became paramount in Katherine Meulenpas's case because abductor and abductee knew one another, and were seen in each other's company even as her family planned her future. The legal category of abduction, as noted earlier, was elastic; distinctions between forced kidnapping and agreed-upon elopement—seduction, in the language of the law—were blurred. The grey area between force and consent, between abduction and seduction, became the site of legal dispute and of social strain, with couples in opposition to families, and with families assailing clandestine marriages

---

90. For an analysis, see Walter Prevenier, "Huwelijk en cliëntèle als sociale vangnetten," in *Van Blauwe Stoep tot Citadel: Varia Historica Brabantica Nova Ludovico Pirenne dedicata,* ed. Josephus P.A. Coopmans and A. M. D. van der Veen ('s Hertogenbosch, 1988), 83–91.

by charging rape or abduction, with the murky matter of consent made the crux of disagreements. Whether abductions were elopements in disguise to evade family opposition or acts of male coercion are still hard for us readers to resolve centuries later, absent the voice of the woman in either witness depositions or the pardon letter itself.

Dirk van Langerode and Katharina Meulenpas, two patricians who sought one another's company even as Meulenpas's extended family planned another future for the widow, were not caught in a unique dilemma. Men and women in love but blocked by families of different social standing were the stuff of popular romance, the Burgundian Netherlands included. Lovers divided by social barriers featured prominently in contemporary literature such as the *Cent Nouvelles Nouvelles*. The theme of the socially impossible marriage also appears some decades later in the play *Spieghel der Minnen (Mirror of Love)*, written about 1480 by a Brussels poet and rhetorician, Colyn van Ryssele. It features Catherine, a poor seamstress who complains that she cannot marry her lover because he is the son of a rich merchant.[91] But the story of concern here does not involve people at different ends of the social spectrum. Rather, Langerode and Meulenpas resemble the protagonists of tale no. 26 of the *Cent Nouvelles Nouvelles*, which recounts the love between the less well-heeled patrician Gérard and the better-off Katherine.[92] Her parents adamantly refuse a marriage between the two, leading to their separation, their attempt to reunite, and their unhappy ending, when Gérard fails to recognize Katherine when she comes to see him in disguise, and when he in turns fails to prevent her subsequent marriage to another man, though he rushes to their wedding. But the Louvain story recounted in the pardon letter here does not perfectly track the tale in the fictional *Cent Nouvelles Nouvelles*, for unlike Gérard, Van Langerode, as a member of a rich family of textile merchants and also active politically in the city, was no less well off than Meulenpas.

Langerode was pardoned for the crime of abduction of which he was accused by the aldermen of Louvain in a complaint filed at the Council of Brabant (letter no. 17). The newly wedded couple were allowed to remain married, but had to pay the enormous sum of five hundred Flemish pounds of forty groats—the equivalent of sixteen and a half years wages of an unskilled

---

91. Margaretha Wilhelmina Immink, ed., *De Spiegel der Minnen door Colijn van Rijssele* (Utrecht, 1913); Marc Boone, Thérèse de Hemptinne, and Walter Prevenier, "Fictie en historische realiteit: Colijn van Rijssele's "De Spieghel der minnen," ook een spiegel van sociale spanningen in de Nederlanden der late middeleeuwen?" *Koninklijke Souvereine Kamer van Rhetorica van Vlaanderen de Fonteyne*, 2d ser., 34, no. 26 (1984): 9–33.
92. Champion *CNN*, 77–86.

worker—in order to do so.[93] Their willingness to pay this sum is strong proof that both had a hand in the staged abduction.[94] So too is the fact that Louvain's archival sources confirm they stayed married, with Katharina outliving Dirk until her death in 1504. The pardon letter itself insists that she consented to the "abduction," even though it admits that when Dirk and his men came to seize her, "she did not respond," to their entreaties to accompany them. Her silence seems to indicate that she was the victim of a forced kidnapping—underscoring the charge of abduction that the aldermen of Louvain had levied against Langerode, probably at the prompting of Meulenpas's natal extended family, who would have considered remarriage of the widow a possible financial loss for them. Yet the pardon recounts:

> in recent times and for a long time Dirk van Langerode was in the habit of visiting and conversing with demoiselle Katharina in her house, and every time with her consent and approval because of the good love and affection he had for her. Occasionally [he] talked to her with the purpose of taking her in marriage, with her feelings [toward him] an argument that could help. By good and gracious responses that demoiselle Katharina often demonstrated and made known to him, Dirk was even more inclined to stay frequently in her company with good hope for a future marriage.

The letter even explains Langerode's decision to abduct Meulenpas as a well-intentioned attempt to evade "malevolent and resentful people," surely meant as a reference to members of her extended family. Fearing what opponents of their relationship would do, Langerode opted to "take her away," with the French verb *emmener* used to indicate an abduction. What awaited the couple was nothing more than a well-wishing priest available in the woods to marry them, then a night spent in his house, services for which he was probably paid.[95] The newly wedded couple spent more than a week in a monastery where Langerode's brother was a lay brother. The couple surrounded themselves with the protective hand of clerical support to stress the peaceful and legitimate nature of their actions, and the fact that their marriage was valid in canon law.

---

93. The payment is recorded in Algemeen Rijksarchief, Brussels, Rekenkamers, Reg 2.108, fol. 62v.

94. Stadsarchief Leuven, 4607, September 4, 1504.

95. This is not certain, however. In fact many priests helped young couples in trouble with their parents or family to marry legally or validly, out of obligation to the stipulation of consent in canon law.

For reasons having probably to do with the Meulenpas extended family, the city's aldermen acted immediately against Langerode, filing charges of abduction against him at the regional court of Brabant.[96] Sticking to the tradition of ducal legislation that stipulated the seizure of assets as punishment for abduction, the Council of Brabant impounded the property and goods of both Langerode and Meulenpas, cutting them off from their own financial resources. Katharina Meulenpas surely had a comfortable estate as a young widow. City records indicate she had previously been married to Vrancke Wilemaer, son of a family belonging the butchers' guild, one of Louvain's top mercantile groups; the family held a whole string of appointments to civic office, including alderman and burgomaster, positions held by two fifteenth-century Wilemaers named Vrancke, the younger of whom, active between 1451 and 1466, was probably Meulenpas's first husband.[97]

As we have already indicated, clandestine marriages, whether they later earned ecclesiastical approval or not, were generally not of concern to legal officers unless children were in dispute, property was contested, or the families involved well-off enough to throw their political weight around in ways that imperiled local political life, if only indirectly. The abduction-cum-elopement of Langerode and Meulenpas clearly involved the latter case, with the aldermen acting immediately, though the ducal bailiff in the town, Lodewijk Pynnock, jumped into the dispute only to muddy the waters by supporting Langerode against the aldermen's efforts.[98] After filing the legal charges of abduction and rape against Langerode, the aldermen sent a messenger after him in Wezemaal a week after the incident. They ordered Langerode dismissed from the position he held as officer of Louvain's parochial organization for poor relief, the Tables of the Holy Ghost; demanded his presence before them to answer the charges; and on October 26, ordered Langerode to undertake a pilgrimage of expiation to faraway Cyprus. But the ducal bailiff countered the next day with a letter from Duke Charles the Bold forbidding Louvain's aldermen from taking these actions. A few

---

96. For the social background of the Langerode and Meulenpas families, see Prevenier, "Huwelijk en cliëntèle," 84–85.

97. On the social, corporate, and institutional background of Louvain, see Raymond van Uytven, *Leuven: De beste stad van Brabant* (Louvain, 1980), and Alfons Meulemans, "Leuvense Ambachten," *Eigen Schoon en de Brabander* 41 (1958): 412–28.

98. Lodewijk Pynnock was mayor of Louvain from 1461 to 1504: Lieve de Mecheleer, "Un officier du prince par temps agités: Les avatars du maïeur Lodewijk Pynnock pendant une période troublée à Louvain (1477 et 1488–89)," in Blockmans, Boone, and de Hemptinne, *Secretum scriptorum*, 351–69; Raymond van Uytven, "Pynnock, Lodewijk," in *Nationaal biografisch woordenboek,* vol. 2 (Brussels, 1966), 715–18; Cools, *Mannen met macht,* 282–83.

days later, Langerode and his new bride Katharina Meulenpas filed for the restitution of their property. Already by November, Langerode had his pardon in hand, though the jockeying between the aldermen and the bailiff continued until January, when the bailiff pressed them to recognize that the ducal pardon had effectively ended the town's efforts against the young couple. Despite this, and despite the legal authority of the pardon letter, the dispute between the bailiff and the town ebbed and flowed until 1479 when legal tensions between the two parties finally wound down, even though Langerode had regained his patrimony and his right to hold public office since winning the pardon.[99]

While Louvain's city records give us the outlines of this power struggle between the town and the ducal officer, we are still in the dark about the exact networks of family and kin that animated the conflict. It is nonetheless obvious that at stake was a conflict between two family factions that spilled over into the world of kin and clientelism that was the stuff of urban and ducal politics. The Langerode pardon is clearly distinct from those of Antoinette de Rambures and Anna Willemszoon even if a rich and vulnerable widow is the common denominator it shares with them. As a narrative construct, it is less strained than the other two, no doubt because it has much less to defend. It makes a fairly coherent case for consent between a couple who wanted to marry and who proclaimed their love for one another as justification, especially because it was filed as a brief on behalf of both of them. Yet the pardon request strains to negotiate the core distinction between abduction and seduction, two terms contained within the legal category of *abductio*. If nothing else, the case shows that sorting out the boundaries between force and consent was no easy task, even in the unusual circumstance of a pardon request prepared for both the abductor and the supposed victim. Langerode's and Meulenpas's narrative starts by implicitly acknowledging an abduction even as it prefaces the seizure of the widow by confirming her personal association with her abductor. Nevertheless, the pardon request posits consent as the basis of the staged abduction, with the couple wed in the woods by a local priest, then retreating to a monastery for more than a week. Their pardon is characterized not only by this consensual posture but also by the speed within which they received it—a matter of weeks—and the large sum they were willing to pay as a penalty, an amount far beyond the few months' worth of wages a pardon normally cost. Theirs was a case where money certainly

---

99. The archival details come from the Stadsarchief Leuven, and are reviewed in Prevenier, "Huwelijk en cliëntèle," 85–86.

lubricated the decision-making process and reinforced the couple's determination to remain married and evade whatever family rivalries their union provoked. The political rift between Louvain's aldermen, eager to freeze the couples' assets and dismiss Langerode from any public offices he held, and the city's ducal bailiff, just as strongly determined to enforce Philip the Good's decision to pardon both Langerode and Meulenpas, confirms these tensions. It also underscores that they were deepened by differences between the city and the state authorities, with Langerode gaining the support of the Burgundian administration. More than anything else, Langerode's and Meulenpas's pardon letter points out the legal blurring between abduction, seduction, and consent. Even though they had conducted a legitimate wedding in the woods of Wezemaal, the couple had to concede that Langerode was guilty of the crime of *abductio*. They admitted this wrongdoing, extenuated it by appealing to the doctrine of consent and the interest of both parties, and paid an enormous price in order to evade the town and family politics that stood in the way of their union. That they had to seek a pardon for a perfectly legal marriage tells us that, no matter how powerful ecclesiastical definitions of marriage might be, the social forces of kin, family, and urban networks were unassailable, and only ignored or breached at social and political costs.

High-profile cases like those of de Rambures, Willemszoon, and Langerode and Meulenpas point up the allure of a widow arising from her mix of property rights and social vulnerability. Such cases involved actors of enough importance that they left footprints in the archives, however light or heavy their tread. These three abductions vary in degree of violence, and include one, the Langerode and Meulenpas pardon, that is better described as an elopement. In the end, these cases are distinguished by the exceptional quality both of the persons involved and by the nature of the crime. Most cases of abductions concerned unsanctioned or clandestine marriages among ordinary people, and regularly involved tensions between the canon law rules of betrothal that permitted consent as a determining criterion of validity and the social power of the family, whose members jealously guarded their rights to determine marriage partners. Our two final cases illustrate these domestic conflicts; though they lack persons of high social rank or political pedigree, they are still of critical importance precisely because they capture the rift between choice and familial constraint, between youthful desire and parental caution, between impulse and social dictates.

Elopement Cases: Wouter Janszoon and Hans van Liesvelt

As ducal legislation made clear, private marriage disputes could be adjudicated if the families involved reached an accord over an elopement or a broken marriage promise, with financial compensation worked out through the process of composition with the help of the bailiff.[100] But achieving such compromise was often difficult given the social breach that had necessitated it. Intractable disputes ended up before the aldermen, the ducal bailiff, or sometimes, ultimately, as was the case with several vendettas, in the procedure of the legal pardon. Such was the case with a conflict with a Romeo-and-Juliet quality to it: the elopement in 1438 of Wouter Janszoon with the sixteen-year-old Jacquemine Willemszoon in Middelburg (Zeeland).[101] It is tempting to read this narrative as a tale of teenage lovers—though we don't know Janszoon's age—eluding parental dictates, and indeed the pardon that Janszoon received makes such a case. In it, the two are described as fleeing together from their parents in Zeeland to a place in Brabant:

> This happened in such a way that the girl left with the supplicant for the country of Brabant to a place called Serboudens Polre.[102] In this place the girl acknowledged before the aldermen that she came to the spot of her own free will, and by the hand of the parish priest they married one another, as made clear and more emphatically by letters about this.

The newlyweds, it's important to note, took the precaution of securing written proof of their mutual consent before the parish priest and the local aldermen:

> After the supplicant and the girl had been together for about three months, she went back to her friends in order to make an accord and arrangement with her father and friends. Nevertheless some of these friends convinced her to change her mind in such a way that she approached the people of our Council of Holland to formulate a complaint against the supplicant, saying that she was abducted by the supplicant against her consent and will.

We may presume that Jacquemine fell victim to machinations from her family and "friends" (the catch-all term for blood relatives and those with connections to the family) who prodded her to accuse Janszoon of abduction.

---

100. On adjudication through *compositio*, Van Rompaey, "Het compositierecht in Vlaanderen," 43–79; Raoul C. van Caenegem, *Geschiedenis van het strafrecht in Vlaanderen van de XIe tot de XIVe eeuw* (Brussels, 1954), 311–19.

101. Pardon for Wouter Janszoon, from Middelburg (county of Zeeland). ADN, Lille, B, 1682, fol. 1v (Lancien, no. 187).

102. Ser Boudens Polre (or Heer Boudens Polder), hamlet near Halsteren, in present-day Bergen-op-Zoom, The Netherlands, prov. Noord-Brabant; see Willem A. van Ham, *Macht en gezag in het Markiezaat: Een politiek-institutionele studie over stad en land van Bergen op Zoom (1477–1583)* (Hilversum, 2000), 38. This village was located just outside the county of Zeeland, the couple's home province, in the medieval duchy of Brabant.

A charge was filed for abduction against Janszoon at the Court of Holland, in whose jurisdiction Middelburg lay. Yet, as the pardon request recounts, friends—precisely who is not known but probably ones other than those already mentioned—wanted to check the young couple's newlywed status, and submitted a request to key ducal appointees and vassals in the area, including the sergeant of Veere, the ducal receiver of Zeeland. These witnesses verified that the couple's marriage was consensual and legal because a priest had officiated at it. Nevertheless, because the charge on the part of Jacquemine and her family was still pending at the Court of Holland, Wouter Janszoon dared not risk returning to Zeeland, though he did prepare a pardon request. On May 7, 1438, duke Philip the Good granted a pardon to Wouter Janszoon. What became of the couple and their marriage is not known, as the people involved are not easily located in the archives, and whether the young couple was able to live together or not is a mystery.

Sixteen was a canonically permissible age for a young woman to marry.[103] It fell below the usual age of eighteen specified by most cities in their local statutes and customs, though this civic age limit had to do with the regulations concerning patrimonies and inheritances and was not a prohibition against marriage itself. Without knowing Janszoon's age, we are in the dark about whether the case was one of teenage lovers or of a somewhat older young adult who seduced an impressionable younger girl into elopement and marriage. Janszoon's pardon implicitly makes the case for the former. The document singles out both Jacquemine Willemszoon's consent and her free will. Jacquemine's actions are hard to understand since they might betoken a sincere desire to patch things up with her family, might indicate the homesickness of a very young girl who regretted what she had done, or might signal either efforts to extricate herself from a seduction or successful pressures from a worried family. In fact, her exact predicament was probably some incalculable mix of all these elements, and various unknown other ones as well. Whatever was at play, Janszoon's pardon is not surprising, even if he had no political weight to throw around. He had married Jacquemine legally before a priest, and she had confirmed her consent before the aldermen in the small town where they eloped. While her family fought him on charges of abduction—Jacquemine's age probably was their principal

---

103. The canonical minimum age for marriage was twelve for girls and fourteen for boys; see Scott L. Waugh, *The Lordship of England: Royal Wardships and Marriages in English Society and Politics, 1217–1327* (Princeton, NJ, 1988), 15–52.

concern—Wouterszoon was guilty only of evading parental consent even if he was later charged by Jacquemine, her father, or other male relatives acting as her legal representatives, with a capital crime. If the court had found a record of her previous consent like the aldermen's certification, then siding with Wouterszoon against Jacquemine and her family carried little or no legal risk, even if it favored exactly the kind of elopement that official legislation decried. In the legal world of the pardon, clemency was all the easier if there were no big social or political ramifications. Proof of a legal marriage was cause enough to dismiss abduction charges even if parental control was traduced and youthful love upheld, however socially irresponsible that might be.

The same argument for free choice is central to our final case, the pardon of Hans van Liesvelt of Dendermonde in Flanders in 1458 for the "abduction" of Katherine Colins. In this instance, the conflict between the family and the supposed abductor resulted, according to the pardon request, from the family's bad faith regarding a matrimonial contract earlier negotiated between them. The pardon also excerpts the original sentence of banishment the bailiff of Dendermonde had imposed on Liesvelt, both in the original Flemish and in a French translation.[104] It is distinctive not for its legal dimension—it once again recounts a seduction turned abduction—but rather for the clear reversal by Colin's family of an original matrimonial contract to which they had apparently agreed. What is clear is that here again a young couple in love is involved. In this instance, the girl is no doubt below the marriage age—not the canonical age of twelve but the typical civic requirement of eighteen:

> the supplicant negotiated in such a way with the father, blood relatives, friends, and guardians of Katherine Colins, daughter of Jehan Colins, that this girl was awarded to him for marriage as soon as she reached the allowable age. On the basis of this a matrimonial agreement and contract was made between the supplicant and Katherine in the month of February 1458 as is proven by a formal document made about this matter.

The specification of guardians may be a reference to the fact that Katherine's mother was already deceased. The pardon does not give Liesvelt's own age, but recounts his closeness to his beloved's natal family and their kin. The

---

104. Pardon for Hans van Liesvelt. ADN, Lille, B, 1688, fol. 22r (Lancien, no. 801). Petit-Dutaillis, 27–29.

letter recounts the shock Liesvelt experienced after he absented himself from Dendermonde for an unspecified amount of time:

> When he returned, it appeared to him that all of a sudden the father, blood relatives, friends, and guardians of the girl regretted the marriage contract, about which he was very unhappy. For this reason, the supplicant and Katherine, who loved one another, had spoken with one another such that Katherine gave the supplicant an hour and day to come find her in her house. She also promised that she would go with him, which she did, and which she admitted and recognized before the aldermen of Saint Mary Baasrode,[105] and for which the supplicant says he has certification from the aldermen of Saint Mary Baasrode.

The marriage's social sanction seemed gravely imperiled, yet it was saved by a post facto reconciliation of the parties in dispute, since "peace" was brokered between them. We cannot know Katherine Colins's precise age, but can reasonably infer she was probably not yet eighteen by the time Liesvelt had returned. One assumes that because of her age—still below the usual civic requirement of eighteen—and because she was deemed the victim of seduction, the bailiff ordered Liesvelt banished. What Liesvelt requested from a ducal pardon was a *rappel de ban,* a lifting of the sentence. Even more than with the case of Wouter Janszoon, this pardon was a low risk for the ducal court. The case had already been resolved on grounds of social peace and domestic reconciliation, and all that was needed was to dismiss the bailiff's order of banishment. This dispute over a young couple and the girl's family, with its language of consent and its reality of broken contracts and supposed amends, begs a denouement. And yet the pardon is our only record of this conflict; Hans Liesvelt and Katherine Colins disappear from the historical record once they are confirmed as man and wife.

Abduction Pardons, Politics, and the Family

Making sense of the pardons for the crime of *abductio,* whether in its legal meaning of a forced abduction, a manipulative seduction, or both, is no easy interpretive task. The pardons are windows into social worries over marriage and property and speak particularly eloquently about women's vulnerability in this realm. Yet they were also grants of clemency—with the exception of Katharina Meulenpas as a copetitioner—to the protagonists, the male aggressors, or, in a few instances, the male lovers. Court and city records, even the

---

105. Baasrode, Belgium, prov. East-Flanders, arr. Dendermonde.

connoisseur realm of elite art and painting, have allowed us a deeper grasp of what befell women like Antoinette de Rambures, Anna Willemszoon, and Katharina Meulenpas, wealthy widows with a shared social condition yet differing personal circumstance. As a subset of the pardon genre, all five cases are microstudies in the strains that marriage and marital property laws brought about in the world of late medieval and early modern Europe. No tension was more polarizing than that between the family, concerned over its social reproduction and its property, and the church, guided by its canonical regulations and its stance of free consent as the basic denominator of marriage. All five cases point out the particular dilemma women confronted in this regard, being at once bearers not only of the next generation but of material property and social and economic prestige. For the sake of these assets women were desired and preyed upon, no matter what their social position or age, from the underage small-town girl Katherine Colins to the cream of the elite: Antoinette de Rambures, a young widowed mother, and Anna Willemszoon, older, dignified, and rich. Their abductions ended up in courts of law, and their kidnappers, whether vicious schemers or rapists or secret lovers, were ultimately pardoned.

As legal texts, the pardon letters afford access to the social phenomenon of violent abductions, ambivalent seductions, and amorous elopements, and to the family reverberations they triggered. Whatever the role of the ducal pardon as the final legal word on these domestic conflicts, town and civic relations often shaped their outcome. The pardons granted to the squire Adriaan Vilain and his accomplices and to the Zeeland nobleman Zweer van Kruiningen and to his violent servant Cornelis Boudinszoon and his helpers belie any assumption that a ducal pardon was an exercise in carefully burnished narratives. Neither the Vilain case's two pardons nor those of Kruiningen, Boudinzoon, and their accomplices show much polish or well-honed exculpatory pleas. This is especially true of Boudinzoon's abduction of Anna Willemszoon, with the crime not only openly admitted but finely described in all its violent detail. The mitigating circumstances recounted are offered not to extenuate Boudinzoon's deeds but rather to distance his employer Kruiningen from anything other than playing the role of helpful mediator. In both of these different letters, all the men involved are pardoned not on the basis of their clever retelling of the abduction but instead out of sheer political expediency: the ducal need to gain a new political client—a perfect illustration of the pardon as a political instrument.[106]

---

106. On this theme, see Prevenier, "The Two Faces of Pardon Jurisdiction in the Burgundian Netherlands: A Royal Road to Social Cohesion and an Effectual Instrument of Princely Clientelism," in *Power and Persuasion: Essays on the Art of State Building in Honour of W. P. Blockmans,* ed. Peter Hoppenbrouwers, Antheun Janse, and Robert Stein (Turnhout, 2010), 183–86.

Politics occupies the foreground also in the resolution of the case of Dirk van Langerode and Katharina Meulenpas, if for entirely different reasons. As our only joint pardon for a man and a woman, consent is explicit as its frame. The pardon offers a coherently assembled account of a canonically valid betrothal performed by a priest outside of Louvain. Civic records have offered us glimpses of a tussle between two urban families, the Langerodes and Meulenpas's natal family, and the political allies each attracted, the ducal bailiff in Langerode's corner, and the town aldermen in Meulenpas's. In the end, Dirk van Langerode and Katharina Meulenpas prevailed, not only because of the heft of the ducal bailiff's support, but because of the enormous sum they were willing to pay to get the charges of abduction against Langerode dismissed. While their case as copetitioners and as a legally wedded couple was almost airtight, the ducal court found occasion to soak them for a large amount to grant their pardon, well aware that both of them sought to reintegrate back into the comfortable fold of money, business, and politics within which they nested in Louvain.

An entirely different order of politics informs our final two pardons, each a story of youthful love and ill-planned elopement. It is not the power politics of ducal ambitions or the civic one of money and political factions that is at work here, but rather the entrenched social domain of the family, and in particular, the steady pressure exerted by "friends and family." Canon law may well have given young people the right to freely chose marriage partners but in reality advice, pressure, and coercion by parents, family, employers, neighbors, and friends were often decisive. As we have seen, the commonly invoked social descriptors "friends and family" are at once more restricted and more capacious in their meaning than their equivalents today. On the one hand, they refer in a precise sense to blood relatives and in-laws (the Dutch term *vrienden en magen*), and not to acquaintances or neighbors. On the other hand, they point to the social network among this kin group, a honeycomb of interests and protection within which the individual was encased and whose goal was to protect children, orphans above all, and widows. In matrimonial choices, too, the weight of "friends and family" was carefully exerted.[107]

The precise circumstances of our two elopements elude us, and we are hard pressed to know whether the two teenage girls were swayed—in fact

---

107. Danneel, *Weduwen en wezen*, 417–422; Buylaert, *Eeuwen van ambitie*, 69–75. Shannon McSheffrey has found similar patterns in late medieval England. Usually young English people were able to chose their partners themselves, if they did not belong to elite social groups. As soon as there was a certain amount of property at stake, fathers, family members, and other important people in the lives of young people exerted control and pressure: McSheffrey, *Marriage*, 76–78.

seduced—by their male paramours, or whether in each instance we have local, plebeian variants of Romeo and Juliet. In both cases, however, one thing is clear: the family was the stumbling block—"father and friends" in the case of Wouter Janszoon and Jacquemine, and "father, relatives, friends, and guardians" in the case of Hans van Liesvelt and the motherless Katherine Colins. Both men were pardoned from charges of seduction and abduction not only because they had had canonically recognized marriages performed, but also because the political dilemmas their transgressions triggered were local domestic ones of no broader consequence. Both cases also offered good additional reasons to favor the petitioner beside evidence of a legal marriage. Wouter Janszoon and Jacquemine had some relatives rebut the charges of abduction filed by other relatives before the Court of Holland; Hans van Liesvelt and Katherine Colins described an actual deal that had been earlier struck between Liesvelt and Colins's father and kinfolk. In both pardon letters, affection and desire are summoned as proof of consent, a far cry from the violent schemings that suffused what befell Antoinette de Rambures or Anna Willemszoon. In the last analysis, the cases of Wouter Janszoon and Jacquemine and Hans van Liesvelt and Katherine Colins render abduction in its most complex meaning. For in these two storylines of families in conflict with their marriageable children, and words and contracts promised, broken, and disputed, the legal category of *abductio* is applied in its fullest sense, incorporating concepts of both seduction and abduction. Resolving the matter of consent in both cases therefore became paramount, but also the question whether a canonically recognized marriage had occurred. What these two stories of young lovers share with our three very different tales of widow abductions—two violent and coercive and one consensual—is not merely the category of abduction as their legal common denominator and the pardon as their means of resolution. It is the social world of family, property, gender, and marriage that they so poignantly evoke, and how, like vendettas and other murderous conflicts, the ducal pardon became their ultimate arbiter.

THE PARDON LETTERS

Letter no. 14

Pardon for Joos van der Slact and the other associates of Squire Adriaan Vilain, from the city of Mechelen (seigneury of Mechelen). Geraardsbergen, August 1481. ADN, Lille, B, 1703, fols. 24v-25r (Lancien, no. 1627).

Maximilian and Mary, let it be known to all those present and to come that we have received the humble supplication of Joos van der Slact, Claeys Boclin, Mangelin de Rouck, Anthuenis van den Merwendicke, Claeys de Riec, . . . de Donckere and Roelkin van Liefvelt, stating that in the year 1477, in the month of December, the supplicants, at the request and prompting of Adriaan Vilain, squire, then staying in our city of Mechelen, waited for and bespied the lady of Humbercourt, widow of the late lord of Humbercourt, at the place of Hanswijk near our city of Mechelen, at the church of Our Lady,[108] as she was entering it. When the lady left the church Adriaan and the supplicants took her and put her in a wagon that Adriaan had brought to Hanswijk.

From there, he took the lady across cities and villages to the village of Rupelmonde[109] in the house of a marshal, where Adriaan and the lady had a meal together, all the while hoping and meaning to make such an impression that the lady of Humbercourt would marry him and take him for her husband. Having been pursued by many people, by noblemen from our house and by her other friends and relatives, Adriaan and the lady were discovered in Rupelmonde after three days. Adriaan was led to jail in our castle of Rupelmonde[110] where he was held for around nine months. From this castle and jail Adriaan, with the supplicants, left without our permission or consent. Although in this matter the supplicants were nothing more than the servants and retainers of Adriaan, and because Adriaan had received a pardon and dismissal of the aforesaid facts from us, nevertheless, the supplicants fear the strict justice that would come to them in our lands and territories if they do not have mercy, remission and pardon from us, which they humbly beg.

Whereupon we, in view of the matter described and having compassion for the supplicants, wishing in this matter to prefer grace and mercy over the rigor of justice, have forgiven and declared dismissed the misdeeds done and perpetuated by them of which mention is made above, and with it all fines and all corporal, criminal, and civil penalties that they may have accrued against our highness and justice for the aforesaid cause. We have therefore restored and returned to the supplicants their goods, fame, and name in all our lands and territories. Their goods shall not be confiscated, and we impose perpetual silence on our procurator general and all the other judges, bailiffs, and officers, rendering satisfaction and a final sentence to those parties involved, and in the civil domain, only in case this has not been done. We order and request our beloved and trusted president and men of our chamber of the Council of Flanders to summon those who were to be summoned, and to proceed fully and completely with the ratification and the *interinement* of this pardon, as required of them. When this has been done, our sovereign bailiff of Flanders, the bailiff of Ghent, Bruges, and all other of our bailiffs, judges, and officers or their lieutenants, whose concern this is for each of them, should proceed with our present grace, remission, and dismissal

---

108. The church of Our Lady was located in Hanswijk, just outside the walls of Mechelen: Jan van Herwaarden, *Opgelegde bedevaarten: Een studie over de praktijk van opleggen van bedevaarten in de Nederlanden gedurende de late middeleeuwen (ca. 130--ca. 1550)* (Assen, 1978), 49 and 706. Illustration in Henri Installé, *Mechelen,* Historische stedenatlas van België, no. 4 (Brussels, 1997), 89–95.

109. Rupelmonde, Belgium, prov. East-Flanders, arr. Sint-Niklaas.

110. The castle of Rupelmonde was the seat of the archives of the counts of Flanders: Maurice Vandermaesen, "Het slot van Rupelmonde als centraal archiefdepot van het graafschap Vlaanderen (midden 13de–14de eeuw)," *Bulletin de la Commission royale d'histoire* 136 (1970): 273–317.

of the supplicants and in form and manner above described, now and in perpetuity, peacefully and fully, refraining from anything against it to the contrary. They should immediately and without delay release their persons or any of their goods from imprisonment or confiscation, restoring and delivering immediately their goods.

Given in our city of Geraardsbergen,[111] in the month of August, in the year of our lord 1481. As signed by my lord the duke, Gougebault. [In the margin:] Without payment of costs.

Letter no. 15

Pardon for Squire Adriaan Vilain, from the city of Mechelen (seigneury of Mechelen). [Ghent], August 26, 1491. Rijksarchief Gent, Raad van Vlaanderen, Reg. 7513, fols. 116v–117v.

In consideration of the *intendit* given by the court to Squire Adriaan Vilain son of lord Colaerts, claimant of a pardon letter, against Lady Antoinette of Rambures, widow of the late lord Guy Humbercourt. Vilain had taken refuge and was recalcitrant before justice, with [all kinds of] pretexts and defenses. The document [the *intendit*] was also given to our lord the procurator general of Flanders. The claimant states how in the year 1477 he had set his mind on and was determined to enter a marriage alliance with the lady Antoinette of Rambures, so that when she left Mechelen to a place named Our Lady of Hanswijk he also went to the same place with some companions on foot and horseback. When she left the church, he seized her and put her in a wagon, going through several places and villages to a marshal's house in Rupelmonde, where he held her without any harm except that he pleaded with her to consent to marry him. By order of our redoubted lord, several noblemen followed them to Rupelmonde, taking the lady in their hands and releasing her and putting the claimant in the castle of Rupelmonde [as prisoner].

After imprisonment in the castle for around nine months, he and his companions left without consent of the castellan to the city of Calais,[112] and from there to the castle of Bohain[113] by the safe conduct of my lord of Saint Pol, count of Romont, lieutenant general of the archduke,[114] to whom he came in service, and received protection in the castle of Bohain. Having spent some time in this castle and fearing ·his ability to return to the county of Flanders because of the strictness of the law, and

---

111. Geraardsbergen, Belgium, prov. East-Flanders, arr. Aalst.

112. Calais, France, dépt. Pas-de-Calais, arr. Boulogne-sur-Mer. Calais was an English enclave on French soil, just southwest of Flanders, and a staple town for the export of all English wool: Wim Blockmans and Walter Prevenier, *The Promised Lands: The Low Countries under Burgundian Rule, 1369–1530* (Philadelphia, 1999), 82–85. Its exceptional strategic position made it "a base for political intrigue," the title of a chapter in Susan Rose, *Calais: An English Town in France, 1347–1558* (Woodbridge, UK, 2008), 73–94.

113. Bohain-en-Vermandois, France, dépt. Aisne, arr. Saint-Quentin, chef-lieu canton. The area of Picardy, as well as this castle, was in the middle of a heated dispute between the French king and Mary of Burgundy following the death of her father: Blockmans and Prevenier, *The Promised Lands,* 177–179, 195; David Potter, *War and Government in French Provinces: Picardy, 1470–1560* (Cambridge, UK, 2002), 48.

114. Jacques de Savoy, count of Romont.

with the reverence he had for our redoubted lord, he beseeched grace and pardon from the facts and misdeeds described above, which [the duke] accorded to him, forgiving and dismissing the facts and misdeeds with all penalties that may accrue to them, corporal, criminal, and civil, as is proved by the expedited letters.

The claimant further stated that because of the wars occurring at that time in these lands where he had traveled, he had not submitted the pardon letter for *interinement* during the required time to do so, but had let it go unregistered so that he saw the necessity to go before our redoubted lord once more and receive from him another letter which ordered that the ratification should proceed as if the pardon letter had not expired . . . .

Letter no. 16

Pardon for Cornelis Boudinszoon and his accomplices, and for Zweer van Kruiningen, squire, from Kruiningen (county of Zeeland). Brussels, March 1449. ADN, Lille, B, 1684, fols. 10r–13r (Lancien, no. 354).

Philip by the grace of God, duke of Burgundy, etc. Let it be known to all those present and to come that we have received the humble supplication and request of Cornelis Boudinszoon, as the principal supplicant, and of Eewoud Boudinszoon his brother, Mathijs Jacobszoon, Adriaen Pieterszoon, called Keint, Jan Ghijsbrechtszoon, Pieter Clariszoon, Goessin Luucxzoon, and Lambrecht Pieterszoon, his accomplices in this affair, and also of Zweer van Kruiningen, squire, as far as he may be involved in the case, all of them our subjects, stating that the aforesaid Cornelis Boudinszoon for many years had faithfully served Zweer van Kruiningen, above named. Because of his faithful service the same Zweer had a good opinion of and goodwill toward him, supporting him with love, and wanted to show this by helping him in all right and honorable things.

Around mid-Lent in the year 1447 [about March 3, 1448] Cornelis, because of the support and faith the aforesaid Zweer his master had shown him, said that he knew a rich widow whom he expected to be able to catch on condition that Zweer would assist him. Whereupon the same Zweer answered him as follows: that because of the good service Cornelis had given him, he would like to provide him, to the best of his ability, with assistance, help, and aid in all proper and honorable matters. He said that when he would return from our county of Flanders, and particularly from the city of Ghent where he had to go on business, he would offer his advice on this problem. After his return he would tell him what he had decided upon as advice and good counsel. But until his return, [Cornelis] must refrain from committing any offenses. Even though Zweer had left the house with these words, one day, perhaps two, later Cornelis took action. With him were his brother Eewoud; Mathijs Jacobszoon; Adriaen Pieterszoon, called Keint; Jan Ghijsbrechtszoon; Pieter Clariszoon; Goessin Luucxzoon; and Lambrecht Pieterszoon, his conspirators and his accomplices in this affair, most of whom were also Zweer's servants. Cornelis had led them, along with Zweer's mother, widow of the late knight Arends van Kruiningen, to understand that he had the permission and the order of their master Zweer to go as a group, with him as the leader, to abduct the widow of the late Christoffel de Winter, living in Hulst.

After that Cornelis Boudinszoon and his accomplices came into our city of Hulst in the Four Offices of our county of Flanders,[115] and abducted the widow, aged sixty years old or thereabouts, in the night, where she was lying in her bed. They wrapped her in her nightgown, and while calling for help and crying forcefully she was taken against her will out of our county of Flanders to Zweer van Kruiningen's house and manor,[116] which lies in our land of Zeeland.

When they came with the widow to Zweer's house, Zweer had just returned home from Ghent. When he found her in his house, he was astonished, and he ordered them to leave his house without the slightest delay. Cornelis and his accomplices took the widow on a boat at the waterfront [of the Honte] in the village of Hansweert,[117] where they threatened the widow with words if she refused to marry Cornelis Boudinszoon. Some of the men threatened to cut the widow's throat, others said they would take her to Scotland, still others said they would take her to England, and other such things in various ways. Frightened by these threats, the widow asked to be brought back to Zweer's house, where she would do everything they asked of her.

Hereupon they returned with her to the same Zweer's house. When they arrived, Zweer once again ordered them to leave. They then went to a tavern in the village of Kruiningen. The next day, Zweer came to the tavern and brought with him three of our vassals from Zeeland. In their presence, the widow was questioned, and she declared that everything that had happened during her abduction was with her goodwill and consent. She said that she would never issue a complaint against Cornelis Boudinszoon and his accomplices, nor against Zweer, nor against anyone else. This is attested in the affidavits of the three vassals which the same Zweer has.

After her testimony happened in this way, the widow, in the presence of Zweer and the vassals and many others who were witnesses, married Cornelis and took him as a legal husband. Cornelis remained with the widow in the tavern for about fifteen days. At the end of the fifteen days, Zweer, working to arrange a peace, led and brought the widow with her goodwill to Hulst. There before the bailiff and aldermen in our same city, without Zweer present, she confirmed again on behalf of Cornelis Boudinszoon and his accomplices, saying that everything that had happened to her during the events had occurred with her consent and goodwill, despite her screaming and her plea for help. Whereupon Zweer asked the bailiff and aldermen for written certification in due form of her statement before them, but this certification and letter was denied. After this had happened, the aforesaid Zweer returned

---

115. The Four Offices (*Vier Ambachten*) were a castellany in the Ghent Quarter, county of Flanders, located north of Ghent.

116. The Netherlands, prov. Zeeland, Zuid-Beveland. According to surveys of 1331 and 1515 they were the richest landowners on that island: Cools, *Mannen met macht*, 242–43; Cornelis Dekker, *Zuid-Beveland: De historische geografie en de instellingen van een Zeeuws eiland in de middeleeuwen* (Assen, 1971), 482–85. The family castle, near the present-day church of Kruiningen, was demolished at the beginning of the nineteenth century; for a picture, see Jacob Pieter van den Broecke, *Middeleeuwse kastelen van Zeeland* (Delft, 1978), 244.

117. Hansweert, *Hennekynszweert,* The Netherlands, prov. Zeeland, Zuid-Beveland; this tiny village is located a few miles from Kruiningen on the Honte (Westerschelde), Dekker, *Zuid-Beveland,* 288.

home to his house with the widow. But the same widow, observing and seeing that Cornelis and his accomplices made no efforts and did not try to win our grace and mercy for their crime and abduction, as they evidently should have done, left and escaped two or three times.

Zweer, who had worked and made efforts with the goal of concluding a peace [between the parties] when the opportunity allowed, retrieved and held the widow in his house in Kruiningen with Cornelis Boudinszoon to whom she had been married for a period of about six months. At the end of this time the widow left the house and went back to Hulst. Cornelis, his accomplices, and even Zweer had not known that the same widow, having returned there in freedom, and leaving all contact with Cornelis, had issued a legal complaint against them for the abduction and violence done against her. Whereupon Cornelis Boudinszoon and his accomplices, because of these misdeeds and violence, were ordered banished by the law of our city of Ghent, each of them fifty years out of our country of Flanders, as is prescribed in the following sentence written below:

> Cornelis Boudinszoon, principal, and his accomplices: Eewoud Boudin-szoon his brother, Adriaen Keint, Pieter Claues Everdieszoon, Lauwerken Pieters Adriaens, Jan Ghysbrechts tVoskin, born in Gelre, Mathys, the nephew of Cornelis Boudinszoon, each banished fifty years out of the country of Flanders because of the vile, horrible and wicked deed plotted and carried out by them in the dead of night against an old woman within our castellany of this city [of Hulst]. They came for this goal with Ector Plasch, citizen of this city, and Pieter Adriaenszoon, brandishing weapons at the woman's house, that is staffs, long knives, bows and arrows. As they had planned, they broke into the widow's house in the dead of the night with force and violence. They went into her bedroom, where she was lying naked in her bed, they wrapped her in her nightgown. They took her out with great force, while crying for help, and dragged her on a wagon and headed toward the sea.
>
> Then in the manner described, the same people took the same woman out of the county. The same people used force to stop those who tried to protect [the widow], putting their lives in jeopardy. Because of these facts the citizen [Ector Plasch, of Ghent] and Pieter Adriaenszoon have been tried in the city [of Ghent]. Even though the malefactors keep themselves outside the territory of Flanders, so that actual justice cannot be rendered, this misdeed should not stay unpunished, bound as we are by the laws of the city of Ghent of the 21 day of June in the year 1448. The same is true for Zweer van Kruiningen, because he lodged in his house and clothed Cornelis, his associates, and also the widow.

Because they [Cornelis Boudinszoon and his men] did not receive in due course our remission and our pardon for this crime and abduction, they feared that they would be hunted down and pursued by us and by our justice with corporal punishment and a penalty. For a long time, they have had great anxiety and fear that they would have to stay away from all our lands and seigneuries and be forced to remain indefinitely away in foreign regions, in great want and poverty, unless we take pity upon them and offer our grace and pardon, which they very humbly beseech.

Having taken these events into consideration, and with the example of our Beloved Lord and wishing to uphold compassion, grace, and pardon over and above the severity and wrath of the law, we favor the appeal for love and goodwill toward several of our faithful servants and pages who have beseeched us. We note that the persons have never previously been accused or condemned for any vile deeds nor shameless crimes, but have always lived courteously and kept company with good fame and in good name. We forgive, remit [any fines] and dismiss them and any parties involved, forgiving, remitting, and dismissing by our grace and legal authority, all the crimes, misdeeds, and violence and the incidents pertaining to them as they happened in the manner described above. And also all the penalties, fines and punishments, both criminal and civil, to which they were sentenced . . .

Given in our city of Brussels, in the month of March, in the year 1448, before Easter [= March 1449].

Letter no. 17

Pardon for Dirk van Langerode and Katharina Meulenpas, and their accomplices, from Louvain (duchy of Brabant). Mechelen, November 1476. ADN, Lille, B, 1698, fols. 80r–81r (Lancien, no. 1460).

Charles, duke of Burgundy, etc. We have received the humble supplication of Dirk van Langerode, a citizen at the time living in our city of Louvain, and demoiselle Katharina Meulenpas, widow of the late Vrancke Wilemaer, a citizen before his death in Louvain on their behalf and in their name, and also in favor and in the name of Henry Vranck, Pieter Speelbergh, a bagpipe player, also living in Louvain, Hennen van der Rest, Jehan Bonen from the Blauwen Putte, Josse de Schepper from the Blauwen Putte, Wouter de Pape, Heyn de Kuster, Jehan Symoens from Wezemaal, and Pieter van den Poele, their accomplices in this matter. They state how in recent times and for a long time Dirk van Langerode, supplicant, was in the habit of visiting and conversing with demoiselle Katharina in her house, and every time with her consent and approval because of the good love and affection he had for her. Occasionally [he] talked to her with the purpose of taking her in marriage, with her feelings [toward him] an argument that could help. By good and gracious responses that demoiselle Katharina, supplicant, often demonstrated and made known to him, the supplicant Dirk was even more inclined to stay frequently in her company with good hope for a future marriage.

Because the supplicant Dirk feared that some resentful and malevolent people would come forward to prevent and distract demoiselle Katherine from her goodwill, he decided to take away (*emmener*) demoiselle Katharina. In fact, on Sunday the 13th of last October, between seven and eight in the morning,[118] this demoiselle left her house accompanied by one of her servants and another female servant, intending to go to mass at the church of Saint Gertrude in Louvain. While nearing the Lombards' house there, Dirk, assisted by Henry Vranck, Pieter Speelbergh, Hennen van der Rest, Jehan Bonen, Josse de Schepper, Wouter de Pape, Heyn de Kuster, Jehan

---

118. Between "seven and eight in the morning'" by the modern reckoning of time. Seven to eight in the old system would run from 12:00 to 1:40 PM in the afternoon; see Egied Strubbe and Léon Voet, *Chronologie van de middeleeuwen en de moderne tijden* (Antwerp, 1960), 15.

Symoens, and Pieter van den Poele, his accomplices named above, came before her on the road and said to her that she must go with them. But she did not respond. As soon as the above-named approached her, they lifted her up and placed her in a wagon hitched to three or four horses. The supplicant Dirk also mounted the same wagon, as did Heynne Bonen, one of his accomplices.

From there, they led her to a certain wood close to Wezemaal,[119] ordering the parish priest of this village to come. In his hands the supplicants entered into betrothal. Around evening, between night and day, they left there and went to the house of the parish priest, where they slept together. Some time thereafter they left for the monastery of Vlierbeek,[120] where the supplicant Dirk has a clerical brother, a monk in attendance of his profession and vows, in whose room the demoiselle was kept for eight or ten days. This became known to the mayor of Louvain, and he placed every and all of the goods, movables, and immovables of the supplicants and their accomplices in our hands, and appointed guards to hold these goods. In response to the things recounted above, the supplicants, together with their accomplices, were summoned before our beloved and loyal president and men of our Council in Brabant, where proceedings against them have already and for some time been carried on. Because of this case, the supplicants have left our lands and borders, and dare not return unless our grace and pity were imparted, as they have very humbly implored and requested.

Upon consideration of the above things and the information about this case provided at our request by our mayor of Louvain, gathered and commented upon by our beloved and loyal councilor and master of requests of our household Master Andrieu Colin,[121] and upon the recommendation of our mayor of Louvain, inclining favorably to the request of the supplicants and their accomplices, and preferring in this case grace and mercy to the rigors of justice, we declare by this letter the case dismissed, remitted, and pardoned, dismissing, remitting and pardoning with our definite knowledge and special grace, together with all corporal and criminal penalties, amends, and offenses . . .

And on condition of the compensation to us of the sum of five hundred pounds, of 40 groats per pound of our money of Flanders, to be paid to the hands of the receiver of our court of the Parlement of Mechelen, which is liable to receive it for our benefit

Given in our city of Mechelen, in the month of November, 1476.

---

119. Wezemaal, Belgium, prov. Vlaams-Brabant, arr. Leuven.

120. The abbey of Vlierbeek is located in Kessel-Lo, Belgium, prov. Vlaams-Brabant, arr. Leuven; see Maurits Smeyers, "Abbaye de Vlierbeek," in *Monasticon belge,* vol. 4.1: *Province de Brabant* (Liège, 1964), 81–110.

121. Andrieu Colin was a ducal counselor and master of requests, president of the Council of Flanders (the ducal court); see Dumolyn, *Staatsvorming,* 32–33, 63, 66; Jan van Rompaey, *De Grote Raad,* 168.

CHAPTER 4

Actress, Wife, or Lover?

Maria van der Hoeven Accused and Defended

The Pardon's Account

At lunchtime on or around June 6, 1475, Mathieu Cricke abducted young Maria van der Hoeven from the company of Jan van Musene in the city of Diest.[1] A former prostitute and actress, Maria van der Hoeven had for four years been the only woman in a small itinerant theater company that Cricke had headed, until she met van Musene in the audience at a performance in Mechelen. Taken with her appearance, van Musene courted Maria, convincing her to leave the theater company and Cricke to cohabit with him, an arrangement that was shattered when Cricke came to take Maria back. Maria van der Hoeven's story is first recounted by Mathieu Cricke in his pardon request to Charles the Bold, in October 1475 (document no. 1). Cricke was in serious trouble only days after seizing Maria, facing charges of abduction and having been jailed with seven of his companions and accomplices by the mayor of nearby Louvain; "as a result of the complaint and accusation of Jan van Musene to the mayor of Louvain and his sergeants, they seized all

---

1. The date of June 6, 1475 comes from a witness deposed about the event, the Diest alderman Godevart de Goesman Geertszoen. See the text of document no. 3, witness no. 5, below. Other witnesses state the time more generally as during summer, and one indicates that it was around the feast day of Saint John the Baptist, June 24. See for example, witness no. 9, the Diest hostel owner Lijsbethe Hekelmakers.

the supplicants and imprisoned them in Louvain's prison . . . ; and the next day he [the mayor] came back again to Mathieu, whom he very inhumanely tortured and tormented." As a result, Cricke and his men asked to be transferred to the custody of the Parlement of Mechelen, the highest court in the Burgundian Netherlands.[2] Cricke and five other associates received the requested transfer, while Copin van der Streke and Josse de Backere, the only other two actors in the company other than Cricke and van der Hoeven, for unknown reasons remained jailed in Louvain. Faced with charges of abduction and rape, the men immediately filed an appeal to Duke Charles the Bold at the court of the Parlement of Mechelen for a pardon, and received it fairly quickly in October 1475.

As with almost all pardons, a ducal notary prepared an account of what befell Cricke and his associates. Cricke and his men opted for a simple legal strategy: to refute the charge of abduction by recounting a fuller story of how they had set out to reclaim a woman they had rescued from poverty and prostitution four years earlier. Cricke and van der Hoeven had first met in Bruges when he was performing with his theater company: "about four and a half years ago, Mathieu, who was used to earning his living by acting in plays, . . . encountered a certain Maria van der Hoeven in our city of Bruges, at the time a young prostitute, and convinced her to leave the dissolute life in which she had been for some time. She entered into their service as an actress in their plays, and served in this role until around last Pentecost [around May 14, 1475]."

Casting himself as a good Samaritan who had rescued a young woman from a "dissolute life" into a new profession, Cricke and his small group began performing with Maria as their sole actress. Their shared life on the urban circuit unexpectedly came to an end in the spring of 1475 when Jan van Musene, married and an illegitimate son of a canon of the collegiate church of Saint Rombault, was so taken with Maria van der Hoeven that he managed to lure her away and make her his mistress: "When at the time of a play in which she performed in our city of Mechelen she exchanged words with a certain Jan van Musene, a married man . . . , who so persuaded her to come with him that she left the supplicant Mathieu, who was forced to stop his plays that were his source of livelihood." A few days later Cricke apparently convinced Maria van der Hoeven to come back to him, a move that so angered van Musene that he tried to shoot Cricke from De Noord, a hostel in

---

2. From 1467 on the High Court of the Parlement of Mechelen started to function as a normal court of appeal for all other courts in the Burgundian Netherlands; see Jan van Rompaey, *De Grote Raad van de hertogen van Boergondië en het Parlement van Mechelen* (Brussels, 1973), 54–72.

Mechelen opposite the Rupelmonde lodging, where Cricke's theater company was staying. The newly reunited company next traveled to Antwerp, but once again van der Hoeven left Cricke for her better-off lover. Cricke faithfully narrates his determination to retrieve van der Hoeven after her second departure with van Musene. At first he couldn't find her, but "about nine or ten days later he was alerted by some people that she was with Jan van Musene at a place called De Pas, just outside our city of Mechelen." Cricke lost his cool, gathering a group of armed men to assist him. A good pardon story need not shy away from an admission of hot temper, especially one justified by the unfair conduct of the opposing party. Cricke failed to find the couple's refuge in De Pas, but finally caught up with the two in a lodging house in the small town of Diest.

The moment of van der Hoeven's abduction serves as the pardon letter's climax, albeit one that comes with a narrative challenge. It was no easy task for Cricke and his men to demonstrate in their pardon request that Maria van der Hoeven had freely consented to accompany them. Cricke and his two fellow actors had secured the help of five other men, and together, they had entered the small town of Diest brandishing lances, swords, and crossbows, resembling exactly the kind of male troublemaking band that caused public disturbance in late medieval European cities. They found Maria van der Hoeven and Jan van Musene eating dinner in the lodging run by the widow Lijsbethe Hekelmakers, bursting into the private setting and unleashing panic. Cricke's narrative of confrontation with the adulterous couple and reconciliation with Maria van der Hoeven leans heavily on the supposition of her free consent and his calm demeanor, but his rendition of the events strains credulity. As Cricke explains it, once in Diest, he remained outside Hekelmakers's lodging house while his companions entered. Cricke followed. When Maria van der Hoeven spotted him, he claims, she stood up and moved toward him: "As soon as Maria saw Mathieu, she came beside him. Mathieu asked her very gently if she wanted to return with him, to which she responded yes." But Jan van Musene suddenly pulled a knife. Confusion ensued as Cricke dropped his scabbard; his companions unintentionally trampled it, and Cricke was left with an unsheathed sword in his hand: "Right then Mathieu, by sheer accident, dropped the sword onto the ground that was in his scabbard and which he had held in his hand . . . ; he was picking up the scabbard and sheathing the sword." Meanwhile, van der Hoeven fled the house shouting for help, much to Cricke's surprise because it contradicted her supposed consent: "Maria also left the house, ran into the streets, and began to shout and cry in front of the men. Mathieu would not have understood what she was saying had someone not told him that she exclaimed that she was a citizen of Diest, and that she was under assault, or words to that effect."[3] Cricke claimed that he approached her in astonishment and offered her the choice to stay or to accompany him with the reassurance that he and his men intended no harm: "'Maria, why do you cry out like that? If you don't want to come with me of your own will, certainly say so, and I will leave you here. If you want to come with me, certainly I will not harm you, and I will forgive you for all the misdeeds you have done to me.' She replied to Mathieu: 'You will not harm me at all ?' He replied no." According to Cricke, van der Hoeven then asked for forgiveness for twice leaving him and the theater company: "Maria addressed several of the men, confessing and saying that she fully did wrong and greatly harmed Mathieu, but she would amend her ways and would help him regain his losses." But as Cricke was speaking with Maria, one of his companions grabbed her. She screamed, Cricke admitted, but only momentarily. His account of Maria van der Hoeven's seizure in Diest therefore denies the role of coercion, even as he admits to violent gestures.

The group departed Diest "peacefully," claimed Cricke, a cocked crossbow in the hands of one of his men. To address the charge of rape, Cricke recounted that he and Maria celebrated the happy reunion of the acting company after the unsettling afternoon in Diest with food, drink, and sex. According to Cricke and other witnesses, Maria van der Hoeven passed the night in the convivial company of Cricke and his companions at a tavern in Ghempe. After dinner, she consented to sleep with him, as she had done in the past when she was his companion: "They arrived at ·the village of Ghempe, where they dined and celebrated in good cheer. Afterward Mathieu and Maria retired together until the next morning when they awoke." The second night, in Louvain, was no less full of celebration and cheer at their happy reconciliation: "After finding lodging, they went to a tavern to dine, with Maria going with them voluntarily. . . . after dining, they returned to sleep in their lodging. The next day they arose and went to lunch in a wine tavern, where they stayed until dinner time." During that night Cricke counseled Maria to return money that van Musene had given her, and the two seemed reunited as companions again. Their camaraderie, he claims, was shattered and rudely interrupted in Louvain with the actors' arrest, torture, and impending prosecution for the abduction and rape of Maria in the Diest lodging house.

---

3. See document no. 1. As a citizen of Diest (if that was the truth) Maria could claim a specific juridical status and the protection of the local authorities, see Philippe Godding, *Le droit privé dans les Pays-Bas méridionaux du 12e au 18e siècle* (Brussels, 1987), 56–61.

Cricke's account in the pardon request is nothing if not strategic. In Cricke's narrative, he and his associates—two fellow actors and five other men he coaxed to help him seize van der Hoeven—implore forgiveness of the duke while presenting themselves as triply victimized: first, by dishonorable men of means, namely Jan van Musene and his allies; second, by local officials who subjected the defendants to torture; and third, by Maria van der Hoeven herself, who abandoned her benefactor without cause. Not surprisingly, Cricke emerges as the unchallenged protagonist in his own drama, a right-minded and hard-working citizen of honorable intentions whose relationship to Maria van der Hoeven is that of an altruistic benefactor, patron, and partner. Maria, by contrast, is a destitute prostitute whom he retrains—and transforms—into an actress in his theater company, a favor that she repays by abandoning him twice for a married man of higher status. In the short space that the pardon letter permits, Maria van der Hoeven appears in succession as a prostitute redeemed, a successful actress, a disloyal employee, and a faithless mistress to a scheming married man.

As he professes his innocence and defends his honor, Cricke presents himself in the text of his pardon as Maria van der Hoeven's patron, mentor, and employer, and their union as one of shared work and interests, sealed by a contract.[4] As in other pardons, such self-presentations are careful narrative choices. Through them, Cricke casts himself as a doer of good deeds whose only legal interest is to reclaim his career and declare his innocence. Cricke certainly was an occasional, even regular, lover of Maria van der Hoeven, but never presents himself in the pardon letter as her husband nor their union as a clandestine marriage. Without the legal rights of a husband over van der Hoeven—rights that would render void charges of abduction and rape—Cricke's strategy is to instead emphasize her transformation from prostitute to actress, a transition he engineered. When Cricke evokes marriage, then, it is not to legitimize his own domestic relationship, but instead to smear his social superior. Cricke paints Jan van Musene as the illegitimate son of a canon of the collegiate church of Saint Rombault, as an angry and violent man ruled by the lower passions, and as a faithless husband and irresponsible father who spends his time cavorting with the actress whom Cricke had redeemed

---

4. See document no. 2, article 45, which refers to a "notarized contract" ("lettres d'instrument" is the technical term for a notarial document), binding Maria van der Hoeven to Cricke's company. The use of a notarial contract between theater employers and actors was not exceptional at the end of the fifteenth century, as has been recently explored for the north of France: Marie Bouhaïk-Gironès and Katell Lavéant, "Les contrats d'acteurs à la fin du Moyen Âge," in *L'acteur et l'accessoire: Mélanges en l'honneur de Michel Rousse*, ed. Marie Bouhaïk-Gironès and Jelle Koopmans (Paris, 2011), 301–18.

from a "dissolute life." Denied the legal prerogatives and masculine privileges of a husband, Cricke pursues, a double rhetorical strategy: to muffle his own ambiguous domestic relationship with Maria van der Hoeven by representing Jan van Musene as an adulterous husband, and to cast her as a fallen woman who found honest employment as an actress only thanks to him.

In the main, Mathieu Cricke's pardon letter attests to his innocence of the charges of abduction and rape. To do this, Cricke presents Jan van Musene as the married man who lures away his actress, then threatens him after Maria van der Hoeven's return with anger and violence. Cricke is the undeserved victim of a cunning van Musene: "Mathieu convinced her to return amiably to him, greatly angering Jan van Musene, who, to carry out his perverse will, came to a hostel De Noord in our city of Mechelen." In sum, Cricke's narrative features him and his men as a cohesive group of working people, men without criminal records some of whom had served the duke as soldiers, that was invaded by Jan van Musene, a married outsider driven by carnal lusts and a vindictive temperament. In his account, Cricke presents van der Hoeven in multiple guises: as a former prostitute, a fellow performer, and, ultimately, a sexual and domestic partner who was seduced and misled by a man's foul designs. Cricke, by contrast, is her redeemer, employer, and lover. In each of these roles, he has leavened affection with a liberal paternalism that forgave her previous work as a prostitute and pardoned her sexual straying. Marginal in status, Cricke casts himself as the morally superior character in this legal tangle, his virtue juxtaposed with the immorality of Maria van der Hoeven, willing to trade sex for higher status as Jan van Musene's mistress, and the duplicity of van Musene.

Multiple Interests, Multiple Voices, Multiple Truths

Our story of the conflict over Maria van der Hoeven is reconstructed entirely from Mathieu Cricke's pardon. In most of the cases we have considered, the supplicant's narrative and its textual strategies are our only access point to what might have transpired. For a few pardons there is valuable external archival information about the activities of the perpetrators and the victims that allows us to broaden our understanding of a particular conflict and contrast narrative with a social field. The Cricke case is exceptional because of the existence of additional internal archival materials that document the successive phases of judicial procedure that took place and the financial penalties that were levied. After Charles the Bold pardoned all eight men in October 1475, the Parlement of Mechelen had to verify the pardon letter with a formal consideration of its legal merits and of possible counterclaims by the opposing party. The archives of the Parlement of Mechelen contain two related documents from this process of certification, making the Cricke pardon the most amply documented case in the Burgundian Audience records.[5]

The first additional document is the supplicants' request before the Parlement to ratify the pardon, the so-called *intendit*—the case file in which the claimants' lawyer enumerates the facts (document no. 2). Here they repeat their arguments as presented in the original pardon petition. The document also addresses the counterclaims of the opponents (van Musene and his party), who vociferously opposed the pardon's ratification, and their responses to the *intendit*. The second additional document transcribes the depositions of eighteen witnesses from Diest and Louvain, summoned to verify the arguments of the *intendit* (document no. 3). This rich harvest permits a fuller consideration of the relationship of a pardon's narrative to its legal and social grounding, and it allows the reader to better grasp the legal jousting between opponent and adversary. Despite a concerted effort against Cricke and the other actors by van Musene that had begun with his original complaint to Louvain's mayor, the Parlement upheld the Cricke party's pardon after it conducted its review and certification.[6] The lower-status actors, remarkably, had beaten back the serious legal case against them by a more prominent townsman. Although Maria was no longer in their camp, the men's freedom was secure, pending payment of the legal fees they owed for the pardon request and for damages to van Musene and his party for the misdemeanor of verbal insults and bodily assault.

The three legal documents, the pardon letter, the *intendit*, and the witness depositions, narrate and document the same abduction tale. Yet although they in part recount similar information, sometimes with identical language, they also diverge from and even contradict one another. Considered together, they present the reader no longer with a *single truth* behind their layers of narrative, but rather with *separate constructions* of what happened, and

---

5. For a critical edition of these texts in their original French, see Walter Prevenier, "Vorstelijke genade in de praktijk: Remissiebrief voor Matthieu Cricke en diens mede-acteurs voor vermeende vrouwenroof in oktober 1476, slechts geïnterineerd na kritische verificatie door de raadsheren van het Parlement van Mechelen," *Handelingen van de Koninklijke Commissie voor Geschiedenis* 175 (2009): 225–58. Case summary in Walter Prevenier, "Een Brugs meisje van plezier, een Brusselse theateracteur en een Mechelse overspelige burgerman in 1475: Emoties en berekeningen van een flamboyant laat-middeleeuws trio," in *Miscellanea in memoriam Pierre Cockshaw (1938–2008),* ed. Frank Daelemans and Ann Kelders (Brussels, 2009), 447–63. For translations of these texts, see documents nos. 2 and 3 below.

6. On pardon letters and the procedure of their confirmation in the fifteenth- and sixteenth-century Low Countries, see Marjan Vrolijk, *Recht door gratie: Gratie bij doodslagen en andere delicten in Vlaanderen, Holland en Zeeland (1531–1567)* (Hilversum, 2004), 39–48, 62–72, 375–406.

therefore with a plurality of views and truths about one reality.[7] The contradictory interests of the opponents in this case result in plural viewpoints, as each person jockeys to stake a claim to innocence. The case's legal outcome in favor of Cricke and his men is confounding and intriguing. How did vulnerable, small-time actors who physically seized a woman with weapons in hand twice defeat a determined, propertied townsman who had the support of the mayor of Louvain and the duke of Juliers, overlord of Diest?[8] And finally, what role did Maria van der Hoeven play in this drama?

The case's central question—whether Mathieu Cricke abducted Maria van der Hoeven and later committed rape or whether later that night, they instead had sex as consenting adults—turns upon Maria van der Hoeven, her intentions, and her actions. In Cricke's testimony, van der Hoeven emerges as a prostitute, among other identities, plucked by Cricke from the streets with her mother's permission following a payment to her pimp. In Jan van Musene's testimony, she appears through a softer lens as a woman in love, the innocent victim of Cricke's lust and greed. No fewer than six eyewitnesses of the events in Diest declared that one of Cricke's companions publicly identified van der Hoeven as Cricke's wife when they seized her in Diest. Cricke's men obviously knew that declaring Cricke and van der Hoeven man and wife gave a cover of legitimacy to their actions.[9] But Cricke's own narrative never claims Maria van der Hoeven as his wife, despite the grave charges against him of abduction and rape. Their union, it appears, was not a formal legal marriage, nor even a valid clandestine marriage, but an informal cohabitation in which vows had never been exchanged in the presence of a

---

7. See the discussion of law and literary artifice in our introduction, and also, on the plurality of truths, Prevenier, "Les multiples vérités dans les discours sur les offenses criminelles envers les femmes dans les Pays-Bas méridionaux (XIV–XVe siècles)," in *Retour aux sources: Textes, études et documents d'histoire médiévale offerts à Michel Parisse,* ed. Sylvain Gouguenheim (Paris, 2004), 955–64, esp. 957–58.

8. The mayor was the representative of the duke of Burgundy in the city, responsible for peace-keeping; see Raymond Van Uytven, "Bestuursinstellingen van de stad Leuven (12de eeuw–1795)," in *De gewestelijke en locale overheidsinstellingen in Brabant en Mechelen tot 1795,* ed. Raymond Van Uytven, Claude Bruneel, and Herman Coppens (Brussels, 2000), 369 and 374. The dukes of Juliers-Berg (Gulik-Berg) became overlords of Diest in the fifteenth century. At the time of Cricke's arrest Duke William II had just succeeded his father Gerard; Aafje Groustra–Werdekker, "Gevaarlijke grenzen: Gelre, Gulik en Kleef in hun conflicten en bondgenootschappen met de Bourgondische vorsten, 1473–1543," in *Staatsvorming onder Bourgondiërs en Habsburgers,* ed. Jac Geurts and Hugo De Schepper (Maastricht, 2006), 143–59.

9. Many witnesses indeed declared that they had heard these words: see documents no. 2, article 41.2; no. 3, witnesses nos. 3, 4, 5, 7, 11, and 12.

priest.[10] This was not unusual because informal unions and clandestine marriages were very common among ordinary folk.[11]

These representations of Maria van der Hoeven would mirror imperfectly, if at all, her own self-identity, and tell us nothing of how she would have described that identity, her motives, and her choices. She had no opportunity to do so; the case was adjudicated on both occasions without her formal testimony. The archive thus reveals less of Maria van der Hoeven than of the two men who claimed her affection and the tumultuous social world that shaped their desires. Yet as our best-documented pardon case, it reveals better than any other the power of the archive to generate its own truths by placing people in categories familiar to the authors of the archival documents, fixing identities within the boundaries of epistemological familiarity. Prostitute, actress, wife, harlot, actor, man of property, prince: such identities provided the lineaments of a logic of justice from which claims of guilt and innocence were constructed. Justice worked, in fact, by assigning these labels to the actors and thus assigning motives, justifications, and culpability. To mine this archive is, then, as much to witness how the categories were defined as it is to discover the "real" story behind the documents.

If the facts of the case are blurred, so too are the ways in which its central actress, Maria van der Hoeven, is represented. Mathieu Cricke, Jan van Musene, and the eighteen witnesses interested in defending their interventions or inaction do so by categorizing van der Hoeven, describing her variously as an actress, a prostitute, a companion, and a wife. These multiple designations are terms of contestation in the legal quarrel, for whether a woman is labeled wife or prostitute, for example, determines the court's, the public's, and even our attitude toward her. But even these terms are imprecise, malleable, and historically contingent. Cricke's characterization of Maria van der Hoeven as a prostitute, however fluid the boundaries of that term, would have evoked a range of responses from his companions and his legal audience, all of which would have tainted her as an unruly and disreputable woman. Cricke, however, emphasizes not just her sin but rather his efforts to redeem her, a stance toward prostitutes that every man from clerical writers to town authorities favored. As early as 1198, Pope Innocent III touted marriage to a prostitute as a pious act, and throughout

---

10. Georges Duby, *The Knight, the Lady, and the Priest: The Making of Modern Marriage in Medieval France* (Chicago, 1993), 119, 181–82.

11. James A. Brundage, *Law, Sex, and Christian Society in Medieval Europe* (Chicago, 1987), 501.

the late Middle Ages, towns established convents for reformed prostitutes, while individuals left bequests to dower prostitutes who were willing to leave their profession and marry.[12] Cricke's self-presentation, in its minor way, echoes this narrative of redemption, though without the larger Christian moral canvas that typically surrounded it.[13] Under his guidance, Maria van der Hoeven rises from fallen woman to actress in the theater, a marginal profession, particularly for a woman, but nonetheless a step toward more respectable employment.

Thus, if the actual chain of events that provoked Cricke's legal dispute is hard to pin down, giving the case an indeterminate quality, so too is its most intriguing person, Maria van der Hoeven. She is both present and absent in its adjudication, fought over through attempts to fix her identity through designations that are anything but stable. Yet her own voice is largely absent from the record. It need not have been, for as an adult single woman, she had authority to bring a suit on her own behalf and to defend her objection to the pardon, as is made clear by her summons to appear before the Parlement of Mechelen.[14] Even a prostitute had a right to legal protection as a citizen of the Burgundian Netherlands in case her physical integrity or her economic condition came under threat.[15] Yet, although she appears as one of the counterclaimants to the registration of Cricke's pardon letter, van der Hoeven has no legal voice in the dispute except for a short declaration. As noted by the Parlement of Mechelen's *intendit,* van der Hoeven declared herself not competent in the legal matter of the suit to stop the pardon letter's registration:[16] ". . . the sworn parties who were summoned but who did not appear, except Maria van der Hoeven, who declared that she was not

---

12. Leah Lydia Otis, "Prostitution and Repentance in Late Medieval Perpignan," in *Women of the Medieval World: Essays in Honor of John H. Mundy,* ed. Julius Kirshner and Suzanne F. Wemple (Oxford, 1985), 137–60; Rebecca Lea McCarthy, *Origins of the Magdalene Laundries: An Analytical History* (Jefferson, NC, 2010), 168–95.

13. John K. Brackett, "The Florentine Onestà and the Control of Prostitution, 1403–1680," *Sixteenth Century Journal* 24, no. 2 (1993): 273–300, argues that the Onestà, the office in charge of controlling prostitution, became an instrument for exploiting prostitutes by the support it gave to the convent of the Convertite, established paradoxically as a refuge for repentant single prostitutes.

14. On the legal capacity of single women to act as witnesses and in judicial procedures, see Godding, *Le droit privé,* 78–79.

15. Guy Dupont, "Des filles de legiere vie: De draaglijke lichtheid van het bestaan als prostituee in het laatmiddeleeuwse Brugge," in *Core and Periphery in Late Medieval Urban Society,* ed. Myriam Carlier et al. (Louvain, 1997), 93–103.

16. The procedure of registration permitted counterclaimants to come before the court to offer their arguments and objections (Vrolijk, *Recht door gratie,* 376–81) but only Maria showed up (document no. 2).

competent in these matters, but stated that she was content that the inquest proceed, as reason commands."

Despite this, van der Hoeven was the only one of van Musene's party to respond when the Mechelen Parlement gave legal notice that witnesses would be deposed to adjudicate the case. Her declaration of "no competence" may have been a tactical move, or an indication of the coercive power of the judicial machinery. Whatever her reasons, in this dispute she preferred to act as a legal dependent and to join her paramour van der Musene as party to his efforts to undo Cricke's pardon and claim damages. Interestingly, her legal interests as a counterclaimant are cast in gendered terms, her claim staked principally around a desire to recover the personal household items of jewelry and clothes that Mathieu Cricke still possessed.

The person with the highest status, Jan van Musene, does not speak on his own behalf in the two main documents in this conflict. The two texts, Mathieu Cricke's pardon and the Parlement of Mechelen's *intendit*, record Cricke's statements and responses. The pardon is his own tightly sequenced narrative of the story, as crafted by a notary, and the *intendit* the enumeration of his party's legal assertions and their counterassertions to van Musene's party's objections to the pardon. Van Musene's original set of legal objections is not separately registered in the *intendit*, though they are easily gleaned from the responses Cricke prepares to them. Our only attribution of a direct quote to van Musene comes from the deposition of the innkeeper in Diest in whose residence he and Maria van der Hoeven had sought refuge. As we shall see, she reports a lovesick man pining for the warmth and touch of his lover who has just been abducted.

The Cricke Case and Society on the Margins

The pardon of Mathieu Cricke and his associates is a remarkable narrative for a number of reasons, none more important than the fact that the case sheds light upon people who rarely appear in the historical record except as a name, a profession, an address, and a vague indication of economic status. The case features a former prostitute and small-time street actors, people hard to locate in the past, whom Bertolt Brecht called "the ones in the dark that one can't see."[17] Archives from many places reveal that sex workers were ubiquitous in the bath houses and public squares of cities such as

---

17. "Die im Dunkeln sieht man nicht." A verse from "Mack the Knife" added to the 1930 German movie adaptation of *The Threepenny Opera*.

Bruges, Brussels, Mechelen, Antwerp, and Louvain, where Cricke's company performed. But while these sources can tell us about the social and financial profile of houses of prostitution and their regulation, they say almost nothing about individual women like Maria van der Hoeven. This is especially the case for fifteenth-century Bruges, a city of some thirty-five thousand with many brothels and public bath houses—around fifteen documented in our period, down from a late-fourteenth-century peak of forty-six at the height of the city's commercial expansion.[18] Municipal officials in Bruges let brothels and bath houses freely operate in an effort to cater to the city's itinerant male population, especially merchants and traders who did business in this banking and trade entrepot from as far away as Italy, Spain, and the Baltic. Local clergymen and local young men like the servant Gillekin Dubois, whose case we considered in chapter 2, were also well known consumers of paid sex. Although officials in Bruges neither licensed nor officially regulated prostitution as officials did elsewhere in Europe,[19] work by Guy Dupont reveals much about the so-called *filles de joye* in Bruges—their geographical and social backgrounds, their prices, their pimps, and the inns and streets where they operated.[20]

In the urban world of fifteenth-century Europe, prostitutes were a common social appearance, mostly poor, young immigrant women, often from outlying rural areas and foreign domains.[21] On the basis of surnames found in tax and legal records of fines, Dupont found that almost half of the brothel owners in fifteenth-century Bruges hailed from Flanders, and 22% of a sample of 166 names came from outside the Low Countries.[22] In the informal and unregulated world of prostitution in Bruges, prostitutes were neither socially nor spatially segregated; there were no red light districts or

---

18. Guy Dupont, *Maagdenverleidsters, hoeren en speculanten: Prostitutie in Brugge tijdens de Bourgondische periode (1385–1515)* (Bruges, 1996), 84–85; the average ratio was one prostitute for 312 inhabitants, which means one woman for every seventy-eight adult men.

19. Peter Schuster, *Das Frauenhaus: Städtische Bordelle in Deutschland (1350–1600)* (Paderborn, 1992), 31–55.

20. On the conditions of prostitution in fifteenth-century Bruges and the absence of regulations and of a separate red light district, see Dupont, *Maagdenverleidsters,* 49–65, 140–57. For the fourteenth century, see James Murray, *Bruges, Cradle of Capitalism, 1280–1390* (Cambridge, UK, 2005), 326–43. Good introductions to the practice of medieval prostitution include: Ruth Mazo Karras, *Common Women: Prostitution and Sexuality in Medieval England* (New York, 1996); Jacques Rossiaud, *Medieval Prostitution,* trans. Lydia G. Cochrane (Oxford, 1988), and Leah Lydia Otis, *Prostitution in Medieval Society: The History of an Urban Institution in Languedoc* (Chicago, 1985).

21. Richard Trexler, "La Prostitution florentine au XVe siècle: Patronages et clientèles," *Annales: Économies, sociétés, civilisations* 36 (1980): 983–1015, based on records of the office of the Onestà.

22. Dupont, *Maagdenverleidsters,* 132.

state-imposed clothing or accessories designed to mark the boundaries between respectable and disreputable women. Bruges' sex workers, unregulated by the state, moved relatively openly in and out of brothels, bathhouses, and sex work, in response to economic exigencies. The magistrates were likewise tolerant about the activities of prostitutes and the services they offered, and only concerned that local women themselves not be lured into the world of prostitution. As long as sexual commerce did not threaten the social or reproductive economy of the urban household, and as long as it served the needs of young bachelors or married men away from home, Bruges' officials allowed the practice to flourish. Significantly, in late medieval Europe, the term "prostitute" had elastic meanings, first, because it encompassed the full range of women involved in commercial sex, from the courtesan of the elite to the young seamstress who occasionally traded sex for a meal, but second, because the term applied not only to those who worked in the organized sex trade but also to sexually active, unmarried women.[23]

The Cricke pardon not only affords a glimpse into the world of the prostitute-turned-actress, but also into that of ordinary actors. Mathieu Cricke headed an itinerant theater company whose livelihood came from performances in the small-time venues of the cities of Brabant and Flanders. He was an actor far removed from the prestigious Chambers of Rhetoric, the official theater companies securely lodged in almost every Low Country city and small town.[24] While the rhetoricians—almost all men of status, education, literary skills, and humanist leanings—received generous support in the form of subsidies from civic officials, Cricke and his three associates scratched out a living from his company's performances, whose repertoire probably consisted of a staple of morality plays, comedies, and bit farces.[25]

---

23. Karras, *Common Women,* 10–12.

24. For a cultural and social analysis of the Chambers of Rhetoric, see Anne-Laure van Bruaene, *Om beters wille: Rederijkerskamers en de stedelijke cultuur in de Zuidelijke Nederlanden (1400–1650)* (Amsterdam, 2008); on p. 20 the author mentions that between 1400 and 1650 about 220 chambers existed in the Low Countries. On late medieval theater companies in the Burgundian Netherlands and northern France, see Katell Lavéant, *Un théâtre des frontières: La culture dramatique dans les provinces du Nord aux XVe et XVIe siècles* (Orleans, 2011); and her "Le théâtre à l'auberge: l'hôtellerie, lieu de représentations dramatiques dans les villes du Nord aux XVe et XVIe siècles," in *Drama, Performance and Spectacle in the Medieval City : Essays in Honour of Alan Hindley,* ed. Catherine Emerson, Mario Longtin, and Adrian P. Tudor (Louvain, 2010), 149–62; Gerard Nijsten, "Feasts and Public Spectacle: Late Medieval Drama and Performance in the Low Countries," in *The Stage as Mirror: Civic Theatre in Late Medieval Europe,* ed. Alan E. Knight (Woodbridge, UK, 1997), 107–43.

25. The pardon letter makes no explicit reference to the company's repertory. It only mentions that Cricke was active by "jouer jeux de personnaige en chambre" (Prevenier, "Vorstelijke genade," 234), a word that does not refer to a specific type of theater. The word "personnaige" may refer to the actor, but also to the character of the play.

Early sixteenth-century drawing of a street theater scene from *Recueil d'airs profanes et sacrés du XVIe siècle* (1542), Médiathèque d'Agglomération de Cambrai. Cliché CNRS-IRHT, ms. 126, fol. 53. Courtesy of Médiathèque d'Agglomération de Cambrai.

While Cricke was not destitute—in fact, his company was busy enough to employ apprentices—his livelihood was modest at best and insecure.[26] Because "chamber companies" like Cricke's did not leave behind the rich records, from statutes of incorporation to membership lists, generated by the official civic, guild, and confraternal organizations, they remain almost invisible to posterity, and actors of Mathieu Cricke's and Maria van der Hoeven's type—local, independent, earning a hardscrabble living by performing crowd-pleasing plays—are a rare find in the archives. Literary historians have identified only one group similar to Cricke's in fifteenth-century Flanders: that of Jacob van der Straten in Ghent in 1477.[27] Itinerant theater companies were not active in the Low Countries before Cricke's, apart from one documented case in 1427.[28] The same holds elsewhere in Europe; in France

26. See document no. 2, article 3, which confirms the presence of "servants" or apprentices in the company.

27. Herman Brinkman, "Spelen om den brode: Het vroegste beroepstoneel in de Nederlanden," *Literatuur: Tijdschrift over Nederlandse letterkunde* 17 (2000): 98–106; Brinkman discusses the Cricke case on the basis of the archival documents provided by Walter Prevenier.

28. Willem M. H. Hummelen, "Performers and Performance in the Earliest Serious Secular Plays in the Netherlands," *Comparative Drama* 26 (1992): 19–33.

and England, they appear only at the end of the fifteenth century, and in Italy, around 1560, with the *Commedia del Arte*.[29]

The Cricke case is important for shedding light on these chamber companies, but the presence of an actress makes it truly exceptional. Maria van der Hoeven is the first recorded actress in the world of small-time drama companies in the Burgundian north, perhaps even in all of late medieval Europe. In France an actress appears only in 1502, in Metz, and in Italy, in 1564.[30] When women are mentioned in association with theater, it is usually in the fulminations of late medieval moralists who denounce their bit roles as dancers, acrobats, and singers as dangerously seductive, making them into modern-day Salomes. Ecclesiastical writers easily conflated the category of actress (*joculatrix*) with that of prostitute (*meretrix*).[31] The actress, thus hypersexualized, shaded so closely into cultural definitions of the prostitute that, in a sense, Maria van der Hoeven still inhabited on the urban theater circuit the same social realm that she had thought she had given up. As a young woman cast in the sexually charged role of performer and entertainer, hers was still the world of the street and the tavern.

Additionally, Cricke's pardon letter and the other court documents take us into a cultural world of late medieval Burgundian sociality, intimacy, and recreation that was usually the preserve of literature, song, and poetry. Cricke and van der Hoeven give us glimpses into hostels, taverns, and the realm of drink and recreation that is the stuff of the ballad, the novella, the poetry of François Villon, and the comic tale like the *Cent Nouvelles Nouvelles*, with its ribald world of intrigue, rivalry, romance, sex, and betrayal. A revealing aspect of this case is the fact that as a honorable burgher van Musene had no

---

29. Stephen K. Wright, "Records of Early French Drama in Parisian Notary Registers," ibid., 24 (1990): 232–54; Madeleine Lazard, *Le théâtre en France au XVIe siècle* (Paris, 1980), 209. Some authors mention an example in England in 1339: John M. Wasson, "Professional Actors in the Middle Ages and Early Renaissance," in *Medieval and Renaissance Drama in England: An Annual Gathering of Research, Criticism, and Reviews*, vol. I, ed. J. Leeds Barroll and Paul Werstine (Cranbury, NJ, 1984), 1–11. But the thesis is rejected by Peter Meredith, "The Professional Travelling Players of the Fifteenth Century: Myth or Reality?" *European Medieval Drama* 2 (1998): 21–34. For Italy, see Margaret A. Katritzky, *The Art of Commedia: A Study in the Commedia dell'Arte 1560–1620* (Amsterdam, 2006), 31–44.

30. Georges Lecocq, *Histoire du théâtre en Picardie* (Paris, 1880), 138; Jane Tylus, "Women at the Windows: "Commedia dell'arte" and Theatrical Practice in Early Modern Italy," *Theatre Journal* 49, no. 3 (1997): 323–42.

31. Wolfgang Hartung, *Die Spielleute, eine Randgruppe in der Gesellschaft des Mittelalters* (Wiesbaden, 1982), 21–40, 65–72; idem, *Die Spielleute im Mittelalter: Gaukler, Dichter, Musikanten* (Düsseldorf, 2003), 194, 224, 231, 245; R. Howard Bloch, *Medieval Misogyny and the Invention of Western Romantic Love* (Chicago, 1991), especially chap. 3.

inhibitions about attending a socially mixed, popular performance. Indeed, Carol Symes's work on medieval Arras confirms that theater performances in such cities often took place in the open air and attracted a socially heterogeneous audience.[32] Jan van Musene is the typical urban burgher who dominates civic property, tax, and political records. A man of property and illegitimate son of a church canon, van Musene appears in this legal case as a socially respected man overcome by his desire for a younger woman who was immersed in the life of prostitution, taverns, and theater that he, at least, found alluring. Although this is a legal case, it affords us a psychological portrait of van Musene as a man driven by sexual passion and intent on revenge and justice—a depiction that is deepened in a pardon he was awarded in 1478 for an entirely different violent confrontation: a barroom brawl over the sale of a horse.[33]

The *Intendit*

Mathieu Cricke's story worked to persuade Charles the Bold to pardon him. However, its inventive narrative was soon contested by Jan van Musene's challenge, a legal maneuver in which he was joined by Maria van der Hoeven and the mayor of Louvain, as well as by the latter's political superior, the duke of Juliers, overlord of Diest, in whose jurisdiction van Musene had originally filed charges of rape and abduction. The Parlement of Mechelen *intendit* retells the story of van der Hoeven's abduction in fifty articles that set forth the Cricke party's legal assertions and the challenges to them by the counterclaimants (document no. 2). The *intendit* does not have the same elements of emplotment and narrative crescendo that the pardon letter typically features; as a legal instrument, its purpose is to enumerate the Cricke party's statements of fact and address the counterclaims filed by van Musene's party. Drawn up by a legal clerk on behalf of the Parlement of Mechelen, the document, like the pardon letter, reflects the vantage point of Cricke and his men. But because the *intendit* addresses the counterclaims of van Musene's party it offers a more complex story. Because Maria van der Hoeven is now explicitly a legal opponent to Cricke and his men, her gendered portrayal at

---

32. Carol Symes, *A Common Stage: Theater and Public Life in Medieval Arras* (Ithaca, 2007), 212. The repertoire of plays offered also was pitched to a socially diverse audience: Walter Prevenier, "Court and City Culture in the Low Countries from 1100 to 1530," in *Medieval Dutch Literature in Its European Context,* ed. Erik Kooper (Cambridge, UK, 1994), 23–24.

33. Pardon for Jan van Musene, bastard, from the city of Mechelen, ADN, Lille, B 1700, fols. 73r–74r (Lancien, no. 1528).

his hands is more sharply drawn and her status as a former prostitute more overtly confirmed.

Articles 1–32 of the *intendit* restate the bare bones facts of Cricke's case. While the story recaps much of the narrative arc of the pardon letter, there are important new items and slight alterations. Articles 4–7 are particularly revealing because they describe Cricke's efforts to rescue Maria van der Hoeven from prostitution and to assist her impoverished mother, painting Cricke as a charitable citizen. Like other cities, Bruges had a convent for reformed prostitutes, the Penitentenklooster established in 1459, and as in the pardon letter, Cricke strives in these four articles of the *intendit* to echo the motif of Christian charity and social redemption that led to the establishment of such cloisters and other acts of charity toward women in prostitution.[34] Cricke paid eight écus to secure Maria van der Hoeven's freedom from her pimp, a not insignificant sum that was the equivalent of 19.2 Parisian pounds, or ninety-six days' wages of an unskilled worker in Bruges. Cricke reports that his good deed had the full support of Maria van der Hoeven's mother. As we saw in the Dubois pardon, women worked frequently as brothel keepers in Bruges, and there was an organized traffic in women, even underage virgins, in which mothers were sometimes implicated, as cases in 1481 and 1503 in Bruges make clear.[35] But there is no indication that Cricke's payment went to Maria van der Hoeven's mother, or that she was either a procurer or a brothel keeper. Indeed, the fact that the mother joined Maria van der Hoeven after they left Bruges, and that Mathieu Cricke supported both, suggests just the opposite, though the name of the brothel owner or pimp who received Cricke's money is not recorded.

These new tidbits about Maria van der Hoeven's release from prostitution in Bruges enhance Cricke's image as a devoted patron of Maria and her mother. In the *intendit,* van Musene is likewise an angrier man than he appears in the pardon letter itself—one who threatened to "beat and humiliate" Mathieu after Maria van der Hoeven had returned to him for the first time (article 11). As in the pardon letter, van Musene is also accused of aiming a cocked crossbow at Mathieu's and Maria's window in Mechelen and pulling a knife on Cricke's men as they enter the kitchen in Diest where he and Maria had sat down to eat. And yet here Cricke and his men are willing to admit to a more complicated confrontation with Maria in Diest. Even though the text still quotes Mathieu as gently asking her consent to

---

34. Dupont, *Maagdenverleidsters,* 40–43, 105–7.
35. Ibid., 96–105.

accompany them, it also admits that Maria was taken by the arm and pulled, and even had screamed "for a short time" (article 22). Once Cricke and his men have left Diest with van der Hoeven, however, the *intendit* details the "good cheer" of their reunion in a tavern and wine bar, and the food, drink, and sexual intimacy of the occasion (articles 24 and 26), before the arrival of the officials carrying van Musene's charge of abduction and rape.

Articles 33–50 of the *intendit* are especially important, for they contain the Cricke party's responses to the specific charges leveled by van Musene's party. Here Cricke turns on van der Hoeven; no longer the companion, she appears again as the prostitute whose very profession absolves Cricke and his men from the charges of rape and abduction, as neither criminal deed applies to women who are engaged in sexual traffic. Article 35 makes the case: "to put it strictly, these claimants have not committed the crime of rape against the person of this Maria, because the aforesaid crime is strictly committed against virgins and other decent women and not against prostitutes, who *more metricio* [in the manner of a prostitute] have abandoned themselves."

The assertion represented a strategy fully in line with cultural perception and legal precedent. In canon law and in municipal statutes in Italy and other European countries the rape of a prostitute was not considered an offense.[36] In the southern Low Countries, rape laws did not apply to prostitutes, as the jurist Filips Wielant made clear in his 1510 legal manual of Flemish law.[37] The perception that prostitutes were easy and acceptable prey was also common. In a legal suit brought by a widow in Paris in 1394 against servants of the Burgundian duke for sexual assault, the victim offered as evidence of her innocence that she had yelled to her aggressors that she was "married and a housewife." The accused, meanwhile, defended themselves with the claim that they had taken her for prostitute, admitting that they had shouted: "You lie, whore, I know exactly who you are. I fucked you twelve years ago!"[38] Reminding the judges of the Parlement court that Maria van der Hoeven had been a prostitute was, therefore, a sound legal strategy that had the effect

---

36. Jeffrey Richards, *Sex, Dissidence, and Damnation: Minority Groups in the Middle Ages* (London, 2002), 129–30. Prostitutes were put on the same legal and cultural footing as other social marginals, for which see Bronislaw Geremek, *Les marginaux parisiens aux XIVe et XVe siècles* (Paris, 1976), 267; Otis, *Prostitution in Medieval Society*, 68–69, 191.

37. Jos Monballyu, ed., *Filips Wielant Verzameld Werk*, vol. 1: *Corte Instructie in materie criminele* (Brussels, 1995), 88–89, 223.

38. ADN, Lille, B, 1276–12.884. The case is recounted in Walter Prevenier, "Violence against Women in a Medieval Metropolis: Paris around 1400," in *Law, Custom, and the Social Fabric in Medieval Europe: Essays in Honor of Bryce Lyon,* ed. Bernard S. Bachrach and David Nicholas (Kalamazoo, MI, 1990), 263–84.

of confirming this professional identity as also her essential legal and social identity. Of course, Cricke's assertion betrays hypocrisy as it contradicts the pardon's presentation of himself as saving Maria from her "dissolute life."

Cricke's counterclaims contain two other vital truth claims wholly absent in the pardon letter's neat recounting of events. Each places Maria van der Hoeven in a social category absent from the first text, even though article 35 had confirmed her as, essentially, nothing more than a prostitute. First, articles 41.2 and 42 alert us to a claim repeated by several witness depositions: that when his men took Maria out of Diest, Cricke publicly asserted that he had a right to do so because he was her husband. As we have pointed out, the pardon letter never mentions the marital status of Cricke and van der Hoeven because they very likely never exchanged vows, either publicly or clandestinely. Even more revealing, in articles 42.2 and 43, Cricke responds to a charge that in the past he had beaten van der Hoeven. In his own defense, he provides the legal retort that no official charges were ever filed and that a private reconciliation brokered by Maria's brother had patched things up over three years later. The revelation, buried near the end of the Mechelen text, casts a new light upon the strains between Cricke and van der Hoeven, and helps to explain her decision to twice abandon Cricke for the status of "kept" woman of an established married man. It might also explain contradictory reports of her behavior with Cricke: her screams and resistance to Cricke's assault, followed by her acquiescence and the couple's reported conviviality and sexual commerce later that same night. If one imagines for a moment that both reports are rooted in reality, and searches for the link between them, one can glimpse a woman caged by sharply narrowed options, alone and subject to Cricke's violent retribution, financially dependent yet psychologically independent, and acutely aware that her livelihood depended upon her ability to play roles that pleased men, whether as prostitute, wife, mistress, or actress.

Eighteen Voices, Eighteen Truths

Our third document, the depositions of eighteen witnesses from Diest and Louvain by Pierre de Gorges, councilor of Duke Charles the Bold, and Thomas Hooft, his assistant, from the Parlement of Mechelen, adds not only multiple perspectives to the case but likewise assigns Maria van der Hoeven different social roles (document no. 3). Although the witnesses' voices come to us filtered through the hands of these two jurists and their legal clerk, they are recognizable as artisans and neighbors, people of the neighborhood. Here, finally, are the accounts of those who witnessed the alleged abduction and the subsequent tavern behavior. Fifteen residents of Diest are questioned directly on articles 18 to 22 that concern the day in the summer of 1475 when Cricke and his men burst into the lodging where van der Hoeven and van Musene had fled, confronted both of them, and led Maria away as she shouted for help. The three remaining witnesses, two tavern owners and a customer in and around Louvain, are questioned on articles 23, 24, 25, and 26 about the issue of van der Hoeven's consent to sex with Cricke. De Gorges and Hooft focus on key questions. What happened in the confrontation between the two parties in the hostel and residence of the widow Lijsbethe Hekelmakers? Was Maria seized by force and was she asked by Mathieu Cricke, as he claims, whether she wanted to come with him or stay behind? Did Cricke and his men exert physical force and violence against van Musene, van der Hoeven, or anyone else? And in the days that followed the conflict in Diest, how did Cricke and van der Hoeven behave in each other's company? The witnesses' answers to these direct questions depended on their proximity to the events as neighbors, casual onlookers, or people somehow inadvertently involved.

The witnesses vary in the fullness of their testimony, but converge around one point of common self-interest: to explain why they watched passively as a group of hot-tempered and well-armed men from outside the city abducted a woman in broad daylight even as she pleaded openly for help. Their inaction is all the more striking since not a single witness heard Mathieu Cricke ask Maria van der Hoeven's consent to depart with his armed companions. Only one, the innkeeper Lijsbethe Hekelmakers, had tried to intervene. After convincing Jan van Musene not to chase after Cricke and his men, she scrambled to locate the town sheriff to stop the abduction, only to find that he and his men were temporarily out of town—a point many other witnesses used in their own defense. Several witnesses claimed that they had failed to intervene because they had thought that van der Hoeven was Mathieu Cricke's wife. The alderman Godevart de Goesman (witness 5), the only town official among the fifteen Diest witnesses, testified that Maria van der Hoeven had directly implored his help as she struggled with her captors. By his account, she ran over to him, sat down directly in front of him, "and cried out to him, asking if he would permit such an abduction done to the daughter of a citizen of the aforesaid town of Diest."

He did nothing, he claimed, because one of the men who surrounded her—surely Mathieu Cricke himself—shouted that a man had a right to take his wife away. The blacksmith Jan Stevens (witness 8) testified that he had heard the same, and that one of Cricke's men had exclaimed that Maria van der Hoeven should be with her husband rather than another married man: "He heard then that the men said to those present that they could very well take her and it would be better that she went with her husband than stay with another married with a wife. Because of this, and also because they did not harm nor misspeak to anyone else other than the young woman, the onlookers did not offer resistance nor did they try to prevent the abduction." Most of the other witnesses confirmed in nearly identical terms the words of Cricke and his men.

The witness accounts, then, construct Maria van der Hoeven as a wife who had strayed into a married man's arms, only to be reclaimed by her husband in full accordance with the law. Her violent seizure was permissible because of the rights granted a husband, and was all the more urgent because she was now an adulteress. Whether as prostitute, actress, or adulterous wife, van der Hoeven embodies carnal excess and moral error, a point reinforced by the last three witnesses, two tavern owners and a customer, who report her cheerful drinking and carousing, and her consensual sex with Cricke over two nights. In these representations, she carries again the stigma of the prostitute, holding money that her lover Jan van Musene had given her, while sharing drinks with and giving her body to another man.

Of the witnesses involved in the fracas, two shed a different light on the motivations of Mathieu Cricke and Jan van Musene. Lijsbethe Hekelmakers, the widow and innkeeper whose house was stormed, and the cobbler Dieric Costers, who led Cricke and his men to Hekelmakers' lodging in Diest, have much to say (witnesses 9 and 11). Lijsbethe Hekelmakers, widow and innkeeper, witnessed the fracas in the kitchen when Cricke's men confronted van Musene and van der Hoeven. Hekelmakers testified that Cricke had entered her home abruptly and summarily seized Maria van der Hoeven. She claimed that she had prevented van Musene from chasing down Cricke and his men, weapon in hand, after they took Maria van der Hoeven. and that later in the evening, van Musene mourned the loss of his lover as he held a pillow between his arms and imagined the two of them embracing:

> Jan stayed this evening in the deponent's hostel, missing Maria terribly, saying to this witness these exact and same words: "I would want to hold Maria, my dear love, here between my arms, and have my heart and hers merge together and grow." That night van Musene took a pillow upon which Maria had slept, saying that with this pillow he would make himself believe that Maria was between his arms, and that with this he would be satisfied. He also expressed several other lamentations and regrets of which the deponent presently has no remembrance.

By contrast, Dieric Costers, who led Cricke and his men to Hekelmakers's lodging in Diest, clearly regretted his involvement in what transpired, for he claimed to have been duped by Cricke and his men when they first exchanged words at the La Croix hostel between Mechelen and Aarschot. Cricke, he said, had led him to believe that Jan van Musene had run off with the wife of a rich man, and that unless he was found and alerted, a search party of some twenty men dispatched by the furious husband would get to him first. Costers's testimony also provides the only physical description of the couple on the run: van Musene is described as a large and handsome young man and van der Hoeven as petite.

Hekelmakers's and Costers's depositions together paint a picture of Cricke as both confrontational and scheming in his efforts to reclaim Maria van der Hoeven. This helps to explain van der Hoeven's zigzag between the two men, quick to return to Cricke, perhaps out of fear of retribution, but quick to slip away when opportunity allowed. No other depositions challenge Cricke's confinement of Maria van der Hoeven to the role of "prostitute" or "wife." But neither do other depositions much support the pardon request, with Cricke condemned by their testimony as a man who came armed into the city and claimed to be a husband out to reclaim publicly his errant wife. It is notable that several slightly amend their testimony before the lawyers of the Parlement of Mechelen, taking back earlier statements to the aldermen of Diest that Maria van der Hoeven was physically dragged out of the gates of their city. Perhaps here too they were worried about exonerating themselves. Perhaps the fact that after her initial cry of help she went quietly with the armed men convinced them that this was, in fact, a private affair and best left alone. Hekelmakers tried to find help, only to discover that the one official of the sheriff in town was sick in bed. The respect medieval judges gave to the testimonies of witnesses should not be underestimated because of the power of oral tradition in this era.[39]

Because of its multiplicity of sources, the Cricke case allows the reader to contrast the pardon request's version of events against parallel legal documents that expose different interpretations of what happened. In doing so, it casts light on how the presentation of what occurred not only differed in each particular source, but also on how each document's ordering of events played into the hands of the protagonists on both sides and the jurists in the

---

39. Daniel Lord Smail, "Aspects of Procedural Documentation in Marseille (14th–15th Centuries)," in *Als die Welt in die Akten kam: Prozeßschriftgut im europäischen Mittelalter*, ed. Susanne Lepsius and Thomas Wetzstein (Frankfurt, 2008), 139–69; Michel Petitjean, "Quelques remarques sur les témoins et leurs témoignages d'après la doctrine médiévale," in *Les témoins devant la justice : Une histoire des statuts et des comportements*, ed. Benoît Garnot (Rennes, 2003), 55–66.

dispute. Yet even the most complete pardon case that we've discovered leaves us with more puzzles than answers. Each document recounts the same set of events and each is a legal instrument on behalf of the party of Mathieu Cricke, but that is where their similarities end. Maria van der Hoeven is the focus around which all three sources narrate the charges of abduction and rape; each legal document—the pardon request, the *intendit*, and the witness depositions—simultaneously writes her centrality and denies her subjectivity, ordering her around the overlapping identities of prostitute, actress, and adulterous wife.

Social Footprints

Of all the questions about the Cricke pardon, one of the most obvious from a legal and a political standpoint is why Mathieu Cricke and his men, minor social types without political or economic importance, were pardoned despite the tenacious campaign by a more prominent townsman who had the support of the mayor of Louvain. Our tangle of contradictions and multiple narratives has left as many questions as it has answered. The fact that this legal case took place in the late fifteenth-century Burgundian Netherlands, an urban landscape honeycombed with cities and towns and ruled by an ambitious prince, Charles the Bold, invites us to investigate whether broader social and political circumstances might have been relevant to its outcome.

It should have been difficult for Mathieu Cricke and his band of itinerant actors to avoid conviction, given the evidence arrayed against them. In other pardon cases, from that of the kidnapper and rapist Cornelis Boudinszoon protected by his influential squire Zweer van Kruiningen to the arrogant nobleman and prominent landholder Clais van Reimerswaal, the rich or well-connected prevail, despite weak legal cases. But Mathieu Cricke and his "poor partners" had no such status, and the evidence was not on their side. They had entered the streets of Diest bearing arms; multiple witnesses had heard Maria van der Hoeven cry out for help. Finally, Jan van Musene was a determined opponent whose social status, whatever it might have been, was certainly higher than that of Cricke and his men in their marginal position. Yet, despite van Musene's challenge, Cricke and company were pardoned by officials of the court of Charles the Bold, their case successfully ratified. We know this because the case has left another set of brief archival texts buried in the account logs of the Parlement of Mechelen: a series of five payments for damages owed to the ducal court for the verbal insults and physical assault against van der Hoeven and van Musene.[40] In short, while Cricke and his men received the duke's pardon, they were subsequently fined for harassment and injury as a private, civil penalty. An entry records a payment for half the penalty's original amount of two hundred pounds of forty groats, paid between January 3 and June 30, 1476, "for certain beatings, assaults and [verbal] injuries" that Cricke and his men had committed during the abduction, followed by four additional payments over the next four years.[41]

Yet, in a sense, Cricke had the last word. Apparently, collecting the remaining damages that he and his men owed to their legal adversaries proved difficult for the local officials, and carried some social risks. That was the case, in particular, with the butcher Jan Gommaer, the father of Cricke's companion Pierre Gommaer, who agreed to come up with the modest balance owed by his insolvent son but in the event proved very troublesome. In 1478–79 a collector balked at securing the outstanding sum, because the butcher was reputed to have "great influence among the popular folk," and to be "extremely dangerous, and full of bad language."[42] In 1479–80 the ducal official was still reluctant to enter Jan Gommaer's neighborhood, because he was "a very feared man in town, due to the bad behavior of the three sons who lived with him, extremely dangerous with their hands and in other ways."[43] The collector was right: social tensions could boil over if he pushed Gommaer, a man with populist associations, too hard.

However culturally laden and legally astute the narratives of the pardon letter and challenges to it, factors external to the narratives of the principals and witnesses in this case likely weighed heavily in the decision to pardon Cricke and his companions.[44] Charles the Bold had become the fourth duke of Burgundy in 1467 after the long reign of his father Philip the Good. His twin goals of territorial expansion and political consolidation had from the outset provoked political and social tensions in the cities of his territories.[45] As with his predecessors, Charles the Bold had to walk a fine line between cultivating alliances with urban elites whose support and tax revenues he needed while restraining their demands for local autonomy in matters of

---

40. Reproduced in full in Prevenier, "Vorstelijke genade in de praktijk," 255–56, from Algemeen Rijksarchief Brussel, Rekenkamers, Reg. 21.438–21.442.

41. Algemeen Rijksarchief Brussel, Rekenkamers, Reg. 21.438, fol. 1v.

42. Algemeen Rijksarchief Brussel, Rekenkamers, Reg. 21.440, fol. 11r.

43. Algemeen Rijksarchief Brussel, Rekenkamers, Reg. 21.441, fols. 13v–14r.

44. Raymond Van Uytven, ed., *De geschiedenis van Mechelen, van heerlijkheid tot stadsgewest* (Tielt, 1991), 83.

45. As detailed in Richard Vaughan, *Charles the Bold* (London, 1973), 1–40.

law, political governance, and finance. He was well aware that these large municipalities were the bedrock of his economic power but also potential tinderboxes of grievances, prone to upheavals and riots, especially among the artisans and their guilds where men like Pierre Gommaer's father made their careers.

Urban records can assist the search for how political context might matter to this case, by offering the possibility of uncovering new social facts about the case's dramatis personae. About Cricke's theater company and its men, we know only what these documents have told us, and as small-time actors, they left no obvious footprint of their lives elsewhere. Maria van der Hoeven disappears from the public record, appearing in neither municipal property records nor the fines and levies occasionally imposed in Bruges on brothels and sex workers charged with disrupting the public peace. By contrast, as a townsman with property, Jan van Musene was the sort whose financial, personal and political doings fill the archives. From the pardon letter and the Mechelen *intendit*, we know that the Jan van Musene of our case was married, had children, and was the illegitimate son of the Mechelen canon Gillis van Musene of the collegiate church of Saint Rombault. As it turns out, the archival records of mid-fifteenth-century Mechelen feature a Jan van Musene, and prominently so. This Jan van Musene had a high profile, serving as an alderman and as dean of the drapery guild between 1444 and 1457, and between 1457 and 1468 as the duke's sheriff, the chief law officer in the city. In fact, in July 1467, this van Musene rode out a thunderous popular revolt in Mechelen fomented by a coalition of artisans led by weavers and brewers angered over the evasion of local grain staple taxes by shippers from Brussels not long after Charles the Bold had made his inaugural visit to the city.[46] Among other grievances, these protestors were convinced that van Musene had secretly sold away the rights to the grain staple to another town and had conspired with the ducal administration against them. To vent their anger, they raided and ransacked his home.[47]

---

46. Hyacinth Coninckx, "Une émeute à Malines en 1467," *Bulletin du cercle archéologique, littéraire et artistique de Malines* 3 (1892): 300–324; Van Uytven, *De geschiedenis van Mechelen*, 63; Vaughan, *Charles the Bold,* 10–11.

47. On the van Musene family, see Van Uytven, *De geschiedenis van Mechelen*, 15. On the career of Jan van Musene, see Victor Hermans, "Le magistrat de Malines," *Handelingen van de Koninklijke Kring voor Oudheidkunde, Letteren en Kunst van Mechelen* 18 (1908): 93–97, 106–12, 19 (1909): 11–15; Henry Joosen, "Dekens en gezworenen van de Mechelse ambachten," ibid., 65 (1961): 145–77, 182–85; Stadsarchief Mechelen, Serie B, Comptes, I, 120r-v, 136r, 121r-v, 133r; 122r-v, 138r; 124r-v, 134r; 125r-v, 134r. On Jan van Musene's position as sheriff between 1457 and 1468, see Louis Theo Maes, *Vijf eeuwen stedelijk strafrecht* (Antwerp, 1947), 502.

Van Musene's prominence in Mechelen, and his administrative relation-ship with the Burgundian court as town sheriff, is a promising discovery from the point of view of analyzing the social background of our case. It is also the source of a major discrepancy. The Cricke imbroglio occurred in 1475. Yet the Jan van Musene who served as alderman from 1444—a post for which a man typically qualified in his mid-twenties at the earliest, when he had established a household and a career—would have been at least in his mid-fifties by the time of the alleged abduction. Our only physical descrip-tion of the Jan van Musene in the Cricke case comes from the witness Dieric Costers, who described him as "ung beau grant jone homme," a large and handsome young man—hardly, by fifteenth-century standards, a description of a man in his fifties. Most likely, then, Cricke's adversary was not the Jan van Musene who held high office in Mechelen, but rather a younger Jan van Musene from the same Mechelen family—a man with kin deeply enmeshed in the duke's urban clientage network. The appointment held by the younger Jan van Musene's father Gillis van Musene as a church canon was a sinecure usually awarded to children of the elite.

The case's legal outcome is thus confusing. Why would Charles the Bold favor a ragtag group of street performers over an urban patrician whose fam-ily had been allied with the ducal administration? How did poor actors who seized a woman with weapons in hand twice defeat a determined urban pa-trician who had the support of the mayor of Louvain and the duke of Juliers, the overlord of Diest? One might be tempted to attribute the verdict to Jan van Musene's status as either illegitimate son or adulterer, identities poten-tially troubling to a prince concerned—whether from self-interest or moral rectitude—that his cities be models of social order. But neither illegitimacy nor male adultery carried a dire social stigma in the late medieval world. Sexual dalliances outside of marriage were the prerogative of propertied men who distinguished between the world of family and household—the realm of property, bloodline, and responsibility—and that of sexual trysts—the arena of pleasure and desire. Members of the male elite were expected to take mistresses, who served both to reflect and to enhance their position. Nor would illegitimacy have provided grounds for van Musene's initial charges to be dismissed and his challenge to Cricke's pardon denied. In the Burgundian Netherlands, as elsewhere in fifteenth-century Europe, socially prominent bastards were everywhere, the children of high church officials, urban patri-cians, and noblemen. Of the countless examples of the time, one need only mention John of Burgundy, bishop of Cambrai, bastard son of the Bur-gundian Duke John the Fearless, who had a luxury residence in Mechelen and all the trappings of a princely lifestyle, including thirty-six illegitimate children and grandchildren.[48] Likewise, Gillis van Musene died in 1491 a well-respected canon at the elite collegiate church of Saint Rombault.[49] The famous jurist Filips Wielant, a highly respected judge at the Parlement of Mechelen, had a bastard daughter, which never slowed his career or blemished his outstanding reputation.[50] In such a context, the representation of van Musene as the illegitimate son of Gillis van Musene could serve as a form of social description and legal identification without besmirching his character or lowering his status.[51]

One final piece of information about the career of magistrate, patrician, and sheriff Jan van Musene offers a clue about the van Musene family that might shed light upon Cricke's pardon. After defending the sheriff during the 1467 revolt against him and other urban elites in Mechelen, Charles the Bold had Jan van Musene removed from this position two years later on February 28, 1469 on charges of embezzlement and corruption. Part of the problem was that van Musene had trouble delivering the financial penalty Charles the Bold had imposed on Mechelen as part of his punishment of the 1467 revolt. There were also complaints in Mechelen that he was collecting the money and enriching himself, not an uncommon practice among government officials.[52] The duke had van Musene briefly imprisoned and fined him the hefty sum of twenty-four hundred Parisian pounds.[53] He apparently never held a ducal appointment again, sold his upscale residence on the Wollemarkt in Mechelen to Filips Wielant,[54] and died in 1477. The Jan

---

48. Myriam Carlier, *Kinderen van de minne? Bastaarden in het vijftiende-eeuwse Vlaanderen* (Brussels, 2001), 128–33, 281–82; Marcel Bergé, "Les bâtards de la maison de Bourgogne," *L'intermédiaire des généalogistes* 60 (1955): 316–408, esp. 321.

49. Emile Steenackers, "Histoire du chapitre Saint-Rombaut" vol. 5 (manuscript in the city archives of Mechelen), 838.

50. Monballyu, *Filips Wielant*, 1:11–12.

51. The history of domestic arrangements, familial practices, and sexual arrangements is the subject of a vast literature, but for an overview of the Burgundian Netherlands see Marc Boone, Thérèse de Hemptinne, and Walter Prevenier, "Gender and Early Emancipation in the Low Countries in the Late Middle Ages and Early Modern Period," in *Gender, Power, and Privilege in Early Modern Europe,* ed. Jessica Munns and Penny Richards (London, 2003), 21–39; and on sexuality see Ruth Mazo Karras, *Sexuality in Medieval Europe: Doing unto Others* (New York, 2005), 59–86.

52. Corruption and financial mismanagement on the part of ducal officials, baillifs, and receivers were so widespread in the Burgundian state that the duke repeatedly issued ordinances and convictions. There were also successive commissions of reform in 1437, 1447, and 1457: Jan van Rompaey, *Het grafelijk baljuwsambt in Vlaanderen tijdens de Boergondische periode* (Brussels, 1967), 439–70; John Bartier, "Une crise de l'Etat bourguignon: La reformation de 1457," in *Hommage au Professeur Paul Bonenfant,* ed. Georges Despy, Maurice Arnould, and Mina Martens (Brussels, 1965), 501–11.

53. Van Rompaey, *Het grafelijk baljuwsambt,* 594 and 598.

54. Monballyu, *Filips Wielant*, 1:9–11.

van Musene from Mechelen of our case is in all likelihood not the Jan van Musene who held high office in that city for the simple reason of the apparent age discrepancy that the witness Costers's testimony has raised.[55] But it is certain that the two men were of the same prominent urban kin group, especially given Gillis van Musene's lucrative canonry. In deciding this 1475 case of abduction and rape, might Charles the Bold have had his erstwhile ally turned embezzler on his mind when his pardoned Mathieu Cricke and his actors and rejected the young Jan van Musene's charges? If so, then more was behind the duke's clemency than Cricke and his men's good story, some previous soldiering in the duke's military campaigns, and their clean criminal records. True, Charles the Bold faced continual urban upheavals during his decade-long reign, but Mechelen's revolt occurred during his inaugural period, and was one of several that rocked his first months as Burgundian duke, including an embarrassing fiasco in Ghent, where he was assaulted by riotous townspeople. So angry was he that he punished Ghent severely, and even threatened to destroy Mechelen, as he did so dramatically Liège in 1468.[56] Charles had deliberately sided with his sheriff Jan van Musene at a critical juncture in the early days of his reign only to have this officeholder let him down, and perhaps in 1475 a van Musene from Mechelen was not a subject worth his attention or favor.

Luck, however, would turn for Jan van Musene, but not with his efforts to have Cricke and his men charged with rape and abduction. Three years after the legal quarrel over Maria van der Hoeven, van Musene would find himself in hot water following the murder of a man during a heated barroom quarrel.[57] In November 1478, he himself would receive a pardon from Charles the Bold's successors, Mary of Burgundy and the archduke Maximilian. His pardon letter is not only an unusual find, but further sheds light on a man who never emerged in full profile in the dispute with Mathieu Cricke since none of our legal documents was from his hand. The criminal narrative of van Musene's pardon in 1478 is not so much compelling as odd: it recounts a drunken dispute in a tavern over payment of a bar tab through the sale

---

55. What is more, the first Jan van Musene died in 1477, while the second Jan was involved in a homicide in November 1478, when he is called a "bastard" just as in the Cricke case.

56. Marc Boone, "'*Civitas mori potest si authoritate superioris damnetur*': Politieke motieven voor het bewust verwoesten van steden (14de-16de eeuw)," in *Destruction et reconstruction de villes, du Moyen Âge à nos jours,* Crédit Communal /Gemeentekrediet, no. 100 (Brussels, 1999), 339–68; on the total destruction of Liège, see Vaughan, *Charles the Bold*, 30–37.

57. Pardon for Jan van Musene, bastard, from the city of Mechelen, ADN, Lille, B 1700, fols. 73r–74r (Lancien, no. 1528).

of a horse. The pardon casts a spotlight on the tavern as a social institution, highlighting it as a space where the well-to-do like van Musene mixed once again with social inferiors.[58] It also presents Jan van Musene, this time, as the protagonist in trouble, fighting charges of murder. In the dispute with Mathieu Cricke, van Musene appears in several guises: as a hot-headed adulterer who shot a crossbow at the actor and as a lovelorn man who pined for Maria van der Hoeven when she was snatched from his companionship in Diest. In the Mechelen *intendit,* we learn that the sheriff of Louvain had to restrain van Musene after his eagerness to have Cricke and his male associates apprehended proved too aggressive. But in all these presentations, he was always the respectable burgher from Mechelen, the bastard son of a well-heeled canon. Van Musene's own pardon does not so much reverse this profile as complicates it. For in it, he appears much as Cricke had been portrayed in the 1475 pardon: a man of the tavern, drinking and socializing with other men. The fact that in this case van Musene's companions are sharing the new wine from Beaune, however, indicates that they are a cut above the average taverngoer, able to buy a more expensive wine for their night of drinking. Trouble brews when there is a dispute over paying the bill; one of the drinking partners offers to sell a horse to Willem de Gortere if he picks up the tab. But Willem changes his mind, and Jan van Musene opts to purchase the horse instead for five Flemish pounds. Unhappy with the deal, van Musene in turn sells the horse to yet another drinking buddy, Girard de Herlaer. As the horse passes through three hands, confusion and disagreement ensue, with Herlaer reneging on the deal and insisting that van Musene, the horse's second purchaser, is its new owner, and therefore the one to pay the drinking tab. Van Musene puts up a protest, and before he knows it, the tone darkens and becomes threatening. Scared—or so he reports—he rushes home to grab a small dagger, and when he returns, he is assaulted by someone new to the group, Jan van Hoeswyc. Van Hoeswyc stabs van Musene in the chest, a scuffle breaks out, and the wounded van Musene is stabbed in the foot by de Gortere, but manages to escape through a window after returning a blow with his dagger. De Gortere dies from the wound the fleeing van Musene has inflicted on him. Van Musene ends up requesting a pardon, pleading his actions as mere self-defense.

---

58. On taverns, see Beat Kümin, *Drinking Matters: Public Houses and Social Exchange in Early Modern Central Europe* (Basingstoke, UK, 2007) and Maarten van Dijck and Anton Vrints, "De kroeg als bron van alle kwaad? Percepties van het openbaar lokaal in Antwerpen 1350–1950," in *Antwerpen bierstad,* ed. Ivan Derijcke (Antwerp, 2011), 180–94.

Passions, Possession, and Politics

The play of these three powerful forces in the case of the abduction and rape of Maria van der Hoeven generated a rich legal archive of testimony by the men who fought for her, the authorities who judged them, and the men and women who witnessed the struggle—an archive rich enough to produce the illusion that we know her. Social and urban context, and the pardon archive itself, have spotlighted the singularity of learning about an actor like Mathieu Cricke and a former prostitute and actress like Maria van der Hoeven. The Cricke case's archival richness has given us multiple perspectives on the pardon letter, and means by which to contrast the narrative text against other legal sources. In doing so, the case has shed light on wider social issues. We learn that the cohabitation of Mathieu and Maria was not a source of concern, that prostitution was a common part of the urban public landscape, and that the sexual whims of married townsmen like Jan van Musene were tolerated, even if moralists frowned on them. More broadly, this case casts a spotlight on both the assumptions and the practices of gender roles and masculinity.[59] Cricke and van Musene both claim a right to Maria, and while it is tempting to assume that they saw her only as a thing to possess, our documents uncover their more complicated perceptions: she is to Cricke a domestic partner, an economic asset, a fellow actress, and, when push comes to shove, always a prostitute; and to van Musene, she is the alluring lover, the opposite of the wife and the household. The men clash over her, and do so with violent words and gestures, pointing to a larger picture of male competition and male groupings—a portrait only deepened by each man's world of the tavern and male companionship. While Cricke accuses van Musene of aggression and physical threats, van Musene reveals Cricke's past domestic abuse. As a supplicant for a pardon, Cricke is one of a tight cohort of actors and hired hands, and their male solidarity forged around work, drink, social identification, violence—the arms they bear and their forceful removal of Maria in Diest—and class antagonism against Jan van Musene are revealing vignettes of larger cultural and social practices. Theirs is a world of the tavern, the street, and collective solidarity, and if Cricke claims Maria as his, they are his collaborators in the effort. But of all the social portraits that emerge from

---

59. On the construction of masculinity in the Middle Ages: Ruth M. Karras, "Sharing Wine, Women, and Song: Masculine Identity Formation in the Medieval European Universities," in *Becoming Male in the Middle Ages,* ed. Jeffrey J. Cohen and Bonnie Wheeler (New York, 2000), 187–202; Clare A. Lees, ed., *Medieval Masculinities: Regarding Men in the Middle Ages* (Minneapolis, 1994); Jacqueline Murray, "Hiding Behind the Universal Man: Male Sexuality in the Middle Ages," in *Handbook of Medieval Sexuality,* ed. Vern L. Bullough and James A. Brundage (New York, 1996), 123–52.

this fully documented case, the person of Maria van der Hoeven stands out. We rarely get access to the biography, however snapshot, of an ordinary late medieval prostitute, or to that of a workaday actress in a theater troupe, since the better-documented Chambers of Rhetoric in the Burgundian Netherlands were male preserves of letters and the arts. While she is multiple things to both Cricke and van Musene, hers is neither a story she can narrate nor a legal suit she opts to pursue by herself. She ends up a party to van Musene's case, and during the depositions that the Parlement of Mechelen orders, she is the sole counterclaimant to Cricke's pardon to appear to the summons, but only to "declare that she was not competent in these matters." She is the recipient of the damages the Cricke party has to pay out, but is denied her right to the clothing and jewelry she seeks because Cricke claims them for his theater company with which she abruptly severed ties. Her abduction story is never told through her voice nor from her viewpoint, and yet the legal narratives are framed around her dilemmas, choices, and constraints, even if through the prism of the two men who contest her and the legal categories and processes that categorize her. Caught between two men, she plays the actress that she, in fact, is, trying to please both, but when seized, asserting her rights. If it is a revelation to find a bit actor defeating a higher-status townsmen in this legal tale, perhaps the even greater historical value is how, inadvertently, this small and forgotten legal suit has foregrounded Maria van der Hoeven and posed questions both about her fate and about the late medieval world of the urban poor and marginal more generally.

DOCUMENTS

Document no. 1

Pardon for Mathieu Cricke, from Brussels (duchy of Brabant), and his accomplices from the city of Mechelen (seigneury of Mechelen). Valenciennes, October 1475. ADN, Lille, B, 1698, fols. 22v–24r (Lancien, no. 1402).

Charles etc. [by the grace of God duke of Burgundy, of Lotharingia, of Brabant, of Limbourg, of Luxemburg, and of Guelders, count of Flanders, of Artois, of Burgundy Palatine, of Hainault, of Holland, of Zeeland, of Namur, and of Zutphen, marquis of the Holy Empire, lord of Frisia, of Salins, and of Mechelen] let it be known to all those present and to come that we have received the humble supplication of Mathieu Cricke, Copin van der Streke, Josse de Backere, Pierre Gommaer, Jan de Weynt, Jan Roetman, Jan Scheye and Sebastien van der Becque, poor men, all prisoners, Copin and Josse jailed in our city of Louvain, and the others in the prison of our sovereign court, the Parlement of Mechelen, stating that about four and a half years ago, Mathieu, who was used to earning his living by acting in plays, as did Copin and Josse, encountered a certain Maria van der Hoeven in our city of Bruges, at the time a young prostitute, and convinced her to leave the dissolute life in which she had been for some time.

She entered into their service as an actress in their plays, and served in this role until around last Pentecost [about May 14, 1475] when at the time of a play in which she performed in our city of Mechelen she exchanged words with a certain Jan van Musene, a married man, and illegitimate son of Master Gillis van Musene, canon in the church of Saint Rombault in Mechelen, who so persuaded her to come with him that she left the supplicant Mathieu, who was forced to stop his plays that were his source of livelihood.

Shortly thereafter, informed about Maria's whereabouts by some in the area, Mathieu convinced her to return amiably to him, greatly angering Jan van Musene, who, to carry out his perverse will, came to a hostel "De Noord" in our city of Mechelen, across from a lodging called "Rupelmonde,"[60] where Mathieu, Copin, and Josse were staying during their performance. Van Musene took a cocked crossbow and aimed to shoot it from the window of "De Noord" hostel at Mathieu as he stood at the window of the "Rupelmonde" lodging, which he would have done had he not been stopped by some others.

Some time thereafter Mathieu and Maria went together to our city of Antwerp. But once there, she secretly left the supplicant Mathieu without his knowledge until about nine or ten days later he was alerted by some people that she was with Jan van Musene at a place called De Pas,[61] just outside our city of Mechelen. The supplicant Mathieu went directly there in the company of the other supplicants and in the company of a man named Boudewijn van Aalst, some of whom were armed with short coats of mail and infantry lances, others of whom carried crossbows and others who had offensive weapons. But once there, they failed to find Maria, and were told that she had left for Aarschot,[62] whereto they departed immediately with the hope of finding her there. But again, they were informed that she had left for Diest,[63] where they next went.

On their way, they encountered a man who told them that he had seen Maria and Jan van Musene in Diest and would show them the hostel where they had taken up residence. They followed the man to the front of the hostel where Maria and Jan van Musene were staying in Diest. At the hostel, two of the men entered and went to

---

60. De Noord (or Fellen Noord), located in the street called the Ijzeren Leen in the city's center, was one of Mechelen's best known hostels, documented since 1429; Archduke Maximilian was given a festive banquet there in February 1486: Adolphe Reydams, "De namen en de korte geschiedenis der huizen van Mechelen," *Handelingen van de Koninklijke Kring voor Oudheidkunde, Letteren en Kunst van Mechelen* 5 (1894): 344. For a watercolor sketch of the house as it appeared in 1764 see Henri Installé, *Mechelen,* Historische stedenatlas van België, no. 4 (Brussels, 1997), 114–15. The Rupelmonde hostel, mentioned since 1346, was opposite of 'De Noord' in the same Ijzeren Leen (Reydams, "De namen," 418). The hostel was apparently a popular tavern. It is mentioned in the 1474 pardon of Gillequin Berssavent in Mechelen, accused of murdering another man during a drink-fueled night of revelry among prostitutes. See ADN, Lille, B 1695, fols. 64v–65v.

61. A bridge in Nekkerspoel (Belgium, prov. Antwerpen, arr. Mechelen) on the road from Mechelen to Heist-op-den-Berg; see print in Installé, *Mechelen,* 43.

62. Aarschot, Belgium, prov. Vlaams-Brabant, arr. Louvain.

63. Diest, Belgium, prov. Vlaams-Brabant, arr. Louvain.

the kitchen where they found Maria and Jan van Musene sitting at a table for a meal with the hostess, saying to Maria that Mathieu was there and that she should go to him. Mathieu, who was standing on the street in front of the lodging, entered inside, and heard his two men say to Jan van Musene, who had stood up from the table and pulled his knife on them, that he should sheath the knife because they had not come to do any harm to him. As soon as Maria saw Mathieu, she came beside him. Mathieu asked her very gently if she wanted to return with him, to which she responded yes. Right then Mathieu, by sheer accident, dropped the sword onto the ground that was in his scabbard and which he had held in his hand. While he was about to pick it up the two men exited the kitchen and stepped on the scabbard, which remained on the ground while Mathieu seized the unsheathed sword in his hand. During the time that he was picking up the scabbard and sheathing the sword, and before leaving the residence, Maria also left the house, ran into the streets, and began to shout and cry in front of the men. Mathieu would not have understood what she was saying had someone not told him that she exclaimed that she was a citizen of Diest, and that she was under assault, or words to that effect.

Upon hearing this, the supplicant Mathieu told his men to give him his scabbard, which they did, and he sheathed his sword in his scabbard, and went to Maria who had fallen down on the ground in the street, saying these words: "Maria, why do you cry out like that? If you don't want to come with me of your own will, certainly say so, and I will leave you here. If you want to come with me, certainly I will not harm you, and I will forgive you for all the misdeeds you have done to me." She replied to Mathieu : "You will not harm me at all?" He replied no. Suddenly some of Mathieu's men and fellow supplicants pulled her up off the ground and took her by the arm. She screamed for a short time but ceased before they came to the city gate to leave. One of the men was armed with a cocked crossbow but he shot at no one. When these supplicants were five or six bowshots outside the city, Maria addressed several of the men, confessing and saying that she had fully done wrong to and greatly harmed Mathieu, but she would amend her ways and would help him regain his losses.

So they traveled, conversing, until they arrived at the village of Ghempe[64] on the road between our city of Diest and Louvain, where they dined and celebrated in good cheer (*firent bonne chiere*). Afterwards Mathieu and Maria retired together until the next morning when they awoke. In the morning, as she was sewing her dress she opened her purse to get some thread, Mathieu saw that she had a Rhenish florin and asked her from whence it came. Maria responded that van Musene had given it to her, but in its place he had gotten a golden ring. Mathieu replied that it would be more honest to give him the florin and take back the said ring than to keep it. For that purpose, she gave the florin to Mathieu.

All the above-named went together from Ghempe to Louvain which they entered openly and not secretly. After finding lodging, they went to a tavern to dine, with Maria going with them voluntarily. After dining, they returned to sleep in their lodging. The next day they arose and went to lunch in a wine tavern, where they stayed until dinner time. During this time, Jan van Musene, who had arrived in Louvain, went to our mayor

---

64. Ghempe, hamlet of Sint-Joris-Winge, part of Tielt-Winge (Belgium, prov. Vlaams-Brabant, arr. Louvain).

of Louvain, and as a result of the complaint and accusation of Jan van Musene to the mayor of Louvain and his sergeants, they seized all the supplicants and imprisoned them in Louvain's prison. After two days of detention the mayor and his lieutenant came to the prison to examine and interrogate Mathieu, accusing him of having taken Maria by force and violently, against her will, so that she cried "murder, violence, and [the rights of] citizenship" against him and the other supplicants. Other charges were leveled against him, and the next day he [the mayor] came back again to Mathieu, whom he very inhumanely tortured and tormented. Because of these charges, and fearing that the mayor would make efforts to proceed even harder against him, Mathieu sought to appeal. The same was done by Pierre Gommaer, Jan de Weynt, Jan Roetman, Jan Scheye, and Sebastien van der Becque. Their appeals were duly ratified in our court of the Parlement of Mechelen. Because of this, they were transferred as prisoners to Mechelen, where they still are detained in closed prison in great poverty and misery.

Although the case stated above is nothing more than what has been recounted, nevertheless the supplicants fear that because of Maria's crying out and because they seized her and led her away with arms, that criminal charges would be levied against them unless we impart our grace and forgiveness to them. This they very humbly beg and request, because, among other things, they have been and still are men of good fame and reputation, never before having been accused or convicted of other criminal charges and reproaches, and given the fact that several of them had served well and loyally as soldiers in our previous wars and armies, and still have goodwill to do so, and, as they say, have suffered in prison and have had a long penance.

Upon consideration of the account given above and the information that has come about this case, and after taking advice from our beloved and loyal men in charge of our court of the Parlement of Mechelen, and having pity and compassion upon the supplicants and preferring in this case grace and mercy to the rigors of justice, inclining toward the demands of each and all of the aforesaid supplicants, we declare the above case dismissed, remitted, and pardoned, pardoning, remitting, and dismissing the above case, offenses and misdeeds. We also dismiss all punishments, amends, and criminal and corporal offenses that each and everyone of them have or could have made against us and our laws.

We restore each of them to their good fame and reputation in [our] lands and restore whatever goods have been confiscated. We impose perpetual silence on this case upon our procurator general and all other of our legal officers, on condition that satisfaction is made to the parties, etc.

On condition that they [the supplicants] make the civil amend required by the case from their assets, and by the terms of arbitration of the qualified people of our court of the Parlement of Mechelen, we command the people of our court of the Parlement, on behalf of those who introduced the appeal, to execute well and properly the verification and the ratification (*interinement*) of this letter, and calculate the amount and the fee of the required civil fine. If all that is done, and if the aforesaid fine is estimated, levied, and paid to the qualified receiver, who is responsible for collecting to our benefit, he and all the other legal officials, officers, and subjects, to whom the case may be, now and later, their concern, or may be the concern of their actual and prospective lieutenants, each of them as it belongs to his legal condition, should allow and permit each and all of the supplicants to enjoy and use fully and peacefully this actual grace, discharge, remission, and pardon, etc.

Given in our city of Valenciennes in the month of October, in the year of grace 1475. Signed by monseigneur the duke. Visa by [Jean] Gros.[65]

Document no. 2

Legal protocol (*intendit*) introduced by Mathieu Cricke and his accomplices at the court of the Parlement of Mechelen, for ratification of their pardon, Mechelen, without date [in or shortly after October 1475]. Algemeen Rijksarchief Brussel, Great Council of Mechelen, Eerste aanleg, no. 2683, a, fols. 1r–12v.

[1] With the intention, my very honorable lords and men of the court of the Parlement of Mechelen, that a judgment be rendered consistent with the legal decision for the benefit and the sake of Mathieu Cricke, Copin van der Streke, Josse de Backere, Pierre Gommaer, Jan de Weynt, Jan Roetman, Jan Scheye and Sebastien van der Becque, claimants of a certain letter of remission and pardon, of the first part, against the procurator general of my most redoubted sovereign lord the duke,[66] Jan van Musene, son of Master Gillis, Maria van der Hoeven, the mayor of Louvain, and the duke of Juliers, lord of Diest, summoned counterclaimants, of the other part.

That for the causes, facts, reasons, and means hereafter declared, the aforementioned letter of remission [would be] reasonably ratified according to its form and tenor, and fully and literally issued and publicized, so that the hand of my lord on the persons and their goods [of these claimants] is released entirely to their advantage, and the pledges and guarantee be dismissed, by this court's proclamation that the claimants are quit, freed, and absolved of the demands, requests, and charges against them by the procurator general and the others summoned [counterclaimants].

[Such action is taken] in order to have the request and proposals proceed with cause and action notwithstanding the charges produced against them by the counterclaimants to disallow them as unfounded proposals and invalid opinions. That Jan van Musene, Maria van der Hoeven, the mayor of Louvain. and the lord of Diest should be condemned to pay all the expenses, and at least the portions thereof already made, in the same manner as the claimants on the occasion of this legal action. On behalf of these ends and conclusion, the claimants pronounce and present as follows:

[2] First, let it be presumed that Mathieu Cricke is a man of good renown, a native of Brussels, who never committed nor was convicted or accused of any villainous deeds.

[3] Item, that for all of his life he used to earn his living by playing characters on a stage, as did Copin and Josse and other of his servants, male and female.

[4] Item, about four and a half years ago, according to the date given in this letter of remission, Mathieu, who was in Bruges with his people, found Maria van der Hoeven in a public area where prostitutes [*femmes de deshonneste vie*] lodged. He

---

65. Jean III Gros, first secretary, official of the ducal Audience ; see Pierre Cockshaw, *Prosopographie des secrétaires de la cour de Bourgogne, 1384–1477* (Ostfildern, 2006), 47–48; Sébastien Hamel and Valérie Bessey, eds., *Comptes de l'argentier de Charles le Téméraire duc de Bourgogne,* Recueil des historiens de France, vol. 4 (Paris, 2009), 301.

66. Thomas de la Papoire, procurator general of the duke of Burgundy since 1473; see Van Rompaey, *De Grote Raad,* 222, 506.

asked her why she pursued this livelihood, and asked her if she would like him to take her out of the dishonorable life that she lived.

[5] Item, the mother of Maria, informed of this, was very happy and strongly requested Mathieu to remove her daughter from the public place and take her with him.

[6] Item, Mathieu took the mother and daughter with him, paying the fee to release her [from prostitution] of eight écus or thereabouts, outfitting her with dresses and other clothing and teaching her how to act in stage plays and histories.

[7] Item, since this time of four and half years ago until the day of Pentecost [about May 14], 1475, Mathieu supported, fed, clothed, and shod at his own expense the mother and daughter, taking care that the daughter not abandon her body publicly, as she had done during time before he had taken her with him.

[8] Item, that some time ago in the past, while Mathieu and Maria were acting in plays in Mechelen, Jan van Musene, a married man with a good and honest wife, with whom he has fair children, came to see the plays.

[9] Item, that he coveted the young woman, exchanging words with her, persuading her and seducing her in such a way that she went with him, leaving Mathieu for some time so that he was forced to stop his plays that were his source of livelihood.

[10] Item, a short while later he was alerted by some people in the area where Maria and van Musene were and he made such overtures to her that she returned amiably with him, which greatly upset van Musene.

[11] Item, he [van Musene] several times threatened to beat and humiliate Mathieu and take Maria back from him. And what is worse, once he came to the hostel "De Noord" in Mechelen, opposite a lodging called "Rupelmonde" where Mathieu, Copin, and Josse were staying during their performances, and from the window of this hostel "De Noord" van Musene tried to shoot a cocked crossbow at Mathieu as he stood at the window of the hostel called "Rupelmonde," which he would have done had he not been stopped by some others.

[12] Item, because of fear of van Musene and to avoid commotion, Mathieu left Mechelen and went with Maria to Antwerp where van Musene came too and again found the means to retake Maria with him and snatch her from Mathieu.

[13] Item, considering and seeing the great damage that he would suffer if he did not have Maria with him and that this situation would prevent him, Maria, and several other people from earning a living, he hastened to find out where Maria was.

[14] Item, that he was alerted by some that she was with Jan van Musene at a place named De Pas outside of Mechelen, whither this Mathieu went in the company of other claimants of this letter of remission along with a man named Boudewijn van Aalst, some of whom were armed with short coats of mail and infantry lances, others of whom had crossbows, and others with offensive weapons, which they continually carried day and night according to the local custom of the land. When they came to this place named De Pas, they did not find Maria there, but were told that she had gone to Aarschot.

[15] Item, that they went to Aarschot with the intention to find her there, but they were alerted that she had gone to Diest, whither they were bound, and on the way there they met a man who told them that he had seen Maria and Jan van Musene in Diest, and would show them the hostel where they were, and they followed the man to the front of the hostel.

[16] Item, that two of the men entered into this hostel and went into the kitchen where they found Maria and Jan van Musene sitting with the hostess at a table to eat. They said to Maria that Mathieu was there and that she should come to him, and also that she should get up from the table to go to Mathieu. Jan van Musene stood up and pulled his knife, attempting to strike the two men.

[17] Item, the men spoke kindly to van Musene, who sheathed his knife, that they would harm neither him nor Maria, and in the meantime, Mathieu entered the aforesaid hostel and as soon as Maria saw him she came to him. When he asked her very gently if she wanted to return with him, she answered yes.

[18] Item, that right at that time Mathieu, by sheer accident, dropped the sword that was in his scabbard and which he had held in his hand, onto the ground. And while he intended to pick it up the two men who had first entered the hostel left the kitchen and stepped on the scabbard, which remained on the ground while Mathieu seized the unsheathed sword in his hand.

[19] Item, that before he was about to pick up the scabbard, sheath the sword, and leave the lodging, Maria went outside into the streets and began to shout and cry, fearing that the men who had come with Mathieu could do something to her.

[20] Item, that Mathieu returned to the street and was told that she had shouted that she was a citizen of Diest, and that she had insisted that violence had been done against a citizen, or words to that effect.

[21] Item, that when Mathieu heard this, he told his men to give him his scabbard, which they did, and he sheathed his sword in his scabbard, and went to Maria who had fallen down on the ground in the street, saying these words: "Maria, why do you cry out like that? If you don't want to come with me of your own will, certainly say so, and I will leave you here. And if you want to come with me, certainly I will not harm you, and I will forgive you for all the misdeeds you have done to me."

[22] Item, that Maria asked Mathieu if he would not harm her at all and he said no, and immediately some of Mathieu's claimants pulled her up off the ground and took her by the arm. She screamed for a short time but ceased before they came to the gate of this city of Diest to leave. At this moment, one of the men was armed with a cocked crossbow but he shot at no one.

[23] Item, that when these claimants were five or six bowshots outside this city of Diest, this Maria addressed several of the men, confessing and saying that she had fully done wrong to and greatly harmed Mathieu, but she would amend her ways and would help him regain his losses, and so they traveled, conversing, until they arrived at the village of Ghempe on the road between Diest and Louvain.

[24] Item, that there they dined and celebrated in good cheer and afterwards Mathieu and Maria slept together until the next morning when they awoke.

[25] Item, that in the morning as she was sewing her dress she opened her purse to get some thread, Mathieu saw that she had a Rhinish florin and asked her from whence it came, to which Maria responded that van Musene had given it to her, but in its place he had gotten a golden ring. Mathieu replied that it would be more honest to give him the florin and take back the said ring than to keep it. For that purpose, she gave the florin to Mathieu.

[26] Item, that the claimants went together from Ghempe to Louvain which they entered openly and not secretly. After finding lodging, they went to a tavern to dine, with Maria going with them voluntarily. After dining, they returned to sleep in their

lodging. And the next day they arose and went to lunch in a wine tavern, where they stayed until supper time.

[27] Item, that during this time Jan van Musene, who had arrived in Louvain, went to the mayor of Louvain, and as a result of the complaint and accusation of Jan van Musene to the mayor of Louvain and his sergeants, they seized all the claimants and imprisoned them in Louvain's prison.

[28] Item, that after two days of detention the mayor and his lieutenant came to the prison to examine and interrogate Mathieu, accusing him of having taken Maria by force and violently, against her will, so that she cried "murder, violence, and [the rights of] citizenship" against him and the other claimants, and leveling other charges against them, after which they departed for the day.

[29] Item, that the next day he [the mayor] came back again to Mathieu, whom he very inhumanely tortured and tormented. Because of these charges, and fearing that Maria would make efforts to proceed even harder against him, Mathieu sought to appeal, as did the other claimants. Their appeal has been received in this court of the Parlement, where the case stands.

[30] Item, that by virtue of these appeals and the letter of relief in the case of appeal, these claimants were transferred to a closed prison in Mechelen in great poverty and misery.

[31] Item, that during the time of their imprisonment they presented a certain letter of remission and pardon to the court obtained by them from our prince, and in order to proceed with its ratification [*interinement*], they summoned the procurator general, Jan van Musene, Maria van der Hoeven, represented by Master Mathurin Thoriau, her procurator, and the bailiff of Diest.

[32] Item, that on the appropriate day, or another day agreed on by them, the claimants presented their letter of remission, and resolved the ratification [*interinement*] of the letter, in line with what is declared in the *intendit* mentioned in this document.

[33] Item, since the summoned [counterclaimants] among whom the mayor of Louvain and the lord of Diest, in place of his bailiff, came to seek litigation, the letter has been attacked and disputed for several reasons and by several means. It has been concluded that the letter should be declared invalid because of concealed facts [*subreptices*] and untruths [*obreptices*] and should be as such revoked and dismissed, in consideration of different conclusions by each of the summoned [counterclaimants] which the claimants rebutted and the counterclaimants made one more reply. It has been decided, among other matters, that the information that was given at that time must be completed, if needed, by renewed hearings and by collecting additional information, in the *intendit* and in the documents that the claimants intend to deliver about the claims for the damages argued by van Musene, and contradictory facts that these claimants intend to argue. While serving a summons, the claimants deliver the present documents to the court.

[34] Item, it should be clear that their intention must be well founded and secure because it is to be noted that our prince has the power and authority to grant remissions and pardon of all crimes, and whoever would dispute this to the contrary commits the crime of sacrilege . . . so that without any doubt our lord prince was able to remit and pardon the aforesaid actions committed by the claimants.

[35] Item, to put it strictly, these claimants have not committed the crime of rape against the person of this Maria, because the crime is strictly committed against virgins and other decent women and not against prostitutes, who *more metricio* [in the

manner of a prostitute] have abandoned themselves *per legem vincam e de rap. Virg., et per glosa dicte legis super verbo honestarum, et per legem quem addulterium, in fine, et ad legem tulli de addulte* [by the laws on the rape of virgins, the commentaries on these laws for honest women, the laws on adultery, and finally, the law on the abduction of adults].

[36] Item, one cannot justly say that the claimants have exerted public violence because they never by force of arms damaged or assaulted any places in order to seize Maria nor did they lead her by force, as was said.

[37] But, supposing that our prince was informed that these claimants had committed violence, abduction, and the crime of rape, in such a case, our prince is unable to remit and pardon the said case with his special grace. This is why the letter of remission must be ratified to their benefit, on the additional condition that the facts included in the letter and above declared are true, and on condition that the civil amends has been paid to our prince as required by this case and within the ability of the claimants.

[38] Item, with regard to van Musene and Maria van der Hoeven, they have no cause to demand any damages; first, van Musene, because the claimants never harmed him. To the contrary, he brought charges against them, had them imprisoned in Louvain, and burdened the claimants with damages and losses, which have accumulated to the sum of three hundred Rhenish florins or more.

[39] Item, similarly, Maria has no cause to request any damages because she is a woman of such condition as we stated before, because against her no violence was committed, but of her own free will she came from Diest with the Mathieu, and slept with him without constraint, etc.

[40] Item, similarly the lord of Diest has no cause to request any reparations or financial sum for common misdeed, for the reason that there is no basis when there is a crime of evil in itself [*crime sessé*] and common misdeed, because a capital penalty surpasses any other penalty; well then, the lord of Diest maintains that the claimants have committed a capital crime, in which case he is not entitled to claim any amends, be it an honorable amends or a financial one.

[40.2] Item, as far as concerns the mayor of Louvain and his request for a fourth of the civil amends that would be imposed on these claimants, upon the adjudication of this present trial, for the profit of our prince, the claimants rely upon the procurator general to support the argument that the mayor has no right to any part or portion of it.

[41] Item, and insofar as it concerns the civil amends, these claimants state that they are poor and that this case is not a great one, so that it should suffice that they all together are condemned to pay the sum of twenty pounds [of forty groats] to the profit of our prince.

[41.2] Item, and that it makes no difference at all that the summoned [counterclaimants] state that at Diest one of the claimants said that Maria was Mathieu's wife so that the sergeants there would let him take her, which thing he and the other claimants kept silent about in their remission request.

[42] Item, because on this point nothing is revealed than what has already been said: that it would have been better had van Musene been with his wife, and thus the aforesaid inhabitants of Diest had neither cause nor ground to prevent Maria from going with Mathieu.

[42.2] Item, and with regard to what the summoned [counterclaimants] say: that Mathieu never mentioned in his aforesaid letter [requesting remission] that he had at a previous time abused Maria.

[43] The claimants answered that this fact does not have bearing at all on the present case. Further, presuming that Mathieu had previously repudiated or abused Maria, he never paid a fine in cash and made restitution to her. In fact, one of her brothers had brought Maria back with her consent, and since then she has lived amiably for about three years with Mathieu; regarding this, satisfaction and restitution appear in the notarized document.

[44] Item, and regarding the dresses and jewelry that Maria requests, she has no claim to make, because all belong to Mathieu, and are used in performing stage plays and are neither hers nor her household's.

[45] Item, and the clothes and jewelry would only have belonged to her if they had been paid to the benefit of Maria, because it was agreed in the past that if Maria departed from him without cause she would own nothing other than that which Mathieu had given her, as appears in the notarized document.

[45.2] Item, and regarding the 160 Rhenish florins that Maria and van Musene demand for their damages and losses, that is, 100 florins to Maria and 60 to van Musene.

[46] The aforesaid claimants answered that Maria and van Musene have neither cause nor occasion for any damages and losses, but to the contrary Maria is the reason why Mathieu fell into great poverty and misery and spent his property. Equally, the aforesaid van Musene is the reason for the great damages and losses imposed on the claimants and Mathieu. To the contrary this van Musene and Maria never had any damage done to them by the claimants.

[47] Item, and in truth, if van Musene had ever spent and distributed his property since he had become acquainted with Maria for the first time and led her away, this happened while having good times with her, against the wishes of Mathieu.

[48] Item, and if van Musene has been detained as a prisoner in Louvain, this is because of his cause and request, as he acted as a civil litigant against these claimants, and by reason of this he should have lived in a closed prison until the time that the trial which he requested against the claimants could take place. However, by the favor that the mayor had toward him, he was immediately released with a security of two hundred écus, with the innkeeper of the "Awe Sauvage" hostel in Louvain as his guarantee, and no matter what van Musene claimed, he never spent one day in prison.

[49] Item, and regarding the legal costs and expenditures which the mayor of Louvain requests, he delivers that by a statement, as has been arranged by the court. The claimants will respond in kind and deliver a rejoinder, but the legal expenditures should not prevent the ratification of the letter of remission.

[50] In this way the claimants conclude, while they present hereabove their deeds, wishing to verify and make clear the proof, if needed, in order to render legal satisfaction. They deny the facts proposed by the summoned, their counterclaimants, as inconsistent and disadvantageous to them, and they make all protests and restrictions in all and for all, until the end of the cause, making claims as above.

[Signature] Vincent[67]

---

67. Jean Vincent, councilor of the duke in the Parlement of Mechelen since 1473; see ibid., 62, 505.

Document no. 3

Depositions of eighteen witnesses in the case of Mathieu Cricke, interrogated by Pierre de Gorges, councilor of Duke Charles the Bold, and Thomas Hooft, his assistant, from the Parlement of Mechelen. Mechelen, February 20–23, 1476. Algemeen Rijksarchief Brussel, Great Council of Mechelen, Eerste aanleg, no. 2683, b, pp. 1–27.

Inquest on behalf of Mathieu Cricke, Josse de Backere, Pierre Gommaer, and the other associates, claimants of a certain [letter of] pardon. Against the counterclaimants, the procurator general, Jan van Musene, son of Master Gillis, Maria van der Hoeven, the mayor of Louvain, and the duke of Juliers, as lord of Diest.

Renewed hearing of witnesses and additional information collected in the city of Diest the 22 of February and the other days which followed in the year 1476 by us, Pierre de Gorges,[68] councilor to my most redoubted lord prince, monseigneur the duke of Burgundy, in his court of the Parlement of Mechelen, and superintendent of this court, charged with this lawsuit, and Thomas Hooft,[69] bailiff of arms of this prince, assistant at the aforesaid renewed hearing and at the collection of additional information in this inquest, so as to pursue to a conclusion this civil action pending in this court between Mathieu Cricke, Copin van der Streke, Josse de Backere, Pierre Gommaer, Jan de Weynt, Jan Scheye, Jan Roetman, and Sebastien van der Becque, claimants of certain letters of remission and pardon, of the first part and the procurator general of our lord, Jan van Musene, Maria van der Hoeven, the mayor of Louvain, and the lord of Diest, summoned and counterclaimants, of the other part.

During the renewed hearings and collection of additional information the following witnesses hereinafter declared were heard on behalf of the claimants as well as the sworn parties who were summoned but who did not appear, except Maria van der Hoeven, who declared that she was not competent in these matters, but stated that she was content that the inquest proceed, as reason commands. As a result, we continued the procedure, and so started the hearings and the collection of additional information from the witnesses whose names and depositions are as follows :

And first on February 20th, in the year above stated

[1] Arnould, sculptor of images, citizen residing in Diest, age sixty or thereabouts, witness produced by Mathieu Cricke, Copin van der Streke and the others named above, claimants of the letter of remission and pardon, sworn in and questioned on articles 18, 19, 20, 21, and 22 of the *intendit* delivered by the claimants, says and deposes under oath that upon a certain day in the past, around the hour of noon, a time that he does not precisely remember, two foreign men, whom the witness did not know, led a young woman by force before the house of this witness to the outside of Diest. The woman cried these words, "death, death" in her plea for help, and other words of complaint, which he does not at present remember. He also says that there followed

---

68. Pierre de Gorges, appointed as councilor in the Parlement of Mechelen in 1473; see ibid., 62, 426, 506.

69. Thomas Hooft, bailiff of arms at the Parlement of Mechelen in 1473; see ibid., 256–57; on this officer's function, ibid., 506.

another man alongside these men who told those present to consider the fact that it was more honorable for the young woman to go with her husband than to stay with another. On account of these words the bystanders did not try to prevent the young women from being led away. He also says further that two others followed straight away behind the companion, one of whom carried an uncocked crossbow on top of his arm and kept a pike on the other arm, and the men said to those assembled there that they would not harm the young woman. Questioned about whether he had seen the young woman fall to the ground when they seized her, he answered yes, and that she was immediately picked up by the men who were taking her away. Questioned about whether he heard one of the men say to this young woman that if she agreed to come with him he would lead her away without any harm and if she did not, that he would leave her there, he says he did not know because he was far away from the men and the young woman, and if these words had been said to the young woman, he would not have been able to hear them. The deponent furthermore confirms his earlier deposition made before the aldermen of Diest, correcting, however, the claim that he saw her taken away, because, as he has deposed above, he only saw her picked back up by the men by force. He knows nothing else pertaining to the aforesaid legal articles. He has been properly questioned, summoned, and examined.

On the aforesaid day

[2] Henry Laurys, shearer with large scissors, citizen residing in Diest, witness produced by the claimants, sworn in and questioned on articles 18, 19, 20, 21, and 22 of their *intendit*, declares and deposes on his oath that about the articles' content he knows nothing except that upon a certain day, which exact day he does not remember, he saw a young woman from Diest led away by some foreign men against her wish and will. Questioned about whether he had heard the men say to the young woman that if she agreed to come with them they would not harm her, and if she did not want to do so they would leave her, he says that because he does not hear well, he does not know how to respond about anything. He has been properly questioned, summoned, and examined.

On the aforesaid day

[3] Pierre Strekers, clothier, residing in Diest, age thirty-six or thereabouts, witness produced for the renewed hearing, sworn in and questioned on articles 18, 19, 20, 21, and 22 of the *intendit*, delivered by the claimants, declares and deposes on his oath that a certain time ago, at the hour of noon, he saw certain foreign men pass in front of his house who were leading a young woman against her wish and will and [who was] shouting for help with full voice and proclaiming her rights as a citizen of Diest. Then the deponent heard one of the aforesaid men say that a man can very well take his wife and impose his will. He saw that some of the men who followed the young woman were armed and carried clubs but which weapons these were he did not know. Asked if he had heard one of these men say substantially the following words to the young woman as she shouted, as is stated above: "If you want to come with me, I will lead you, and if not, I will leave you here," he said he knew nothing because he was not close enough to them that he could hear the words. Questioned about why the residents of Diest did not prevent the young woman's seizure, he says that it was largely because the incident happened at the noon hour and that it occurred so close to the city's gate that the men went immediately with the young woman outside the city. And also that the bailiff, the aldermen, and other officers

were not in this city [at this time]. He knows nothing else concerning the aforesaid articles. He has been properly questioned, summoned, and examined, and refers in addition to the deposition he made before the aldermen of Diest which he upholds.

On the aforesaid day of February 20

[4] Matheus van Bosche, marshal, residing in Diest, age thirty-six or thereabouts, witness produced by the claimants, sworn in and questioned on articles 18, 19, 20, 21, and 22 of their *intendit*, declares and deposes on his oath that a certain time ago, which presently he does not remember, at lunchtime, he heard a great commotion and murmur in the streets of Diest which caused him to come out of his house and then see that between certain foreign men was a young woman, whom they wanted to take with them but which they did against the wish and will of this young woman, who was shouting in a full voice, but the deponent did not know what she was crying. He says also that he heard one of the aforesaid men say—which he does not know—that he could very well take the young woman because she was his wife. Questioned about whether he had heard one of the men say to this young woman that if she agreed to come with him, he would not harm her, and if she did not want to do so he would leave her there, he said no. He says further that the foreign men were armed with uncocked bows, and other weapons which at present he does not remember. He says further that the widow with whom the young woman resided and from whom the men led her away had gone into the town to request the sheriff to stop the abduction. And because the sheriff was not in the city and because the widow had waited a long time before being informed of this fact, the young woman was taken away from the hostel and outside of the town, before she [the widow] had returned. The deponent believes that it was because of this that the citizens of Diest did not prevent the abduction. He knows nothing else concerning the aforesaid articles. He has been properly questioned, summoned, and examined.

On the aforesaid day

[5] Godevart de Goesman Geertszoen, aged forty-three or thereabouts, alderman of Diest, witness produced for the renewed hearing by Mathieu and his fellow claimants, sworn in and questioned on articles 18, 19, 20, 21, and 22 of the *intendit*, delivered by the claimants, says and deposes on his oath that on the 6th day of June, 1475, certain foreign men came to Diest, where they took a young woman and led her outside the house of a certain widow named Lijsbethe Hekelmakers, against the wish and will of the young woman, who immediately when seeing the deponent sat down on the ground and cried out to him, asking if he would permit such an abduction done to the daughter of a citizen of Diest. When the deponent spoke to one of the men, saying that they were doing harm, he responded that a man could very well take along his wife, and that no harm would be done to the young woman. Questioned about whether she was dragged by the aforesaid men, as he earlier had deposed, he says under oath no, correcting his deposition, but [she] was led away as he says above. Questioned whether he heard any of the men ask the young woman for what reason she cried out, saying that if she wanted to go with them they would lead her away, and if not they would leave her there, he says and deposes on his oath that he knows nothing because he did not see the men except in passing. Says further that he saw that two of the men were armed, one with an uncocked crossbow on top of his arm and the other with a pike, and he does not know what weapons the others had. Questioned why when these men committed the abduction in the city

the residents or officers of the place did not stop this abduction, he says on his oath that at that time there were no officers in the city except one lying sick in bed. Another cause was that in Diest nobody but officers could apprehend them, everyone being convinced that they would be seized by the officers. One more reason was that the men did not do anything nor misspeak against anyone in the city except the young woman about whom they said she was the wife of one of them. The deponent believes that because of this the men were left in peace and were not prevented from the abduction by anyone in Diest. He knows nothing else pertaining to the legal articles. He has been properly questioned, summoned, and examined, referring in addition to the deposition he previously made, except for the correction made above.

On the aforesaid day

[6] Henry de Akele, furrier, residing in the Diest, age forty-three or thereabouts, witness produced, sworn in, and questioned on articles 18, 19, 20, 21, and 22 of the *intendit* of the claimants, says and deposes upon his oath that a certain time ago which presently he does not remember, he saw certain men enter the hostel of a widow named Lijsbethe Hekelmakers in Diest, where Jan van Musene of Mechelen, son of Master Gillis, was with a certain young woman from Diest. He saw this because he was living opposite on the right of the hostel into whose kitchen two of the men entered while the others stayed outside. They entered and said to Jan van Musene not to move from there and that they would do no harm to him. The men shouted to the others who stayed outside that they should not strike anyone who was in the hostel. And then the men took the young woman out to the street. While the deponent heard this young woman cry out something that he did not understand he had the feeling that she was being taken away by force and against her wishes. He says also that some of the men were armed with bows, others with pikes, and others with saws which, however, they never used, nor misspoke to anyone, except to the young woman. Questioned whether he heard any of the men say to the young woman that if she did not want to come with them then she should stay and that no harm would come to her, he says that he does not know. He says further on this point that if the officers of Diest had been in the city they would have prevented the young woman from being taken away by force outside this city. About other things he does not know. He was properly questioned, summoned, and examined.

On the aforesaid day

[7] Govaerd Goesman, shearer with large scissors, residing in the aforesaid Diest, age forty-six or thereabouts, witness produced for the renewed hearing by the claimants, sworn in and questioned on articles 18, 19, 20, 21, and 22 of their *intendit*, says and deposes on his oath that on a certain day which he actually does not remember, he saw certain men take a young woman by force, against her wish and will, passing in front of his home in Diest. Upon seeing this, the deponent asked one named Godevart Goesman, his cousin and alderman of Diest, what he was going to do about it, to which one of the men responded with these words in substance : "What do you want to do about it? Can't a man very well take his wife?" Because of this there was no attempt to prevent the abduction and also because the officers of Diest were outside of the city. Questioned about how the men were armed, he says that he saw two of the men, one with an uncocked crossbow and the other with a pike. He does not know what the others had as weapons. He says further in this interrogation

that he never saw nor heard any of the men do or say something wrong to someone of Diest, except to the young woman. He also said, questioned on this point, that he did not hear one of the men say to the young woman that if she wanted to go with them he would lead her, and that there would be no harm to her, and if not he would leave her there. He knows nothing else pertaining to the aforesaid legal articles. He has been properly questioned, summoned, and examined, and refers in addition to the deposition he previously made in front of the aldermen of Diest, correcting the part where he said that the young woman was dragged by the men, saying at present that she was led by force and against her wish.

On the 21 of the aforesaid February

[8] Jan Stevens, shoeing smith, residing in Diest, age thirty-five or thereabouts, witness produced for the renewed hearing by the claimants, sworn in and questioned on articles 18, 19, 20, 21, and 22 of their *intendit*, says and deposes on oath that this past summertime, on which day he does not remember, he saw certain foreign men lead a young woman outside the house of a certain widow named Lijsbethe Hekelmakers, living in Diest very close to the home of the deponent. At that time he saw the young woman let herself fall to the ground on the street, crying that she had the right of citizenship in Diest, and [he saw] the men pull her up and lead her by force and against her wish, saying to her that should go ahead with her husband. Questioned about whether the men were armed and carrying clubs, he says he does not know. He heard then that the men said to those present that they could very well take her and it would be better that she go with her husband rather than stay with another married with a wife. Because of this, and also because they did not harm nor misspeak to anyone else other than the young woman, the onlookers did not offer resistance nor did they try to prevent the abduction. Questioned whether he had heard one of the men say to the woman these words in substance when she cried out about her citizenship: "Why do you cry out, if you want to come, I'll lead you, and if not, I'll leave you here," he says and deposes that he knows nothing, nor anything else about any or all of it. Diligently questioned, summoned, and examined, he refers in addition to the deposition he previously made in front of the aldermen of Diest, correcting the part where he said the young woman was dragged by the men, saying at present that she was led by force and against her wish and will without being dragged.

On the aforesaid day

[9] Lijsbethe Hekelmakers, widow, residing in Diest, age forty-four or thereabouts, witness produced by the claimants, sworn in and questioned on articles 16, 17, 18, 19, 20, 21, and 22 of the *intendit* of the claimants, and first questioned on articles 16 and 17. She says and deposes on her oath that around Saint John's feast day of the past summer—and anything more about this time she does not remember—Mathieu Cricke and certain others of his men came into her hostel in Diest, and entered the kitchen, where they found Jan van Musene, son of Master Gillis, Lijsbethe who is speaking, and Maria van der Hoeven. Mathieu entered there together with two of his men and said to van Musene that he should not move from there and that there would be no harm done to him. Immediately afterward he asked Maria, who came up to him, if she wanted to go with him, and suddenly he took Maria by the dress and pulled her outside the hostel without the deponent knowing whether this Maria had made any response to Mathieu. Questioned on articles 18, 19, 20, 21 and 22, first to

know if Mathieu had let his sword fall to the ground of the hostel and whether one of his men stepped on its sheath, and Mathieu, intending to pick up the sword, pulled it out of its sheath, she says and deposes upon her oath that when the men entered in her hostel, they had no drawn sword, but she, the deponent, then saw that one of the men had an unsheathed sword, but she did not know which one nor in what manner [it was held]. Questioned if Jan van Musene pulled a knife when the men entered the deponent Lijsbethe's hostel and kitchen, she says that she did not see that van Musene pulled a knife. But after Maria was taken outside of the hostel and outside Diest, van Musene dressed to go out and put on his small hauberk and took his crossbow on his arm and other weapons to follow after the men, intending to recover Maria. But van Musene was detained and delayed by the deponent and by another female neighbor here. Jan stayed this evening in the deponent's hostel, terribly missing Maria, saying to this witness these exact and same words: "I would want to hold Maria, my dear love, here between my arms, and have my heart and hers merge together and grow." That night van Musene took a pillow upon which Maria had slept, saying that with this pillow he would make himself believe that Maria was between his arms, and that with this he would be satisfied. He also expressed several other lamentations and regrets of which the deponent at present has no remembrance. The next day van Musene left Diest and then took leave of this witness, who does not know where van Musene went, nor anything else about everything. She was diligently questioned, summoned, and examined.

On the aforesaid day

[10] Art van Gulden, furrier, residing in Diest, age forty-six or thereabouts, witness produced by Mathieu and his associates, claimants of the letter of remission and pardon, sworn in and questioned on articles 18, 19, 20, 21, and 22 of the *intendit*, produced by the claimants, says and deposes on his oath that he knows nothing concerning the content of these articles, except that he had heard it said that Maria van der Hoeven was led away by force outside Diest by some foreign men against her wish and will. He knows nothing else, and was diligently questioned, summoned, and examined.

On the aforesaid day

[11] Dieric Costers, cobbler, residing in Diest, witness produced for the renewed hearing by the claimants, sworn in and questioned on articles 18, 19, 20, 21, and 22 of their *intendit*, says and deposes on his oath that, around last Pentecost, this witness was in a certain lodging named La Croix, between Mechelen and Aarschot, and this deponent encountered Mathieu Cricke and his accomplices there, the present claimants, who asked him if he had not seen in Diest a young man with a young woman. He answered yes, that he had seen them the day before in front of his house as they passed through Diest, and that the aforesaid person was a handsome and large young man and the young women was small, though he does not know if they were the people about whom he is being questioned. Then Mathieu requested the deponent to take him to where they [van Musene and Maria] were, and the claimants went together with this witness to Diest and they went to drink at a tavern close to the gate through which they had entered. The claimants had said to the witness that the young man who was leading the young woman was named Jan van Musene, and they wanted to accompany and lead him [van Musene] back to Mechelen. Because some of them had made the deponent believe that van Musene had taken away the

wife of a rich man who had dispatched twenty men to take back his wife, the witness went to inquire about the whereabouts of van Musene and the young woman for their well-being. After this witness found out where they were, he revealed it to the claimants, and took them there without entering the house where they were, but instead gave them a sign, that is throwing a little stick down at the hostel where van Musene and the young woman were. Then the deponent left. After he had sheltered far from there, he saw that the men and claimants led the young woman away against her wish and will without seeing Jan van Musene among them. He then realized that the men had not come to escort van Musene. He wished he had been in his home and had never gotten mixed up in this because it seemed to him that those men took the young woman by force, against her will. Questioned about whether he had heard one of the men say to this young woman that if she wanted to stay he would leave her there, and if she agreed to come with him, he would not harm her, he said he knew nothing. But he heard some of the men following this young woman say to onlookers that what they were doing was not abduction, for a husband can very well take away his wife. For this reason the deponent believes that the onlookers did not prevent the abduction. It is also true that the sheriff and officers of Diest were at that time out of town. Questioned about whether the men carried clubs and were armed, he says and deposes on his oath that the men were all armed, or the majority, with small hauberks and others with pikes, and others with swords, and two of the men each had uncocked crossbows. He says that they never threatened nor misspoke to anyone whomsoever in Diest, except to the young woman. He says further that when the men had led the young woman away to the Wood Market [Houtmarkt] in Diest, he heard, from whom he does not know, that one of the men said to the young woman that if she wanted to go with him he would lead her away and if not he would leave her there. For the rest he refers to his deposition earlier made before Diest's aldermen, correcting the written part where he said that the young woman was dragged by the men, saying at present that she was led by force and against her wish. He knows nothing else about the content of the articles and about the event. He was diligently questioned, summoned, and examined.

On the aforesaid day

[12] Maria le Patissiere, residing in Diest, age sixty-two years or thereabouts, witness produced on behalf of the aforesaid claimants, sworn in and questioned on articles 18, 19, 20, 21, and 22 of their *intendit,* says and deposes on her oath that a certain time ago, which date she does not remember, there came seven or eight foreign men to the aforesaid Diest, of whom one thrust his head into the house of this witness. At that time, because this deponent has a daughter who lives in Mechelen, she asked him what he wanted, and if he had come from Mechelen. Suddenly, she heard noise coming from the hostel of Lijsbethe Hekelmakers, her neighbor next door, and soon after saw some of the men come out of her house, leading by force and against her will a young woman crying out and asking for the assistance owed to a daughter of a citizen. Some of the men said to the onlookers that a husband could very well take his wife away, and for this reason no one came to help, nor gave aid to the young woman, suspecting that she was the wife of one of them. The deponent heard that some of the men, being outside of Lijsbethe's hostel and close to it, said to the other men who were there not to strike anyone who was inside the hostel with the young woman, and those inside said to Jan van Musene who was sitting there not to move

and that they would not harm him. They asked the young woman if she wanted to come with them and they would not harm her in any way. As soon as the young woman was led away, van Musene put on his small hauberk. When questioned, the deponent said she never heard the men say to the young woman that if she wanted to come with them they would lead her away and if not that they would leave her there. About the articles she does not know anything more. She was diligently questioned, summoned, and examined.

On the aforesaid day

[13] Gauvaerd, son of Jan, furrier, residing in Diest, age twenty-six years or thereabouts, witness produced for the renewed hearing on behalf of the claimants, sworn in and questioned on articles 18, 19, 20, 21, and 22 of the *intendit* delivered by these claimants, says and deposes on his oath that a certain time ago, which date he does not remember, he saw certain foreign men lead a young woman by force and against her will out of the house of Lijsbethe Hekelmakers, a rather close neighbor of the deponent. He never heard any of the men say to the young woman that if she wanted to go with him he would lead her away without harming her, and that if she did not want to, he would leave her there. But he heard well the men say that they would not harm the young woman, nor Jan van Musene, who was with her in Lijsbethe's hostel. He says further that the men were armed, some with swords, others with pikes, and others with uncocked crossbows. About the articles he does not know anything more. He was diligently questioned, summoned, and examined, referring in addition to the deposition he previously made in front of Diest's aldermen correcting the part where he says the men had cocked crossbows, saying at present that they were not cocked.

On the 22 of the aforesaid February

[14] Henry vander Spicque, residing in Diest, age fifty or thereabouts, witness produced on behalf of the claimants, sworn in and questioned on article 22 of their *intendit,* says and deposes on his oath that last summer, which exact date he does not remember, he saw certain men take away a young woman. They passed in front of his house close to the gate of Diest and he did not hear the young woman cry or make any noise. But he heard that some of the men said that they were taking her to her husband whom she had abandoned. The deponent saw that one of the men had a bow, but he did not know if it was cocked or not. He knows nothing else, and was diligently questioned, summoned, and examined.

On the aforesaid day

[15] Henry Layekijns, residing in Diest, age forty-eight years or thereabouts, witness produced on behalf of the claimants, sworn in and questioned on article 22 of their *intendit*, says and deposes on his oath as the previous witness had. He knows nothing else on the oath that he took, and was diligently questioned, summoned, and examined.

Witnesses heard in the city of Louvain, the 23d of February, by us, Pierre de Gorges, councilor and commissioner, and Thomas Hooft, assistant deputed as above, on behalf and on request of the aforesaid claimants.

And first

[16] Gossin de Villers, owner of the "Homme Sauvage" ["Wild Man" inn] at Ghempe near Louvain, age thirty-two years or thereabouts, witness produced on behalf of the claimants, sworn in and questioned on articles 24, 25 and 26 of the

intendit of the claimants, says and deposes on his oath that on a certain day, which he does not presently remember, there came eight foreign men to his hostel, around dinnertime, and they were accompanied by a young woman. They took dinner there, making good cheer, laughing and drinking with one another, without the young woman showing any sign that she was there by force. After they ate the young woman went to sleep with Mathien Cricke, at present a claimant, in a separate room, without any coercion, and the men in another room. Questioned about articles 25 and 26, he says and deposes on his oath that he does not know anything about their content, except that the next day, very early in the morning, the men left his hostel after they had eaten breakfast and had had cinnamon and milk caudle. The deponent does not know where they went. But he heard them say that they went to Louvain. He knows nothing else concerning the articles, and has been diligently questioned, summoned, and examined.

On the aforesaid day

[17] Andrieu de Roesmere, residing in Louvain, age forty-seven years, witness produced on behalf of the claimants, sworn in and questioned on article 26 of their *intendit*, says and deposes on his oath that last summer, on which day he does not remember, certain men came into the hostel of the deponent, and they had a young woman with them and they had dinner there together with a sergeant from Louvain named Jan de Voistre. They made good cheer, without this young woman making any complaint to the sergeant or anyone else, but she had good cheer like the others, and went as she wished, without being guarded or detained by the men. The young woman slept with Mathien Cricke, the present claimant, of her own will as it seemed to this witness whose hostel it was. The next day the men went together with the young woman to drink in a wine tavern and stayed there until dinner time. This deponent does not know where they next went, but he heard that they were taken prisoner that same day. He does not know anything else concerning the article, and was diligently questioned, summoned, and examined.

On the same day

[18] Guillaume de Buchelt, owner of the "Auwe Sauvauge" ["Wild Water" inn] at Louvain, age forty years, witness produced on behalf of the claimants, sworn in and questioned on article 48 of their *intendit,* says and deposes on his oath that a certain time ago, which he does not remember at present, when certain men, that is Mathieu Cricke and his other accomplices, the present claimants, had come to Louvain, and brought with them a young woman, Jan van Musene, son of Master Gillis, also came to Louvain and lodged in this witness's hostel. Van Musene had Mathieu and his accomplices arrested and taken prisoner. Because Jan van Musene issued charges against the men, the mayor of Louvain commanded him to go to his hostel and stay there. Notwithstanding this order, van Musene took action to help the mayor and his officers apprehend the men and claimants. Because of this, this deponent believes that the mayor took van Musene into custody. He was held for about two days in prison, but was set free following the intervention of this witness and another person, and released without this deponent having paid the bail. He knows nothing else about the article, and was diligently questioned, summoned, and examined.

[Signatures] Pierre de Gorges   Thomas Hooft

People and Their Stories

It was August 10, 1449, the feast day of Saint
Lawrence, in the small town of Château Chalon in the county of Burgundy
when Pierre Cornet and Simon Chantereau, "two poor men who earn
their daily bread as laborers" got unexpectedly into trouble.[1] The nearby
little town of Brery was the site of a summer festival attended by the visiting
Provost of Voiteur and Toulouse-le-Château. A local prostitute named Jolye
caught the provost's eye, and he ordered his men to track her down and bring
her back to him. The Provost's sergeants tapped Pierre and Simon to assist
them, but the two men refused. As a minor official of the region, the provost
wouldn't take no for an answer, threatened to break down their doors if they
didn't help out, and even outfitted Cornet with his sword and coat. They
consented grudgingly and set off to locate the young woman upon whom
the provost had trained his eye. They found her easily in nearby Beaumes-
les-Messieurs, though she happened to be in bed with a monk. Needless to
say, the monk was not pleased, and scuffled with the men who had unexpectedly interrupted his time with Jolye, cutting himself on Cornet's borrowed
sword. Fearing for his life, the monk made it clear he wanted no trouble, and
reminded his intruders that he had to celebrate mass the next day. Jolye was

---

1. ADN, Lille, B, 1684, fols. 2r–3r, Lille, January 1449 (Lancien, no. 3259).

also distressed, adding that she needed to bring the consecrated bread to mass. But the men had an order to carry out, so seized Jolye forcibly, taking her back to the provost. As they did so, they also confiscated some of Jolye's and the monk's possessions, as customary law allowed when a couple was found dishonorably *in flagrante delicto*. But that didn't stop Jolye from submitting a complaint to her local bailiff that Cornet, Chantereau, and their accomplices had abducted her and confiscated her goods, forcing them to flee for fear of punishment. Concerned about their livelihood and their "honor," the two men requested a pardon with this tale of a lascivious provost and monk in competition for the same prostitute.

Cornet and Chantereau's pardon recounts a typical story of two petitioners who proclaim themselves innocent of the crimes of which they stand accused and who point the finger at others for the misdeeds that landed them in hot water. Like many of the other pardon letters we have considered, it also pulls the curtain back on a world turned upside down, recalling the carnivalesque motif that was so much a part of the festive mental scaffolding of late medieval culture. Men whose duties it is to be sober and responsible—the secular authority, the provost, and the religious authority, the monk—are just the opposite, governed by their lust. The provost hankers after a prostitute, and conscripts two humble laborers to carry out his designs on her. The prostitute is in bed with a monk, shattering the illusion of clerical celibacy, and when discovered, both invoke sacred obligations: to say mass and to bring bread to be blessed. All is the opposite of what it should be. Our consideration of pardon letters has interpreted these sources as both narrative constructs assembled by petitioner and notary but also mirrors, however mediated, of a larger social world, ones that grant us privileged access to people and places not otherwise easily accessible, and to social conditions that are often unsettled.

As an urban society, the late medieval Low Countries is rich in municipal sources—city laws, guild regulations, financial records—that might lead readers who immerse themselves in them to gain the impression that the era was a perfectly ordered, neatly controlled realm of interlocking social groups, from family and kin to political and social collectives, like guilds, confraternities, religious brotherhoods, and other institutions, secured by countless careful decrees to ensure social order and harmony. This pardon letter, from the rural territory of the Franche-Comté with its well-regulated villages and small towns, suggests just the reverse: a society that is both fragile and untethered, vulnerable to sudden and threatening eruptions of violence that fray established social and political institutions. Families war with one another, youth fight in bloody dust-ups, men like our randy provost and monk are prey to sexual appetites, while key social sites like taverns and public squares become spaces of drunken squabbles and outbursts of deadly conflict. In an important sense, these two contrasting images of late medieval society—the well-ordered world and the world turned upside down—were established motifs in the larger late medieval cultural imagination itself, a result of the sense that people of this era had of the fragility of the world in which they lived.[2] Pardon letters confirm the vulnerability of the late medieval social order, exposing how often the established order that was such a preoccupation of urban magistrates and regional and princely authorities could be frayed, torn, and shattered. But the letters just as readily point out that wrongs could be righted, that sudden eruptions of chaos could be tamped down, that vendettas could be settled, and, more than anything else, that there was a mechanism in place—the pardon procedure itself—that permitted the supreme authority in the Burgundian territories to make executive decisions about these matters. Indeed, that very princely authority permitted the duke not only to flaunt his power but to reconstitute the social good, repairing chaos and setting the world right anew after violence had destabilized it.

Our consideration of Burgundian pardon letters has embraced these sources as social texts and shown their potential for accessing larger questions of social order and political authority. No doubt, as Natalie Zemon Davis has explored, pardon letters challenge our traditional positivist understanding of the archives as repositories of durable historical facts. Despite all the legal and procedural language they embody, pardons are stories, micronarratives of misfortunes and misdeeds whose truths are tailored to the self-interest of the petitioner behind them. Our cases have showcased the storytelling ambitions and strategies of the ordinary people who scripted them with the help of a notary. We have affirmed the structural similarities and resonances between legal text and fiction, made all the more obvious in the Burgundian Low Countries because of the *Cent Nouvelles Nouvelles,* whose tales approximate the language and incidents in pardon narratives. Yet our interest in these cases has extended into the extratextual realm, and brought us back to the primary sources themselves in a search for the place of the archives in the "fiction"—the imaginative dimension—of the pardon genre. In this book's pardons, we have tried to unearth, where possible, additional archival details about a particular case in an effort to compare and contrast the pardon letter with the social world. We do so not in an attempt to locate and fix a single

---

2. For the Low Countries see Herman Pleij, *Het Gilde van de blauwe schuit: Literatuur, volksfeest en burgermoraal in de late middeleeuwen* (Amsterdam, 1983), and his *Dreaming of Cockaigne: Medieval Fantasies of the Perfect Life,* trans. Diane Webb (New York, 2001).

truth—the elusive goal of what really happened—but rather to single out the textual and rhetorical strategies of the pardon letter by juxtaposing them with hard social facts. Comparing internal discursive elements of the pardon letter with the social context strengthens rather than weakens an appreciation of both, for it at once underscores the pardon letter as a constructed and strategic text and grounds it in a verifiable social realm.

While our approach has focused on individual cases and the relationship between text and social world, we have been equally concerned with the political dimension of the pardon as a princely tool. The Burgundian administration, and the Burgundian duke above all, capitalized on the pardon to sidestep and overrule customary and urban laws and the civic officials and magistrates who enforced them. The pardon had an executive purpose, allowing an ambitious prince like the long-reigning Philip the Good to cultivate clients and allies while presenting himself as a judicious lawgiver and forgiving father. The duke's standard language in the pardon award of favoring mercy over the "rigors" of justice, as we have seen, was a routine invocation that conceals the most important reason that a pardon was granted. A few letters, however, are exceptions as they feature protagonists with ties to the ducal administration, like Philippot de Boneffe, who ran the manorial oven on ducal property. But men like Boneffe have such a tenuous connection to the court and its interests that it's hard to peg his pardon's success to favoritism. The clientelism argument is clearer with important families such as the nobleman Jan van Gavere, who enjoyed concrete ties with ducal officials and with the court. More obvious are those pardons that reference prior political and military services to the court such as those of Braeyman and the citizens of Hulst. Likewise, recall the case of hot-tempered Adriaan van Reimerswaal in Zeeland, who proclaimed his allegiance to the Burgundian duke in his pardon request: "All my life I risked my life and property for him. Should he require my service I would still risk my life and goods for him."[3] In a few cases we have considered, ducal favoritism is explicitly linked to a financial incentive, like the unusually high fees the nobleman Jan van Gavere and the townspeople Dirk van Langerode and Katherine Meulenpas had to pay for their pardon letters. But more than offering concrete, specific political advantages, pardons burnished the image of the prince as fair and forgiving by underscoring his monopoly on absolving felons and resolving legal logjams; a prince's decision to pardon was, more often than not, less about a specific political favor than about broader political and social goals.

---

3. ADN, Lille, B, 1710, fols. 10r–11v, Brussels, January 1499 (Lancien, no. 2228).

Narratives of Self-Defense

Despite the right of a prince to grant a pardon summarily and even without explanation, the narrative pleas petitioners made in their requests often mattered more than anything else, for a good argument could make murderous aggression a matter instead of self-defense or righteous anger. Jan Rutghers in Bruges, for example, presented himself as the victim of an ambush, killing his opponents only to defend himself bravely after his servant was brutally cut down. The city bailiff's account, however frustratingly succinct, reveal that Jan Rutghers and his friend Jossequin Richart were more troublesome men than he admitted in his request, involved in other disputes and, in Richart's case, even other murders. Yet they told a good story in the pardon request, and it is this self-presentation and the sequence of events it narrates that the duke's chancery lawyers heard, considered, and adjudicated. Self-defense was the common denominator of almost all pardon requests. We have repeatedly seen petitioners claim to have resorted to violence purely out of self-defense, admitting to the crime but simultaneously padding the narrative with justifications and mitigating circumstances. The plea for clemency is built around the absence of premeditation; the contrast between an innocent person and an intemperate opponent who shows unpredictable, vengeful, and unreasonable behavior; and the resulting provocation to "hot anger" of someone like Jan Rutghers, who bravely defended himself by wounding an opponent who had ambushed him. In the small town of Deinze, Christiaen van der Naet was violently attacked, despite his efforts to diffuse his conflict with his opponent. Parcheval van de Woestine in Ypres, to take another example, presented himself as an innocent young boy, recalling how his mother's death led him and his family to minor wrongdoing.

Rare, as we have seen, is a case in which a petitioner does not explicitly invoke some variety of the self-defense argument. But it is one coupled with other exculpatory motifs, none more important than assaults upon one's honor and "hot anger" resulting from a sudden provocation that triggered a loss of reason that often led to a murderous reaction—an internal emotional eruption that our petitioners routinely invoked. Christiaen van der Naet in war-weary Deinze reacted violently to Rogier de Marscalc's provocations. Alberto Spinola in Antwerp solicited clemency for his hot anger because he was "troubled and affected" by the injurious words of his opponent. The small-town schoolboy Jan Melnairs "became so infuriated and enraged that with hot anger he took a small knife" to kill his young taunters. The entire town of Hulst cited the threat to its very livelihood and safety in 1485 by the English captain sent by Ghent's militia when they asked for a pardon on the basis of admitting to collective hot anger. Sudden anger was just as readily stirred up by verbal insults. Vincent Zoetart was called a "false traitor," and a "son of a whore," Francesco Spinola was insulted as a "ribald, ruffian, traitor, and bad man."

When Jacot Barcueille discovered his neighbor in his spouse's bed and killed him "de chaude colle," he alluded to the assault on his male honor. In many pardon letters we have gauged how notions of honor govern self-worth, and how assaults upon it were the principal reason behind the flash of hot anger that provoked trouble. Christiaen van der Naet, dining at the terrace of the hostel where he lived after his house was burned down in 1489 during a war, got a chamber pot dumped on his head from a window above by the young daughter of Rogier de Marscalc. It was an act of dishonor made all the worse because his friends were with him in a public setting. Rogier de Marscalc's honor was also at stake, resulting in his daughter's double punishment, once by the embarrassed Christiaen and again by Rogier himself, who exerted his patriarchal authority. The case opens a window onto how honor was typically gendered, defined by a man's ability to exercise authority over women, especially his wife and daughters. When this authority was transgressed, especially in cases of adultery, the results were scandalous, with honor ruined, sometimes doubly so. In the case of Pieter de Scelewe the initial humiliation sprang from the public rumors about his neighbor Christian de Cloot's dalliance with his wife, but was deepened by de Cloot's taunting of Scelewe's masculinity, "that the supplicant was a mongrel and had no balls and that he was hardly fit to be a man." Scelewe's pardon request for homicide hinged entirely on the affront to his public honor. In a related case we explored, Jacot Barcueille's killing of Estevenin d'Escoste occurred after he found d'Escoste in his bed with his wife—a discovery worsened by the fact that d'Escoste had "bragged many times and in many places that he had had sexual intercourse with the wife of the supplicant." Confronted by the betrayal of his master Jan, Ywain Voet in his pardon invoked how a friendship betrayed led to public shame and therefore murder.

Gender Themes

Honor's invocation was as gendered as it was commonplace, with men overwhelmingly claiming the burden it imposed on them to act. Women are everywhere in the pardon letters, but rarely as petitioners, though we sampled a few of the less than 1 percent of cases in which they acted in that role. In almost all the pardons, the petitioner is the male perpetrator of the crime. It is his narrative we read, and it is his ordering of events that frames the storyline.

The archive of Burgundian pardon letters chronicles men's and women's lives, but it cannot recover their voices in any balanced way and offers instead revealing instances of the construction of gender roles in late medieval society. Women are regularly featured in pardon letters in ways that conform to gender expectations. There are the hysterical innkeeper Margareta van de Mote; the loving mother who wraps her dying son Hacquinot Nollet into her apron, in the case of the murder by his angry father; the pious widow and good mother Antoinette de Rambures; and the alluring prostitute and actress Maria van der Hoeven, among others. There are the rich widows Antoinette de Rambures and Anna Willemszoon, wealthy because of their assets yet vulnerable without a husband; the assertive and transgressive women, like the young girl from Deinze who threw the chamber pot; and the partners in crime, like young Jacquemine Willemszoon from Middelburg, evading parents and kin in an elopement staged by her lover Wouter Janszoon. On the more tragic side we document two infanticide cases in which the petitioners, facing conviction for one of the most harshly punished crimes in early modern Europe, are pardoned with the justification that they were young, poor and naively irresponsible. Less clemency was found for the serial adulteress Jehanette, wife of Pierre Monié, engaged in adulterous affairs before turning to prostitution, and the victim of a murderous ambush by her outraged husband's associates. The Burgundian adultery cases more generally reveal gender distinctions in very sharp relief. In the narratives of Barcueille and Scelewe the focus is entirely on their male adversaries and not their wives, their pardons predicated on male outrage and male rivalries. In the ordinary procedures of urban and ecclesiastical courts, however, adulterous wives are not absent in the texts; they mostly pay exactly the same fines as adulterous husbands. In most of the late medieval Low Countries adultery was certainly not considered socially dangerous or destabilizing. Yet revenge by duped husbands was accepted because male honor demanded it.

Between Text and Social World

Pardon letters have long drawn the attention of historians as archival sources, for they serve as mirrors of ordinary people in the past and recount stories that expose the social landscape of late medieval Europe, inviting us into taverns, public squares, festive celebrations, people's houses, and other public and interior spaces. The Burgundian archival collection is particularly rich and yet underused for historical purposes, and if nothing else, we hope this book has pointed the way for a fuller appreciation of this remarkable late medieval and early modern source. As inviting as they are, pardon letters, we have cautioned, are not transparent sources, nor methodologically the equivalent of letters of other kinds, diaries, or other types of documents, for they involve a notary's hand and a legal culture, both of which shape their narrative structure and choices. A petitioner's letter is penned with a strategy in mind and employs a particular ordering of events to shape a favorable outcome. Pardon letters are texts like other archival documents, but ones that bear their constructed armature more fully and obviously. While we have acknowledged their compliance with the rules of the legal game both in narrative and procedure, we have also insisted that they nevertheless afford access to a larger social canvas, especially in cases where they can be compared with other archival documents in a process not unlike the process of verification that they were themselves required to undergo for their legal registration. In doing so, however, our purpose has not been to replay the role of the judge who evaluated the pardon letter's veracity but instead to reclaim the social world of family, kin, neighborhood, countryside, and city from which the pardon request issued. Without this remarkable archive, we would never learn so much about taverns and inns, street theater and street musicians, desperate acts of infanticide among young women both poor and wealthy, brawling youth, erring priests, romantic young couples, vulnerable widows, and warring families. The pardon letters' value lies not in the truths they expose but in the lives they recount and the people they bring back to life for readers willing to explore their many stories.

BIBLIOGRAPHICAL NOTE

General overviews in English of the territories of the Burgundian Low Countries and their cultural, social, economic, and political history include the following works by Richard Vaughan: *Philip the Bold: The Formation of the Burgundian State* (London, 1962); *John the Fearless: The Growth of Burgundian Power* (London, 1966); *Philip the Good: The Apogee of Burgundy* (London, 1970); *Charles the Bold* (London, 1973); Boydell's new edition in 2002 (Woodbridge, UK) updates all four books to 2002 with introductions and supplementary bibliographies (as long as the original ones) by Malcolm Vale, Bertrand Schnerb, Graeme Small, and Werner Paravicini respectively. Also consult Walter Prevenier and Wim Blockmans, *The Burgundian Netherlands* (Cambridge, UK, 1986); Wim Blockmans and Walter Prevenier, *The Promised Lands: The Low Countries under Burgundian Rule, 1369–1530* (Philadelphia, 1999).

The pardon as a legal instrument and set of juridical procedures is explored in Natalie Zemon Davis, *Fiction in the Archives: Pardon Tales and Their Tellers in Sixteenth-Century France* (Stanford, CA, 1987); Robert Muchembled, *A History of Violence: From the End of the Middle Ages to the Present* (Cambridge, UK, 2012); Claude Gauvard, *"De grace espécial": Crime, état et société en France à la fin du moyen âge* (Paris, 1991); Jean-Marie Cauchies and Hugo de Schepper, *Justice, grâce et legislation: Genèse de l'état et moyens juridiques dans les Pays-Bas, 1200–1600* (Brussels, 1994); Marjan Vrolijk, *Recht door gratie: Gratie bij doodslagen en andere delicten in Vlaanderen, Holland en Zeeland (1531–1567)* (Hilversum, 2004); Bernard Dauven and Xavier Rousseaux, eds., *Préférant miséricorde à rigueur de justice: Pratiques de la grâce, XIIIe–XVIIe siècles* (Louvain-la-Neuve, 2012). On regulations concerning property, inheritance, and marriage in the Low Countries see Philippe Godding, *Le droit privé dans les Pays-Bas méridionaux du 12e au 18e siècle* (Brussels, 1987).

On the pardon letter as a political instrument see Claude Gauvard, "L'image du roi justicier en France à la fin du moyen âge d'après les lettres de rémission," in *La faute, la répression et le pardon : Actes du 107e congrès national des sociétés savantes*, vol. 1, ed. Pierre Braun (Paris, 1984), 165–92; Frédéric Lalière, "La lettre de rémission entre source directe et indirecte: Instrument juridique de la centralisation du pouvoir et champ de prospection pour l'historien du droit," in *Violence, conciliation et répression*, ed. Aude Musin, Xavier Rousseaux, and Frédéric Vesentini (Louvain-la-Neuve, 2008), 21–65 ; Walter Prevenier, "The Two Faces of Pardon Jurisdiction in the Burgundian Netherlands: A Royal Road to Social Cohesion and an Effectual Instrument of Princely Clientelism," in *Power and Persuasion: Essays on the Art of State Building in Honour of W.P. Blockmans*, ed. Peter Hoppenbrouwers, Antheun Janse, and Robert Stein (Turnhout, 2010), 183–86; Willem P. Blockmans, "Patronage, Brokerage and Corruption as Symptoms of Incipient State Formation in the Burgundian-Habsburg

Netherlands," in *Klientelsysteme im Europa der frühen Neuzeit,* ed. Antoni Mączak (Munich, 1988), 117–26.

The dukes of Burgundy and other medieval rulers issued pardons for a wide variety of crimes and acts of violence of which people had been convicted. On medieval violence, including domestic violence, see Hannah Skoda, *Medieval Violence: Physical Brutality in Northern France, 1270–1330* (Oxford, 2013). On anger and "hot anger," see Barbara H. Rosenwein, ed., *Anger's Past: The Social Uses of an Emotion in the Middle Ages* (Ithaca, 1998). On murder and homicide: Pieter Spierenburg, *A History of Murder: Personal Violence in Europe from the Middle Ages to the Present* (Cambridge, UK, 2008). On vengeance: Susanna A. Throop and Paul R. Hyams, eds., *Vengeance in the Middle Ages: Emotion, Religion and Feud* (Farnham, UK, 2010). On urban disputes: Lorenza Vantaggiato, "Civil Disputes in Fourteenth-Century Ghent: The Case Study of the Feud between the Rijm and Alijn Families," *Handelingen der Maatschappij voor Geschiedenis en Oudheidkunde te Gent* 64, no. 1 (2010): 57–85. On prostitution: Jacques Rossiaud, *Medieval Prostitution,* trans. Lydia G. Cochrane (Oxford, 1988); Leah Lydia Otis, *Prostitution in Medieval Society: The History of an Urban Institution in Languedoc* (Chicago, 1985); Ruth Mazo Karras, *Common Women: Prostitution and Sexuality in Medieval England* (New York, 1996). On taverns, gambling, and popular games: Katelijne Geerts, *De spelende mens in de Boergondische Nederlanden* (Bruges, 1987); Beat Kümin, *Drinking Matters: Public Houses and Social Exchange in Early Modern Central Europe* (Basingstoke, UK, 2007). On charivari: Jacques Le Goff and Jean-Claude Schmitt, eds., *Le Charivari: Actes de la table ronde organisée à Paris, 25–27 avril 1977* (Paris, 1981). On honor: Thomas J. Kuehn, "Honor and Conflict in a Fifteenth-Century Florentine Family," in *Law, Family, and Woman,* ed. Thomas Kuehn (Chicago, 1991), 129–42; Walter Prevenier, "The Notions of Honor and Adultery in the Fifteenth-Century Burgundian Netherlands," in *Comparative Perspectives on History and Historians: Essays in Memory of Bryce Lyon,* ed. David Nicholas, Bernard S. Bachrach, and James Murray (Kalamazoo, MI, 2012), 259–278. On infanticide: Joanne Ferraro, *Nefarious Crimes, Contested Justice: Illicit Sex and Infanticide in the Republic of Venice, 1557–1789* (Baltimore, 2008). On sodomy: Marc Boone, "State Power and Illicit Sexuality: The Persecution of Sodomy in Late Medieval Bruges," *Journal of Medieval History* 22 (1996): 135–53.

Other important studies in a comparative context of pardons and mercy include Helen Lacey, *The Royal Pardon: Access to Mercy in Fourteenth-Century England* (Woodbridge, UK, 2009); Geoffrey Koziol, *Begging Pardon and Favor: Ritual and Political Order in Early Medieval France* (Ithaca, 1992). On verbal violence: Karen Jones, *Gender and Petty Crime in Late Medieval England: The Local Courts in Kent, 1460–1560* (Woodbridge, UK, 2006). On rape: Caroline Dunn, "The Language of Ravishment in Medieval England," *Speculum* 86 (2011): 79–116. On forms of marriage and companionship: Martha Howell, *The Marriage Exchange: Property, Social Place, and Gender in Cities of the Low Countries, 1300–1550* (Chicago, 1998); Shannon McSheffrey, *Marriage, Sex and Civic Culture in Late Medieval London* (Philadelphia, 2006); Ruth Mazo Karras, *Unmarriages: Women, Men, and Sexual Unions in the Middle Ages* (Philadelphia, 2012). On adultery: Peggy McCracken, *The Romance of Adultery: Queenship and Sexual Transgression in Old French Literature* (Philadelphia, 1998); Leah Otis-Cour, "'*De jure novo*': Dealing with Adultery in the Fifteenth-Century Toulousain," *Speculum*

84 (2009): 347–92. On clientelism: Gunnar Lind, "Great Friends and Small Friends: Clientelism and the Power Elite," in *Power Elites and State Building,* ed. Wolfgang Reinhard (Oxford, 1996), 123–47. On theater: Alan E. Knight, ed., *The Stage as Mirror: Civic Theatre in Late Medieval Europe* (Woodbridge, UK, 1997); Carol Symes, *A Common Stage: Theater and Public Life in Medieval Arras* (Ithaca, 2007). On minorities: Jeffrey Richards, *Sex, Dissidence, and Damnation: Minority Groups in the Middle Ages* (London, 2002).

Index